The MARCEL NETWORK

Related Titles from Potomac Books

Doctor to the Resistance: The Heroic True Story of an American Surgeon and His Family in Occupied Paris, by Hal Vaughan

Harvest in the Snow: My Crusade to Rescue the Lost Children of Bosnia, by Ellen Blackman

Needle in the Bone: How a Holocaust Survivor and a Polish Resistance Fighter Beat the Odds and Found Each Other, by Caryn Mirriam-Goldberg

Witness to Annihilation: Surviving the Holocaust, by Samuel Drix

The MARCEL NETWORK

How One French Couple Saved 527 Children from the Holocaust

Fred Coleman

Potomac Books
Washington, D.C.

Library of Congress Cataloging-in-Publication Data

Coleman, Fred.

The Marcel network : how one French couple saved 527 children from the Holocaust / Fred Coleman. — 1st ed.

p. cm.

Includes bibliographical references.

ISBN 978-1-61234-511-6 (hardcover : alk. paper)

ISBN 978-1-61234-512-3 (electronic)

1. Abadi, Moussa. 2. Abadi, Odette, 1914–. 3. Jews—France—Nice—Biography. 4. Jewish children in the Holocaust—France—Nice. 5. World War, 1939–1945—Children. 6. World War, 1939–1945—Jews—Rescue—France—Nice. 7. Holocaust, Jewish (1939–1945)—France—Nice. 8. Nice (France)—Ethnic relations. I. Title.

DS135.F9A334 2013

940.53'18092244941–dc23

2012031568

Printed in the United States of America on acid-free paper that meets the American National Standards Institute Z39-48 Standard.

Potomac Books

22841 Quicksilver Drive

Dulles, Virginia 20166

First Edition

10 9 8 7 6 5 4 3 2

To my children, Eric and Cynthia,
born, thank God, into a better world

Adapted from Eric Gaba and Rama, "Occupation zones of France during the Second World War," courtesy of Wikimedia Commons.

CONTENTS

1

CHILDREN

Julien Engel saw his parents for the last time when he was barely nine years old. They stood on one side of a barbed-wire fence. Julien and his little brother, George, then not yet four, stood on the other. It was September 1942, during the German occupation of France in World War II. Their parents, David and Rosa Engel, had been arrested because they were Jews, and detained at an internment camp in the southwest. Soon they would be deported to the gas chambers at Auschwitz. Their small sons understood none of this. The boys had been arrested with their parents, housed in separate barracks inside the camp, and then brought out along the fence to say good-bye. Unlike their parents, the children would be spared. It was one of the last times anywhere in occupied France that Jewish children were released.

Julien and George could not hug or kiss their parents good-bye. They managed only to touch hands through the narrow slits between rows of barbed wire. Along the fence other families also made their farewells, with tears and wails. The last words Julien heard his parents say were "Take care of your little brother."

✦

After the Nazis arrested her parents, Marthe Artsztein hid with neighbors, the Weiss family, on the ground floor of her building. Monsieur and Madame Weiss gave Marthe her own bedroom at the back of the apartment. Their two daughters played with her and made her feel like a member of the family. One morning, Marthe awoke to find everyone else gone. The Gestapo had raided during the night and arrested the Weisses. They never looked for Marthe in the room at the back because her name was not on their list of people living in the apartment. Frightened and not knowing what to do, Marthe somehow understood that she had to hide somewhere else. She climbed out of her ground-floor window and down onto the Paris streets, where German soldiers and French police ruthlessly rounded up Jews, children included, and deported them to the death camps. Now Marthe's survival depended on herself alone. She was eight years old.

✦

Françoise Knopf and her family trembled in the rundown hotel for Jewish refugees in Nice. They heard boots on the stairs and German voices. Her mother made Françoise, fifteen, and her younger sister, eleven-year-old Paulette, hide in the closet. "No matter what happens, don't say a word," she told the girls. The parents then opened their hotel room door partway, sat on the bed, and waited to be arrested, hoping that if they offered no resistance the Germans wouldn't look in the closet. The Knopfs heard more boots, this time in the hall on their floor. But no one ever entered their room. Every family in the hotel was arrested except theirs. The Germans took the partly opened door to mean that the room had already been searched and that no one was left inside.

The Knopfs left the hotel, but their ordeal was far from over. They had no place to stay. They had no ration cards to buy food legally, and with their money running out, they could no longer cope with black market prices. Worst of all, they knew they could not continue to provide for their daughters. In the most difficult decision for any parents, the Knopfs decided to give up their children to someone who was able to hide them safely, so at least their girls might live. They had the name of a couple who could help. It was their last chance.

✦

He was a graduate student—she, just out of medical school. Together, the young Jewish couple in German-occupied France had nothing—no money, no influence, no protection. For Moussa Abadi, an immigrant from Syria, and Odette Rosenstock, his French companion, transport meant a borrowed bicycle, a meal was often only a hard-boiled egg, a shared cigarette was a luxury. And yet, improbably, these two stood up against Nazi atrocities. At the risk of their lives, they dedicated themselves to saving Jewish children from the gas chambers.

Moussa Abadi was only thirty-three and his future wife twenty-eight when they formed the Marcel Network to hide children in Catholic convents and boarding schools, or with Protestant families. Their clandestine network became one of the most successful operations of Jewish resistance anywhere in Europe, although, inevitably, not without tragic losses. The fate of hundreds of young people would ultimately depend on the Abadis, among them Julien and George Engel, Marthe Artsztein, and Françoise and Paulette Knopf.

The true story of the Marcel Network has been drawn from a multitude of sources, and is now told in full for the first time in this book. Moussa and Odette admitted that the odds were overwhelmingly stacked against them. And still, they persevered. Armed only with courage, brains, and a moral compass, they defied one of the most brutal dictatorships in history to save 527 young lives. As an example of what only two people of goodwill can accomplish when confronted with crimes against humanity, their story is a lesson for all time.[1]

2

MOUSSA AND ODETTE

Moussa Abadi arrived in France on a graduate student scholarship in 1933, determined to stay forever. He loved the French language, culture, and, most of all, the theater. In Paris, at the Sorbonne, Moussa worked toward a doctorate in literature, with a thesis on French theater in the Middle Ages. He also trained to become an actor, winning a leading role in a French professional troupe that performed in New York for five months in 1937. The young Abadi was short and stocky, with a full round face, outsized glasses, dark hair, and a Mediterranean complexion. The actor in him made Moussa a dazzling storyteller, from his humble origins in the Jewish ghetto of Damascus, to his glory days on the American stage.[1]

Still only in his twenties, Moussa's life in Paris already showed a remarkable progression. Jews in the Damascus ghetto, where Moussa was born on September 17, 1910, lived in abject poverty—families of seven or eight in one room, with appalling conditions of hygiene. As a small boy Moussa awoke each day at 5 A.M. The house had no running water. Often Moussa found that a layer of ice had formed overnight in the washbasin. He broke the ice with a stick in order to clean himself, and then went off to the synagogue for daily prayers, before breakfast and school.

Jews in Damascus were required to live in the city's ghetto, one of the oldest in the world. But they could leave during the day to work at menial jobs on survival wages. Prospects for a better future were bleak, as Jewish education in the ghetto ended at primary school. Moussa's mother died when he was twelve, leaving his maternal grandparents to raise him, a sister, and a brother, with help from their father. Still, Moussa was luckier than most boys. His family agreed to let the bright and ambitious boy part with ghetto tradition and attend a Catholic secondary school in the city, run by French Lazarist priests, to continue his studies. For them, the promise of a higher education was worth the risk of placing a Jewish boy in a Catholic school.

As a boy, Moussa owned only three books, one of them a French history called *Our Ancestors the Gauls*, which was the genesis of his passion for France. He loved the ghetto for its sense of community, beguiling naivete, and extraordinary friendships. But, as a teenager, Moussa dreamed of a life of literature and ideas, and of being surrounded by great books. He longed to get away from the ghetto's suffocating ancient rituals. His escape route came through studies, scholarships abroad, and eventually, graduate work in Paris.[2]

In Paris for seven years, the young Abadi lived frugally, at first on a student stipend. It was enough to rent a small room, feed and clothe himself, buy books, and occasionally attend the theater. Later on, earnings from his acting, and favorable reviews, increased his capacity to enjoy life. Moussa was well on his way to earning a PhD and fulfilling all his childhood hopes. Then his world collapsed.

In 1940, the Germans invaded France. Moussa borrowed a bicycle from a friend and fled Paris with little more than a change of underwear. The first night, he stopped on the side of the road and fell asleep. When he awoke, the bicycle was gone. With what remained of his stipend, Moussa kept on heading south.

The armistice that the Germans imposed on France in June 1940 split the country into two nearly equal parts. Hitler's forces ran the northern half, the "Occupied Zone," from Paris. But the southern half, including

Nice, became a so-called Free Zone run by a French government at Vichy, which was supposedly autonomous. Indeed, Vichy had diplomatic relations with forty countries, including the United States, all recognizing it as independent. Despite that, however, Vichy gradually increased collaboration with the Germans in the mass deportation of Jews to the death camps.

Moussa headed for Nice in the early days of the Vichy regime, when Jews were often harassed but were not yet being arrested. He arrived nearly broke. Fortunately, his professor at the Sorbonne, Gustav Cohen, was another Jew who had been forced to flee Paris. Cohen eked out a living in the South of France by giving lectures on Medieval French Theater. The professor hired his former student to illustrate his lectures by acting out some of the roles.

Cohen managed to leave for the United States and take up a post at Harvard University. Varian Fry, an American in Marseille, secured Cohen's safe passage. Fry represented the New York–based Emergency Rescue Committee, a private group that helped European intellectuals and artists, many of them Jews, escape from Nazi-occupied France, among them Marc Chagall, Max Ernst, Hannah Arendt, Jean Arp, and Marcel Duchamp. Fry could have done the same for Moussa Abadi. Indeed, Cohen wanted Moussa to join him in America, but Moussa preferred to stay and take his chances.

✦

Odette Rosenstock was born in Paris on August 24, 1914. Her parents ran a garment factory and provided a comfortable upbringing for Odette and her younger sister, in contrast to Moussa's childhood of extreme poverty in the Damascus ghetto. Unlike Moussa, Odette grew up with two loving parents present, in a home where there was no excess of tradition or ritual. Although Jewish, Odette's family was not religious. But like Moussa, Odette developed a wanderlust for travel. She dreamed of an international career, and entered law school with that goal in mind. However legal studies did not interest her and after a few months, she decided to study medicine.[3]

Even as a teenager, Odette was outraged by injustice. She did not join any political party, preferring instead to discreetly attend debates and meetings. The rise of Hitler and the threat of fascism alarmed her. By her early twenties, Odette had already turned to political activism. She started with the Spanish Civil War of 1936–39, supporting the doomed Republicans against the Fascist forces of General Francisco Franco, aided by Hitler. A year before finishing medical school, Odette went to the Spanish border region to work in internment camps where Republican refugees were held prisoner. Some of them she freed, smuggling them out in ambulances.

Odette met Moussa Abadi in 1939 at the Paris apartment of Olga Fink, another medical student. Moussa, who was a friend of Olga's family, dropped by one day and Odette opened the door. "It all happened by chance, nothing premeditated," Olga recalled. Odette was "a charming girl, very beautiful"—a thin blonde with sparkling blue eyes, a warm heart, and a zest for life.[4] Moussa was smitten the moment he first saw her. Odette quickly fell for him, too. "Moussa was a raconteur with great charm, and Odette was certainly captivated by him," said Marie Gatard, a friend of both of them.[5] Jeannette Wolgust, the couple's closest friend, put it more succinctly: "They fell in love immediately."[6]

Odette was twenty-five years old when they met, and Moussa twenty-nine. "But there was no talk of marriage yet," Olga explained. Both had studies to finish and a future fraught with wartime uncertainty, especially for Jews. By then Hitler had invaded Poland and World War II had begun.

Odette and Moussa never told any of their friends about their early romance. "They were very discreet," said Jacqueline DeNechère, a friend of forty years. "They considered that their affair had no importance for others so they never said anything about it."[7] Jeannette Wolgust thought more than discretion was involved. "They were very protective of their private world," she said. "They never let anyone else in." Jeannette recalled that in later life Moussa and Odette insisted that even their best friends phone first before visiting them. "That gave the Abadis the chance to say 'yes' or 'no.' If you just showed up and knocked at their door, they wouldn't open it," Jeannette said.[8]

Less than a year after they met, Moussa and Odette had to part for a time. Odette became a doctor and went to work in the state hospital system in Montargis, sixty miles away. Moussa remained in Paris until he fled during the German invasion.

In the chaos that followed, Odette's father, Camille Rosenstock, left Paris for the south to arrange a hiding place for the family in a remote village. But her mother, Marthe, and younger sister, Simone, were arrested before they could join him. Both eventually lost their lives at Auschwitz.

In the German-occupied north of France, Jews working for the state, like Odette, lost their jobs. Then to avoid arrest, they had to hide, but fleeing to the south was fraught with danger. Using armed patrols and a Line of Demarcation, the Germans closed off access to the Free Zone. Moussa arrived in Nice in July 1940 in the first weeks of the armistice, before the seven-hundred-mile long line was completed. By the time Odette decided to join him the next year, she had to sneak across the line, wading through a river at an unguarded point. She reached Nice in November 1941 to begin a partnership with Moussa that would last for the rest of their lives, ultimately as a married couple decades later.

When Odette arrived in Nice, Jewish charities still operated openly in the south. Odette went to work in a medical clinic for children run by one such charity, an organization known by its initials as the OSE, or l'Oeuvre de Secours aux Enfants (Help the Children Fund). The clinic provided an income for the Abadis, as well as contacts with the Jewish families who would later want to hide their children. Moussa supplemented the couple's meager finances by giving French language lessons to immigrants.

Soon after Odette arrived, Vichy began escalating the arrest of Jews in the southern Free Zone, starting with those born outside France. The arrests threatened thousands of refugees who had fled from Nazi oppression before the war, leaving Germany, Austria, and Eastern Europe for what they hoped would be a safe haven in France. The Vichy policy of hunting down foreign-born Jews, including a massive roundup in Nice in August 1942, put Moussa in grave danger. He survived by getting false identity papers that eliminated his Jewish origin. Odette, as a French-born Jew, had less to fear, but she too obtained false papers with a Christian name.

Fortunately for both of them, the situation in the south actually improved three months later, in November 1942, thanks to the presence of Italian troops, there under an agreement between Hitler and his ally, Benito Mussolini. Italian forces already stationed just inside the French border at Menton moved farther inland to occupy the area around nearby Nice, a city that was once part of the Roman Empire.[9] The Italians still called it "Nizza" (NEET-sah). Moussa and Odette watched the Italians march in, "tired and dragging their feet," Moussa recalled. "Some of them flirted with French girls. There was nothing threatening about them."

In effect, Nice became an island of relative safety for Jews while the rest of the Free Zone in the south suffered from increased repression. Unlike Vichy, the Italians opposed deporting civilians—even Jews—to death camps. The Italians could not stop Vichy police from arresting Jews in Nice, but they slowed them down. Among other things, Italian soldiers protected synagogues in the city from raids by Vichy.[10] Italian generals and diplomats, among them Count Gian Galezzo Ciano, the foregin minister who also happened to be Mussolini's son-in-law, were appalled by Hitler's final solution—his plan for the total destruction of Europe's Jews. Eventually Joachim von Ribbentrop, the German foreign minister, complained to Mussolini that Italian military circles lacked a proper understanding of the Jewish question. Despite that, Italian commanders in Nice continued their efforts to stall deportation of Jews to the gas chambers.

Nonetheless, as Moussa said, "it was a time of fear." As the Allies pushed victoriously up through Italy, it became increasingly clear that Mussolini would soon fall and the Italian troops would have to withdraw from France, leaving the Nice region open to Vichy repressions at the very least, or even the worst-case scenario of a German occupation. "We feared the worst," Moussa said.[11]

Two incidents convinced Moussa he was right to be so frightened. The first occurred in April 1942, before the Italians arrived, during a walk on the Promenade des Anglais, the palm-shrouded avenue lining the magnificent arc of the beach at Nice. "It was a radiant morning," Moussa recalled, "under a postcard-blue sky." Suddenly he stopped at a scene that took his breath away.

A young woman lay on the ground, covered in blood, as a French policeman stomped her head in with his heavy boot. A crowd of about twenty people watched the woman die, among them her sister, who stood nearby holding the hand of the victim's six-year-old son. "Mama, Mama, Mama," the little boy screamed. No one dared to intervene.

"What's happening?" an incredulous Moussa asked.

"Can't you see?" a man in the crowd replied. "He's disciplining a Jew."

Shocked, Moussa turned and walked away, so upset that he cried out in the street, "God, why have you abandoned us?"

Moussa could not stop thinking about the little boy. "What would happen to him? Tomorrow he might be arrested. That was the day I decided I would not just sit idly by and watch the parade," Moussa said. "I was going to do something. I didn't know how, but Odette and I were going to help."[12]

The second incident, in early 1943 during the Italian occupation, increased Moussa's resolve. There could be no delay. The time to organize a rescue effort for Jewish children was running out.

A friend had introduced Moussa to an Italian priest who had served as a chaplain to Italian troops fighting alongside the Germans on the Soviet front. The priest, Dom Giulio Penitenti, had just returned from Ukraine and wanted to speak to local Jews. He met Moussa in a hotel in Cimiez, in the hills above Nice, overlooking the sea.

Penitenti was tall, bearded, tanned, and dressed in a long, black cassock. He invited Moussa to sit. "Monsieur, you are not going to believe me," Penitenti began. "But I have to tell you. I have just come back from the front and I want someone to know what is happening there.

"Do you know what the Nazis do to Jewish children? They are massacred to the last one, without regard for age or sex."[13]

Penitenti told Moussa he had watched SS troopers line twenty children up against a wall and slaughter them with machine guns. The priest said he had also seen German soldiers make children run, only to fire their rifles at the fleeing youngsters—as in a skeet shooting contest—with the best shot winning beer money for the most kills.

"Father, I don't believe you," Moussa said. "Barbarity has its limits."

By then, people in the south of France had heard rumors about gas chambers in Nazi death camps. Jews tended to dismiss such stories of atrocity as Allied war propaganda. Moussa, like many others, was skeptical.[14]

Penitenti unbuttoned his cassock, took out a wooden crucifix, and said, "I swear on the blood of Christ that what I have told you is the truth."

Moussa's doubts collapsed. "You have to believe a priest when he swears on the crucifix," he told Odette later. "It was not a military act the Germans were conducting. It was a game."

Moussa thought he knew how Odette would react to that, but he decided to ask her anyway: "If the Germans come tomorrow, do you think the same thing will happen here?"

"Absolutely," Odette replied.

So they agreed, "We have to do something—urgently."[15]

Neither had the faintest idea where to begin.

3

The Bishop

Given the attitude of Pope Pius XII, the Catholic Church looked like the last place the Abadis would start. For most of World War II, the Pope stood silent in the face of Nazi atrocities against Jews. Allied diplomats and Jewish leaders continually implored him to exercise his moral authority, to condemn publicly the horrors of the mass deportations to the gas chambers. Pius XII refused, often arguing that the Vatican had to remain neutral during the war. Only when it became clear that Nazi Germany was heading for defeat did the Pope soften his stand. By then it was too little, too late.[1]

There are abundant examples of the difference the Pope could have made across Europe by speaking out—in Spain, in Lithuania, in Germany itself. But one example, from France, stands out. Marshal Philippe Pétain, the head of the French collaborationist government at Vichy, asked the Pope if the Vatican would object to anti-Jewish laws. Among the laws Pétain had in mind—and would implement—was a requirement that all Jews had to register with local authorities so their national identity cards could be stamped with the word "*Juif*" (Jew). The cards had to be carried at all times, meaning Jews could be stopped by police at any time, identified, and arrested. Pius XII replied that the Church condemned racism, but did not repudiate every rule against the Jews. One can only wonder what influence the Pope might have exercised in heavily Catholic France, had he warned Pétain that anti-Jewish laws were unconscionable?

The overwhelming majority of the Catholic hierarchy in France, from archbishops down to local priests, followed the Pope's lead whatever their private beliefs. With rare exceptions, they refrained from speaking out against Nazi atrocities from their pulpits, and they maintained cordial relations with Vichy. Nothing on the public record suggested that the Catholic hierarchy in France would come to the rescue of the Jews. To Moussa Abadi, ironically, that was a plus. For him, it meant the Church was beyond suspicion as far as the Germans were concerned. After much thought, and after taking the advice of an influential friend in the French resistance, Maurice Brener, Moussa decided to turn first to the Catholic Church for help.[2]

Despite the odds, Moussa always knew he might succeed. He knew the Catholic priesthood was full of men of goodwill, men who often helped Jews. Moussa's own life was proof of that. Moussa finished his secondary education at a Catholic school run by French priests. It was thanks to them that he learned French, grew intellectually, and won his scholarship to Paris. They helped him on a human level, never trying to convert their Jewish student to their faith. Moussa knew that at least in theory it should be possible to hide Jewish children in France at Catholic boarding schools, convents, and other institutions, and have them remain Jews.

He also knew a lot about Catholic lore, both from his school days with the priests and from his graduate studies on the French theater of the Middle Ages—essentially plays based on Catholic Bible stories. These experiences helped Moussa break the ice with Catholic prelates.

Most important, Moussa knew the man to see. Monseigneur Paul Rémond, the bishop of Nice, ran dozens of institutions where children could be hidden throughout the diocese—in Nice, Cannes, Grasse, and other towns. Fortunately, Moussa had met him once. Bishop Rémond attended one of Gustav Cohen's lectures, and afterward praised Moussa on his supporting role. Given the atmosphere created by Vichy and the Pope, it took courage, Moussa thought, for a Catholic bishop to appear in public at a lecture given by a Jewish professor. But would Rémond remember him? And even if he did, could a Jewish nobody like Moussa arrange a private audience with such a high official of the Catholic Church? In the spring of 1943, Moussa asked a Jesuit priest he knew to set up an appointment with the Bishop of Nice—and hoped for the best.

Monseigneur Paul Rémond received Moussa Abadi at his residence, a three-story beige villa on a hill near the center of the city. The bishop, dressed in his robes of office, was a short, corpulent man, nearing his seventieth birthday. Moussa noticed several pairs of eyeglasses spread across his desk, one of them broken. When troubled, the bishop had the habit of holding eyeglasses in his hand and squeezing them, sometimes until the lenses cracked.

Moussa began by reminding Rémond that they had previously met through Gustav Cohen. "Do you have any news of him?" the bishop wanted to know. Moussa did not. "Well," the bishop said, "what have you come to tell me?"

"Monseigneur, I come to you in all confidence," Moussa replied. "I belong to a religion that is not yours. There is nothing in common between you and me. Still, Monseigneur, I am here to ask you to help us in a perilous task.

"We are only two, my companion, Odette Rosenstock, and me. Will you help us at the risk of your life and ours?"

"What do you want me to do at the risk of our lives?"

"Only to save children."[3]

He didn't know it then, but Moussa was hitting all the right notes.

Monseigneur Paul Rémond was a man of exceptional courage, ready to risk his life for a noble cause. He had proved that in World War I when, as an ordained priest, Rémond would normally have served as a chaplain. Instead, he fought at the front as a combat officer in the trenches, rising to the rank of commandant, a captain commanding a battalion. Five times he was cited for bravery on the battlefield for being "an officer of high moral value" ready to take on "the most dangerous missions." Rémond received

France's highest honors for his military service, including the Légion d'Honneur and the Croix de Guerre, with two silver stars and two gold stars.[4]

As a good Catholic, the bishop regarded killing as a sin. But he also believed it was justified in the wartime defense of his country. Paul Rémond had no problem explaining his philosophy. First, he based his moral judgments on the teachings of the Church. Then he let his conscience play a role in his decisions, even if that sometimes meant stretching the limits of what the Church permitted. Thus, in war, he was prepared to kill.

Rémond never went further, however. He might put a more independent interpretation on Church teachings, but he would not defy them. He apparently kept his vow of chastity, for example, sometimes with humor. During the war, after the liberation of a village, an exuberant young Frenchwoman threw her arms around Rémond and tried to kiss him in thanks, awkwardly bumping her head into the visor of his cap. "Excuse me, mademoiselle," the soldier-priest told her, "but I don't have much practice at kissing."[5]

In peacetime, the bishop continued to demonstrate courage, independent thinking, and high moral values. He was one of the first French prelates to speak out against Nazi persecution of the Jews. In a sermon at the Sacré-Coeur Church in Nice in 1933, the year Hitler took power, Rémond denounced religious persecution. He expressed sympathy for the Jewish community and his "desire to ease their pain with moral and material support."[6]

The bishop loved children and believed he had a moral obligation to try to save them, whatever their faith. He followed the lead of Pius XII where possible, but felt he had a higher duty to God. As in World War I, Paul Rémond was again ready to risk his life for a righteous cause. But first he needed more specifics.

"And just how do you plan to save children?" Rémond asked.

"The only way is to hide them," Moussa said.

Moussa told Rémond he would need a list of all the Catholic institutions in the diocese—schools, orphanages, and convents—capable of doing just that.

"What else will you need?"

"An office," Moussa said, "here at your residence. I have no office and a place is needed to falsify documents for the children."

Moussa would not have to forge national identity cards because children under the age of sixteen were exempt from carrying them. But he would need to produce baptismal certificates and ration cards, both in false names, so the Jewish children could masquerade as Christians, hide in Catholic institutions, and survive. The whole operation would be clandestine, against the law, and punishable by death if discovered.

The bishop wanted to make sure he had heard correctly. "You mean you want to falsify documents here in my house?"

"Exactly," Moussa said.

The bishop held a pair of eyeglasses in his hand, Moussa noticed. This time he did not break them, but his double chin shook, another sign of his grave concern.

Rémond had only one further question. "In your clandestine work, will you carry arms?"

"No. Never," Moussa said.

"Very well," the bishop concluded. "I will reflect on your proposal. Come back to see me in forty-eight hours."

As he escorted Moussa to the door, the bishop hinted of the answer to come. "I believe you have converted me," he said, although he stopped short of giving his consent at that time.[7]

The bishop was already convinced. But he needed the forty-eight hours to consult his closest aides—among them his private secretary, Father Auguste Rostan—to see if they would agree to be brought into the secret operation, inevitably at the risk of their lives too. He wanted to weigh with them the risks to the Church, and to the institutions in the diocese. In the end, he expected, they would concur.

When Moussa returned, Rémond told him, "Consider my residence as your home. Because you want to save children, it is my duty as a Christian to give you a helping hand."[8]

The bishop said Moussa could start right away, in an office conveniently located on the ground floor of the residence, with a window looking out on a huge garden. If the Vichy police raided the residence, Moussa could jump out the window and run.

Once the bishop's new Jewish associate had been installed in the ground-floor office, he had to be introduced to Father Rostan and other senior aides to Rémond. All agreed Moussa would have to take a new false name for his clandestine life. The bishop asked him his choice.

"Monsieur Marcel," Moussa said.

"Marcel what?"

"Just Marcel," Moussa told him.

And with that, the Marcel Network was born.

4

THE PASTORS

Years later, looking back on his first meetings with Bishop Rémond, Moussa Abadi would say, "I came to him as a beggar, asking him to help me, to give me something. But, call it pride if you like, I had the feeling that I had given him something—me, a Jew. I had given him the opportunity to live the Gospel."[1]

For his part, the bishop had given Moussa and Odette a start. But they would have to do all the detailed and dangerous legwork to get the Marcel Network up and running. They would have to find secure hiding places and manufacture false papers in Christian names for hundreds of children. They would have to alert Jewish families in secret on how to contact them if and when the Nazis occupied the Nice region, and explain to them that the only way to save children would be to hide them. They would need financing. And they would have to do all this by themselves, just the two of them.

Moussa and Odette did not know how much time they had, only that it was alarmingly short. Beginning in the late spring of 1943, after securing the bishop's support, both worked day and night, in a frenzy of activity, to get the job done. All the while they always kept one eye on the military situation in Italy, where, ironically, the prospect of an Allied victory posed the greatest danger for them.

American and British troops invaded Sicily on July 10, 1943. Mussolini was ousted from power in Rome on July 25, and the Italian military crumbled. Clearly, the Allies would soon move up through Italy and force the nation to surrender. Italian troops in the Nice region would then go home. And after that, almost certainly, German forces would replace the defeated Italians. In the end, Moussa and Odette would have only three months, from late June to early September 1943, before Nice fell under the boots of Nazi troops.

During daylight hours, Moussa prospected for hiding places in Catholic convents, boarding schools for boys, and in other institutions. He carried credentials signed by Bishop Rémond identifying "Monsieur Marcel" as an inspector of schools. Usually the priests and nuns he called on throughout the Nice region agreed to his request to take in Jewish children should the need arise. Many did so because they regarded the request as coming by proxy from the bishop himself. When Moussa arrived they would say "Welcome, Monseigneur," taking him for a priest in civilian clothes. Because it suited his purpose, Moussa did nothing to correct them. The actor in him made that easy.[2]

Moussa's prospecting covered hundreds of miles, by bicycle or public transport buses, from schools within the city of Nice to more remote convents in all corners of the diocese. Inevitably, he encountered disappointments, among them a mother superior at a convent near Grasse. When Moussa asked her to take in three or four girls, she replied:

"Why? Do they have a vocation to become nuns?"

"No, it is not a question of vocation. They are Jewish girls and they are in danger."

"Why are they in danger?"

Moussa was incredulous. The mother superior knew nothing about the world outside the gates of her convent, not even that in Nazi-occupied France Jewish girls lived in fear for their lives. Moussa could only thank her for her time and leave in frustration.

There were other disappointments in Nice. Early on, Moussa tried to find additional hiding places with families in the city, sometimes successfully but often not. Some people slammed doors in his face. One woman told him she might be able to take a little girl, provided he could find her a blonde. After that, Moussa rarely sought out individual families in the city and focused his search almost entirely on Catholic institutions around the diocese.

In the evenings, he forged papers at the bishop's residence. One night Rémond himself came down to Moussa's office, said, "Let me help you," and began to fill in false ration cards and baptismal certificates.

"What you are doing is crazy," Moussa told the bishop. "Your handwriting is known throughout the diocese. You'll be arrested, tortured, maybe shot."

"Then you will go to heaven with me," Rémond said. "You won't be such bad company."[3]

Undeterred, the bishop often came down to help. When he left to return to his own quarters, Moussa would tear up all the papers Rémond had filled in—though he never told the bishop he had done so.

The two men quickly established a mutual respect. Intrigued by Moussa's background as an actor, Rémond asked him to give elocution lessons to priests training at a Nice seminary, hoping to improve their performance in Sunday sermons. Moussa took on the job initially, but dropped it when he learned that one of the priests was suspected of reporting to the Vichy Milice, a paramilitary force with its own uniform—khaki shirt, black beret, black tie. Unlike the regular police, the Milice were often recruited from ex-criminals and other ruffians to do Vichy's more brutal work, including rounding up Jews. The bishop told Moussa he had done the right thing.

Odette also worked well into the night during the three frantic months before the Germans arrived. "From this point on," she said, "I was Sylvie Delattre," her undercover Christian name in the Marcel Network. She traveled throughout the Nice region, often to distant mountain villages, returning after dark. Fortunately, during the Italian occupation, it was relatively easy to move around the area, although Odette still had to worry about the Milice. "I wasn't bothered," she recalled. "I don't have a very Semitic-looking face."[4]

False credentials for Sylvie Delattre provided protection. The bishop gave Odette a signed letter identifying "Sylvie" as a social worker employed by the Catholic Church. In case she was stopped by the police, that would help. Odette, however, spent her prospecting time within the Protestant community.

While Moussa looked for hiding places in Catholic institutions like convents, Odette focused on individual Protestant homes. "I would go to see the pastors and find out which families would help," she said. The pastors also recommended mayors of mountain villages who were likely to receive Odette favorably and put her in touch with additional families.

In general, Moussa and Odette discovered, the poorer, more humble peasant families proved more willing to hide Jewish children than were city residents. It wasn't a question of faith, of Catholic versus Protestant attitudes. People of both faiths helped. Indeed the Abadis hid a few children with nonsectarian couples as well. The real difference was rural versus urban attitudes. Often those most ready to open their homes were older, childless couples in poorer pockets of the countryside.

The peasant response could be remarkably generous. Odette never forgot a certain Madame Belliol, who told her, "Give me your ugliest child, the most miserable, the one that nobody wants, and I will cuddle him. I will love him." When Odette later brought her a six-month-old Jewish boy straight from the hospital—a baby painfully thin, sickly, covered with scabs, and so weak he could hardly move—Madame Belliol said, "Look at this little baby Jesus, how beautiful he is. I want him."[5]

All those agreeing to hide Jewish children took enormous risks. If discovered, they could be deported east to the Nazi death camps, or tortured and shot in France.

Two Protestant ministers became essential to Odette's efforts. The first, the Rev. Pierre Gagnier, was pastor of the Reformed church in Nice, just down the road from the Jewish synagogue on the same street, the Boulevard Dubouchage. Leaders at the synagogue formed a Dubouchage Committee, which arranged to help Jewish refugees from abroad and from German-occupied France, by welcoming them to Nice and directing them to charitable institutions such as the clinic where Odette worked. Through the Dubouchage Committee, Odette often met families whose children she would eventually hide. In looking for Protestant ministers to help shelter these children, Moussa inevitably turned to the church down the street from the synagogue. He made the first contact with Pastor Gagnier, then introduced him to Odette. She maintained the link, calling on the Protestant families and mayors recommended by Gagnier.

As with Bishop Rémond, Moussa had once again found in Pierre Gagnier a man of remarkable courage. The pastor had studied at the Sorbonne and for a year in Germany, receiving a degree in German before taking up his preparations for the clergy. He would soon prove himself unafraid to march into Gestapo headquarters in Nice, and, in fluent German, demand the release of prisoners he insisted had been arrested by mistake. Sometimes he succeeded, sometimes not.

"For two years, half our time was taken up helping the Jews," Pastor Gagnier recalled after the war. "This began well before the arrival of the Germans. Jews were flooding into Nice from all corners of France in the belief that they would be protected by the Italians."[6] During the Italian occupation, the pastor helped Jewish refugees find food and housing, and, through Odette, hiding places for their children if and when the Germans came.

The other Protestant minister Odette worked closely with, the Rev. Edmond Evrard of the Nice Baptist Church, had a well-deserved reputation for helping Jews long before the war. As early as 1930, Pastor Evrard began receiving Jewish refugee children from Germany and Austria and arranging for their care in France. In 1940, in a rare act for a French clergyman, he proclaimed his opposition to the Vichy government's anti-Jewish measures in a sermon from his pulpit and urged his parishioners to follow his lead. Pastor Evrard would later hide Jewish refugees in his home and let them conduct a service for the Jewish holiday of Purim in his church, with his two sons standing guard outside to warn of any potential troublemakers in the area. He proved himself indispensable to Odette by finding hiding places during the Italian occupation. After the war he would say modestly, "We did what we could to help the Jews."[7]

During the three months Odette crisscrossed the region searching out hiding places with Protestant families, she still managed to retain her job at the children's clinic in Nice where she offered a potential lifeline to worried parents. Most of them, of course, wanted to keep their children as long as possible, especially since no one yet knew for sure if the Germans would occupy Nice. Jewish parents did know, however, that if Nice fell under the Nazis they would have to run or hide, with no realistic way to support or protect their children. In that case, Odette's offer would be a godsend. Her work at the OSE clinic was absolutely essential to the success of the Marcel Network. Parents who visited Odette's clinic told their friends about the Abadis and they in turn informed other friends by word of mouth. Only by such discreet contacts could the word go out to Jews in Nice that a channel had been put in place to save children.

Jeannette Wolgust and her family, Jewish refugees from Paris, were a prime example of how Odette saved lives. Jeannette, then fourteen, and her brother Jean, aged five, arrived in Nice with their parents in July 1943. Soon afterward, Jeannette needed a doctor's care. Her mother took her to the OSE clinic where she was treated by Odette.

Jeannette remembers Odette telling her mother, "In case of trouble we can send your children to the mountains and hide them with a family that can care for them."

Her mother thanked Odette for the offer, but said, "As long as it is safe, I will keep my children with me."

Odette understood. "If the situation worsens," she said, "you can leave your children for us at this pharmacy." Odette then wrote out an address on a piece of paper. Jeannette watched her mother put the paper in her pocket.[8]

Finding the hiding places and alerting parents about them was only the beginning for Moussa and Odette. Children have to eat, and in wartime Nice, no one could buy milk or bread or any other food for a child without a ration card in the child's name. Catholic institutions or Protestant families could take in a Jewish youngster and hide him or her as a Christian with a false baptismal certificate, but they still had to fill an extra plate at the dinner table. Convents, boarding schools, and individual families had no way to get extra ration cards for the Jewish children they hid. Somehow, Moussa had to find a solution, or the children he hoped to hide would starve.

He took a chance and called on Raoul Brès, the Vichy bureaucrat who served as head of the general supply office for the Nice region. It proved to be a risk worth taking. Brès put Moussa on to a subordinate in charge of ration cards, and instructed the man, identified by Moussa only as Monsieur Broch, to help. Brès was one of those lifelong French civil servants, a minority to be sure, who on finding himself working for a Vichy regime he regarded as repugnant, did what he could in secret to oppose collaboration with the Nazis. In coming to the aid of Moussa and others, Brès put his life on the line. A few months later, he was shot by the Germans for helping the French Resistance.

Understandably, when Moussa first told Broch that he needed false ration cards for hidden children, the supply officer panicked. He replied, "Impossible. Falsification of ration cards by state officials is an act punishable by imprisonment."[9]

All right, Moussa thought, if they won't falsify ration cards for me, maybe they will give me blank ration cards and let me fill in the names. He knew that even blank cards presented problems, since each card was numbered and could be traced. If Moussa was given two hundred blank cards, numbered for example 11,300 to 11,500, the police might somehow trace the two hundred missing numbers to Moussa and learn that officials had supplied the blanks.

Still, Moussa thought it was worth the risk, and made his request. Broch agreed to hand over blanks, but warned Moussa, "If we are ever questioned, we will say that you stole the cards to sell them on the black market."

Moussa took the deal, gratefully. He didn't have much choice.

The other false papers needed were less of a problem. Moussa obtained the baptismal certificates with the help of the bishop and the Protestant pastors.

Even with all the false papers, however, Moussa and Odette were still far from ready. It would take money, millions of francs, for the hidden children to survive. The ration cards meant food could be bought, but it still had to be paid for. The hidden children, hundreds of them, would also need clothing, school fees and supplies, perhaps medical care—and all of that for God only knew how long. The Catholic institutions and Protestant families that agreed to hide Jewish children at great risk were already doing more than their share to help and could not be asked to pay the bills as well. Moussa and Odette would have to arrange funding—lots of it.

They could hardly help financially by themselves. Moussa and Odette had no money saved, only barely enough to get by each month. Their savior turned out to be Maurice Brener, a friend of Moussa's from his days in Paris. Once again, Moussa demonstrated his knack of going to the right man. Brener was a miracle worker, a one-man Mission Impossible, a hero of the French Resistance, and a sometimes spy for the United States. Incredibly for such a man of action, he could barely walk.

5

Zazou

Childhood polio left Maurice Brener crippled for life. "I never saw my father walking normally," his son, Thierry, said. "He limped on the right leg and walked with great difficulty." Brener hardly looked like a man of action. "Most of the time I remember him sitting on a couch," Thierry added. "His eyes showed suffering from the constant pain in his legs."[1]

Apart from his physical disability, Maurice Brener enjoyed an enviable life before the war. Home was a large bourgeois apartment literally in the shadow of the Eiffel Tower. Brener never had to work. His wife came from a wealthy Iranian family and her money allowed her husband to indulge himself in such pastimes as collecting rare books and paintings, among them a first edition of *A la Recherche du Temps Perdu* (*Rembrance of Things Past*) annotated and signed by Marcel Proust, and oil paintings by Pablo Picasso, Georges Braque, and Salvador Dali.

Brener impressed friends as a distinguished-looking gentleman from an earlier age—a dapper dresser, always in a jacket and tie, with elegant manners. His straight nose and lack of any Semitic features hid his Jewish origins, an asset in his later clandestine life.

When war broke out, Brener immediately volunteered for military service. Inevitably, the army rejected him because of his handicapped legs.

But Brener refused to take no for an answer. "Once the Germans occupied France in 1940," Thierry said, "my father threw his crutches into the Seine and decided to walk with a cane."

He and his cane walked straight into the arms of the Resistance. There were two Resistance movements in France. The first—larger, and better known—carried out sabotage and other military operations against the German occupiers. The second, unarmed, was a Jewish Resistance dedicated to the survival of Jews in France, especially by hiding children safely. Maurice Brener worked for both.

In the south of France, Brener provided liaison services between the two Resistance movements and false papers for each of them. When agents of the armed Resistance blew up the old port of Marseilles, Brener assured their escape route. Thierry said his father took part personally in other sabotage operations. The French government eventually awarded Brener a Medal of the Resistance, citing him as "an officer of great valor."

Brener also had ties to the American Office of Strategic Services (OSS), the wartime spy agency that was the precursor of the CIA. He spoke fluent English and was well informed about the French Resistance. Clearly, he would have been a valuable source of information, if not a full-time agent for the Americans. His son said that once, when listening behind a closed door as a small boy, "I overheard my father say he had to do something for the OSS." Thierry never learned the details. "My father was a secretive man who rarely spoke about the war," he explained. "All he told me was that he had done his duty."

The Gestapo hunted down Brener as a known Resistance agent and once came within a whisker of catching him. At the time, Brener ostensibly worked for a sugar company, a cover for his clandestine activity. As he hobbled down the staircase of his office building, nearing the ground floor, Gestapo officers going up the stairs stopped him and asked the way to Monsieur Brener's office. Realizing he had not been recognized, Brener told them that the office they wanted was on the sixth floor. While the Gestapo continued going up, Brener kept going down—and out. After that, he went into hiding under the wartime alias of "Zazou."

Ultimately, Maurice Brener's most important clandestine work came with the American Joint Distribution Committee, an umbrella group for Jewish charities in the United States. The committee, known in France simply as "the Joint," financed the struggle to save Jewish children. Brener, as Zazou, secretly became the Joint Committee's representative in France, working without pay. Funding for the Marcel Network, as well as other organizations within the Jewish Resistance, came through him.

American Jews contributed generously to the cause. The problem was getting their money to the needy in France. At first it seemed simple. The funds came through banks in Lisbon, as Portugal was neutral during the war. Then the U.S. government closed down that channel as part of a ban on transferring dollars to German-occupied France. The Americans feared—rightly—that any international bank transfers sent to France would end up in Nazi hands.

After that, Brener appealed to rich Jews in the South of France. He convinced many of them to lend to the Joint Committee. Their money had the advantage of already being in France, where it would be put to use. The lenders were to be repaid from America in dollars after the war, at an attractive rate of interest. But this ingenious funding method also proved short-lived. For the most part, the rich Jews in the Free Zone, fearing that the Germans would soon occupy all of France, left the country and took their money with them.

So Brener turned to Switzerland. Like Portugal, Switzerland was neutral, but unlike Portugal, it bordered on France, making the job of smuggling money much easier. American contributions went to Switzerland, where leading figures from the Jewish Resistance in France arranged to get the money across the frontier. Often Swiss schoolteachers carried the cash in their knapsacks on vacation hikes through mountains of the border region. Other funds came in under the floorboards of cars, in bicycle tubes, or even stuffed into bras.

Still more money arrived, parachuted into France from British warplanes. Zazou, always the dandy dresser, had himself a silk shirt made from one of the dropped chutes. It almost cost him his life. Vichy police questioned him, suspecting that the shirt he wore came from parachute silk. Somehow, he talked his way out of the danger.

There were other close calls. The Gestapo nearly arrested Brener on a bridge in Lyon. While crossing the bridge with a colleague from the Resistance, he stopped to tie a shoelace. The colleague continued on and was arrested at the end of the bridge. Brener turned back and escaped.

It was critical for Moussa Abadi that Brener remained free, and not only for the money he raised. Brener also proved essential in helping Moussa organize the Marcel Network.

Maurice Brener and Moussa Abadi had met in Paris. Moussa was just one year older and they had much in common besides their youth. Love of books and the arts drew them together in a friendship they renewed when both found themselves in the south of France after the German occupation of the north. The timing of the second phase of their friendship could not have been better. Moussa's meeting with the Italian priest Dom Giulio Penitenti, in early 1943, was a turning point for him. Penitenti's account of German soldiers inventing games to slaughter Jewish children spurred Moussa to action. But at first he had no practical idea of what to do. In July his friend Brener provided the crucial guidance to get the Marcel Network up and running.

Moussa had turned to Brener for advice because he knew his friend worked for the French Resistance, helping to organize and run its operations. Brener proposed that Moussa organize a clandestine network in the Nice region and that he arrange to hide Jewish children in Catholic institutions or with Protestant families. Brener advised on how to procure false documents. And he promised that the "Joint" would fund the entire operation.

Maurice Brener knew what he was talking about. All the ideas he suggested had been tested, and worked well. For two years this strategy had formed the basis of a secret operation to save Jewish children in the occupied north of France, financed by Brener and the Joint Committee. In the north, Brener channeled the money for the rescue effort to the OSE, a Jewish charity that had been forced underground by Nazi rule.

In Nice, while the Italians held sway, the OSE still worked legally in such places as the medical clinic that employed Odette. But Brener understood that if the Germans ever took the region, the OSE would have to set up a secret arm there as well. In fact, Georges Garel, who led the OSE's clandestine rescue operation in the north, was already expanding it to cover all of France, and looking for the right man to run operations in Nice. Brener suggested to Garel that Moussa should take on the job.

Garel, a French engineer born into a Lithuanian Jewish family, had created the model containing everything Moussa would use in organizing the Marcel Network.

Garel pioneered the approach to the Catholic Church. He contacted Monseigneur Jules Salièges, the Archbishop of Toulouse, the first French Catholic prelate to speak out openly against the Nazi deportation of Jews to concentration camps. Salièges opened Catholic institutions in the Toulouse area to hide Jewish children for Garel and the OSE, a precedent for Bishop Rémond's later assistance to the Abadis in the Nice region. Garel's model also included using pastors to find Protestant families willing to take in Jewish children, as Odette was doing in the south.

Garel arranged for false papers—baptismal certificates and ration cards—to protect the children in hiding and keep them fed. Moussa would do the same.

Garel used the French-Jewish version of the Boy Scouts, the Eclaireurs Israelites de France, as messengers and to escort younger children in safety to their hiding places. Moussa adopted this practice too. Like all Jewish organizations, the Eclaireurs were shut down under the Nazi occupation. But former scouts continued to work clandestinely for the Resistance.

In addition to hiding children, Garel arranged for some to leave France. OSE guides regularly smuggled youngsters to safety across mountain borders to Switzerland or Spain. Moussa tapped into this exit strategy as well.

Maurice Brener passed Garel's ideas on to Moussa, helped him organize the Marcel Network, and suggested that the network would benefit from links to Garel's OSE. Then Brener arranged for Moussa Abadi and Georges Garel to meet face-to-face for the first time at an ice-cream parlor in Nice in August 1943. Their talks went well. But Moussa insisted that he run his operation independently—for security reasons, he said—for Garel's sake as well as his own. "I could be arrested and tortured," Moussa explained. "At such a moment, I should not be able to tell the Gestapo where they could find Georges Garel." Furthermore, Moussa added, if he worked for the far larger OSE, any security lapses in Garel's organization risked leading the Gestapo or the Vichy Milice to him and Odette.[2]

Garel understood all this was a smokescreen. Moussa was genuinely concerned about security, of course, but his real reason for wanting to be his own boss was that he disliked taking orders from anyone. Garel later described Abadi as "an Oriental, a proud and independent man, a thoroughbred racehorse sensitive to the slightest kick of the spurs, a strong personality who would never allow himself to be a second in command." In short, Garel liked Abadi, and wanted him to head the rescue operations in the Nice region, but he realized that any accord between them would depend on Moussa running his own show.[3]

For his part, Moussa regarded Garel as "a man of courage, lucidity, and tenacity." He liked Garel from the start. In recalling their first meeting in a letter after the war, Moussa wrote to Garel, "One little phrase was enough for me to know that I could count on you. You looked me in the eyes and said: 'Go ahead, do what you have to do. As far as instructions go, I have only one to give you: Don't let a single child fall into the hands of the Gestapo.'"[4]

Georges Garel was one of the great heroes of the Jewish Resistance. By the end of the war, his OSE had saved 1,600 children throughout France, and had helped the Abadis to launch the Marcel Network. No one can minimize his contribution. Still, what Moussa and Odette Abadi accomplished is all the more remarkable because they had none of the advantages that Garel enjoyed.

Garel had more time. He saved more children than the Abadis, but he did so over a period of three years. Moussa and Odette had only one year.

Garel also had a head start, an infrastructure in place. Before the German occupation, the OSE had fourteen homes in France that cared legally for 1,200 Jewish children, most of them from refugee families that had fled Germany or Eastern Europe. When Nazi forces invaded France, the OSE homes became traps. They had to be closed and the children smuggled into hiding. But Garel at least had the significant advantage of starting with children already assembled in OSE homes, in effect large collection points. Moussa and Odette instead had to improvise on the run, taking in children dropped individually at pharmacies, on doorsteps, or with concierges—a slower, more dangerous, and far more complex task.

Most important, Garel had far more help, in the form of a nationwide organization. Some fifty people worked full time for Garel's clandestine service, finding hiding places and making sure children were safe and well. Moussa and Odette were responsible for all of those problems almost entirely by themselves.

By the time the Germans marched into Nice, the Abadis were as ready as they would ever be. They had hiding places and false documents ready for 140 children between the ages of one and sixteen. But they had no backup plan, no room for mistakes. The slightest error could cost young lives.

6

THE GERMANS

On September 10, 1943, under the command of Alois Brunner, SS troops goose-stepped into Nice to the strains of martial music. Adolf Eichmann, the architect of Hitler's Final Solution, had sent his most trusted aide, his "best man" as he called Brunner, to rid the South of France of Jews. Brunner held the rank of Haupsturmfuhrer or captain in the SS, Hitler's praetorian guard. As commander of the Drancy internment center outside Paris, the departure point for the trains to the Nazi death camps, Brunner personally sent an estimated 73,000 Jews—men, women, and children—to the gas chambers. He arrived in Nice determined to deport and exterminate all Jews from what had been the Free Zone.

"The Germans marched in sternly," Odette remembered, "nothing like the Italians who smiled, waved, and whistled at the girls."

In the weeks that followed, with the help of French Milice, German troops terrorized the Jews in a massive wave of arrests. They blocked intersections in Nice and patrolled streets, hunting down their quarry. They raided apartments, hotels, and train stations. The Gestapo hauled men out of cars or seized them on street corners, pulling down their pants in the middle of a crowded city. Those men found to be circumcised were assumed to be Jewish. They got thrown into trucks and taken away, never to return. Among the French, even non-Jews closed their shutters and hid in their homes, terrified that they might be arrested by mistake. Nights were filled with the sounds of boots bashing in doors, and the cries of victims hit by truncheons.

Despite the dangers, "Odette and I were out in the streets all the time," Moussa said, skirting roadblocks and checkpoints, hurrying to contact parents, and collecting children, often from untried drop points. "It was like working in a laboratory on a vaccine, and then having to use it without testing it first," Moussa recalled.[1]

Although their methods were untested, the three months of preparation paid off well. Moussa and Odette first sheltered children at a secret assembly point in a Nice cellar, readied their false papers, and drilled them on their new, Christian identities. Then children were taken to hiding places at Catholic institutions or with Protestant families, traveling over back roads, often at night. Sometimes Moussa or Odette took them personally. Sometimes children hid under blankets and rode to safety in fiacres (horse-drawn carriages) hired by Moussa. Jewish Boy Scouts escorted the younger children on the fiacres.

The need for the Abadis' rescue operation could not have been greater. By the time the Germans occupied Nice, the city was one huge trap for Jews. In only two years, the Jewish population of the Nice region had more than tripled to 50,000 as refugees poured in from northern France and other European countries in the mistaken belief that the corner of the south occupied by the Italians would be safe for them. The situation in Nice was unique. No other French city experienced such a huge influx of Jews. It made the Abadis' attempt to save young lives in Nice far more complicated than anything Garel faced elsewhere in France.

The Demarcation Line that separated the Free Zone, including Nice, from the rest of France had proven to be a porous obstacle, despite the death penalty for those who crossed it illegally. The line, some seven hundred miles long across the middle of the country, was watched but far from hermetically sealed. Only a few hundred soldiers and police manned it, with sporadic patrols and at distant checkpoints not even connected by telephones. They regularly arrested Jews trying to cross the line. But thousands of other determined refugees made it across at unguarded points, often with the help of French guides who knew when patrols passed and where barriers operated. Some guides took fees for helping Jews. Others worked for nothing, as their way of fighting the Nazi occupation. Relatively few guides betrayed Jews to the authorities. So the flood of refugees got through.

Virtually on the eve of the Nazi arrival in Nice, an ambitious plan to save thousands of Jewish refugees took shape. Angelo Donati, a rich Jewish businessman with contacts in high places, arranged for four ships to take between 20,000 and 30,000 Jews from Nice to safety in North Africa, via Italy. The Italian-born Donati worked out his plan with the Italian occupation authorities in Nice. He got it approved by both the Western Allies and the Italian government that succeeded Mussolini.

On September 3, 1943, the new Italian government signed a secret armistice with the Allies at Camp Fairfield in Sicily. Donati understood from the Italians that the armistice would be kept secret for another four weeks, until early October, to give him the time needed to pull off his evacuation. Not so. The text of the armistice agreement said clearly that it would "not be made public without the approval of the allied commander in chief," Gen. Dwight Eisenhower.[2] In other words, Eisenhower would decide on when to announce the armistice, based primarily on the military conditions on the ground in Italy among other things—on the positions of Allied, Italian, and German troops rather than on Donati's concerns. As a result, on September 8, only five days after the signature, Eisenhower publicly announced the armistice, without consulting the Italians. Donati's plan collapsed before it could be carried out. In the next two days Italian troops left Nice and the Germans marched in.

Thousands of Jews remained behind, trapped in Nice and waiting in vain for Donati's ships. Many of them were foreign refugees stuck in small hotels with nowhere to go. Often they did nothing to hide their Jewishness, refusing to remove the telltale signs, such as the traditional long beards or skullcaps that marked them as Jews. The Germans systematically went through these hotels, arresting all the guests, mostly Jews but some non-Jews as well. To this day, survivors of the Holocaust blame Eisenhower's early announcement for the deaths of loved ones trapped in Nice.[3]

Remarkably, in the first weeks of the German takeover in the Nice region, Moussa and Odette rescued more than a hundred children, by hiding them in France or by smuggling them abroad, without one falling into Nazi hands. But, inevitably, they could not always prevent a loss of life. Two of their closest collaborators perished early in the struggle to save children, a constant reminder to the Abadis of the dangers they faced themselves.

The first victim, a young Jewish woman called Nicole Weil, took the Christian cover name of Nicole Salon in joining the Marcel Network. Nicole was barely twenty-one when she agreed to help Jewish children escape to Switzerland.

"Why would you want to risk your life?" Moussa asked her. "You are pretty, happy, just married."

"Yes, I am happy," Nicole replied. "But I cannot remain happy if I know these children are suffering, if they are dying every day."[4] Like Moussa and Odette, Nicole would not stand idly by in the face of Nazi atrocities. She was determined to resist them.

Nicole joined the Marcel Network in early October 1943, barely a month after the arrival of the German forces in Nice. Three weeks later, an anonymous informer denounced her to the Nazis as a Resistance agent. The Germans arrested Nicole on her own, between trips to the Swiss border. They sent her to Drancy and on to Auschwitz, but even then she remained dedicated to helping children. While at Drancy, Nicole took three abandoned Jewish orphans under her wing. When their train arrived at the death camp, the Germans separated the Jews. The elderly, the infirm, and the children went immediately to the gas chambers. Those able to work survived. Nicole understood none of this as the selections were being made, only that she must steadfastly refuse to leave the children. She was judged fit to work, so she could have lived. But Nicole hung on to the hands of the children and was gassed with them.[5]

The second victim, Huguette Wahl, took the cover name of Odile Varlet. Like Nicole, Huguette had been a Jewish social worker at OSE, sent by Georges Garel to help the Abadis. Huguette joined the Marcel Network in November 1943, a month after Nicole's arrest. She lasted only a few days. The Gestapo arrested Huguette as she was carrying a bundle of clothing intended for hidden children. She too perished in Auschwitz.

After that, Moussa and Odette were on their own. The brief aid provided by Nicole and Huguette had lasted just over two months. From then until the end of the war, all efforts by the Marcel Network depended almost entirely on the Abadis alone.

Fortunately for Moussa and Odette, the Germans were slow in finding Jewish children. Their determination to stamp out the Jewish race meant that they had to target the youngest. Often French Christians, outraged by such brutality, refused to cooperate. The Germans first offered the equivalent of two dollars a head for information on where Jewish children were living. They found some takers, but not enough, and had to raise the ante. After the war a letter was discovered in German archives in which a Frenchwoman in Nice working as a concierge pointed the Gestapo to the addresses where a Jewish boy, aged ten, a girl of eight, and another boy aged three were sheltered. She demanded and got five dollars a head.[6] But despite the increased offers, the Germans still found relatively few Frenchmen willing to sell out children. None of the youngsters hidden by the Marcel Network were captured through bribes.

French Christians helped the Jews both passively and actively: passively by refusing to take money for revealing hiding places, more actively in a number of ways, from warning Jews of the timing and location of upcoming German raids to the sheltering of Jewish refugees. Hatred of the Nazi occupiers, patriotism, and the moral teachings of the Church all motivated the French to help Jews.

It can be argued that wartime France began to stand the nation's long tradition of anti-Semitism on its head. The anti-Jewish measures of the Vichy regime—forcing Jews to register, denying them jobs, arresting and deporting them—testified to the continued strength of old thinking. So did the indifference to the plight of the Jews by large segments of the French population. But, at the same time, the significant help from ordinary Frenchmen for the survival of the nation's Jews, especially the children, demonstrated the new thinking.

This new thinking slowed down the Nazi hunt for Jewish children, a godsend for Moussa and Odette. It gave them what they needed most, more time to save young lives, among them babies only a few months old. For the Abadis there was so much to do, so little time, as desperate parents on the run, no longer able to protect their children, gave them up to anyone who might help. In a letter to Garel after the war, Moussa described their task from the first days of the German stranglehold on Nice this way:

> Every day in the sinister month of September, more abandoned children were brought to us, collected by neighbors, corner grocers, concierges. We had to take them in all haste and place them as best we could. The poor little kids came to us, their eyes red, their faces drawn, able to say only poignant phrases like "Where did Papa go?"
>
> Every day brought a new cargo. Every day we had to do our best to place them, dress them, care and console these little ones who had such a thirst for tenderness and affection. Their parents had to flee precipitously, and left us children without food, clothing, or ration cards. All that had to be provided urgently.[7]

And all that was still not enough. Once the children were properly hidden, fed, clothed, and provided with false papers, they often remained disturbed by emotional problems.

Moussa particularly remembered the case of a six-year-old boy that he housed with a family of railway workers in a Nice suburb. He called on them one day to see if all was going well and the wife said to him, "Monsieur, I can't take it anymore. Since you left him to me this child says only one thing, 'Where is Mama? Where is Mama? Where is Mama?'"[8]

She pushed Moussa into a little room that served as a dining room, living room, and kitchen all in one. The child sat in an armchair, all shrivelled up. Moussa approached him, caressed his cheek, and said, "How are you, my little one?"

"Where is Mama? Where is Mama? Where is Mama?" the boy yelled.

Situations like that, Moussa said, "were our daily bread."

Odette especially remembered a boy of three from a German refugee family. The mother put the child in her hands. "I never saw a woman tremble as much as this woman did," Odette said. She placed the child with a French peasant family. She knew he would have problems—here was a little German boy torn from his parents and suddenly housed in a family that did not speak his language—but there was no other way to save him. Odette returned a few days later to check on the boy. She found him sullen, sitting under a table, and refusing to budge. Whenever he was approached, with food, with tenderness, whatever, all he would say was "Nein. Nein."

On another occasion, Moussa tried to explain to a boy of six that he had to be separated from his four-year-old sister. Families would take in one child, but not two. The boy refused to listen. He pushed his sister down on the floor and lay on top of her to protect her. "I won't let my sister go," the boy yelled. "I promised my parents I would take care of her." Somehow, Moussa found a family willing to take both of them.[9]

All the hidden children had adjustment problems, from minor ones like getting used to new surroundings to major ones such as not knowing when or if they would see their parents again. Moussa's strict security rules made it harder for them. Jewish parents were not allowed to know where their children were hidden. That way if parents got arrested they could not reveal their children's whereabouts. Children could not mail letters to their parents, even if they knew where they were, because mail opened by French police and the Gestapo could expose the hiding places. The Catholic institutions and Protestant families, often ill equipped to handle the adjustment problems of young children, did the best they could and soldiered on.

In the first few days after the Germans occupied Nice, the Abadis and their Marcel Network faced an atmosphere of terror and chaos with courage and luck. Perhaps nothing illustrated these days better than the improbable story of Georges Isserlis, a schoolboy messenger for the network.

Georges had just turned eighteen and was finishing his high school studies when the Germans arrived. His mother, a doctor, headed the OSE medical clinic where Odette Abadi worked. His father helped Jewish refugees settling in Nice. Georges, dressed in shorts and a T-shirt like any camper in the south of France, looked innocuous on his bicycle while running errands for the network. Pastor Pierre Gagnier tested the teenager by sending him to nearby Monaco with the equivalent of $1,500 in a knapsack to help smuggle Jewish children into Switzerland. He carried off the mission without a hitch. Georges had long known Odette, ever since he had met her on a skiing vacation as a kid on the slopes years before. But when it came to the Marcel Network, Georges worked for Pastor Gagnier. Unlike the bishop, the pastor had no staff, and unlike the Abadis, he could not work virtually full time for the Jews. He needed all the help he could get, so Georges was assigned to him.

In the first week they occupied Nice, the Germans set a trap at the OSE children's clinic. Soldiers occupied the office and arrested any Jews coming there for help. A Gestapo agent speaking fluent French answered the telephone, telling callers, "No. I cannot talk about that over the phone. Come in this afternoon and I will give you the information you want." The caller would be arrested on arrival. The ruse worked for a few days. Then the clinic was shut down.

Georges Isserlis fell into the trap. The day the Germans took over the building Georges was on a mission for the Marcel Network, which also did what it could to help Jewish adults. His task: deliver a stack of false identity cards to the clinic for Jewish parents seeking help there. He obtained the forged cards from Pastor Gagnier and put them in one of the two knapsacks he was carrying. The other knapsack contained his books.

A friend accompanied Georges to the clinic and offered to carry one of the knapsacks. "I didn't remember which one carried the cards, but I was a gentleman so I gave him the lighter one," Georges remembered.[10] The friend stayed outside when Georges entered the clinic and was arrested; fortunately, it turned out, with the knapsack containing only the books. Had Georges been caught with the forged cards, all the families for whom they had been prepared would have been endangered.

The friend ran off safely with the other knapsack containing the compromising cards. He went immediately to Pastor Gagnier to report Georges's arrest. Gagnier in turn demanded and got an urgent meeting with Alois Brunner, the Nazi commandant, at his headquarters in the Hotel Excelsior. In those first few days of German occupation the official policy of the Vichy government in the south was still one of arresting foreign Jewish refugees, but not French-born Jews. Gagnier hoped he could use that to their advantage, claiming that Georges had been arrested by mistake.

"I explained to Brunner in vain that Georges was born in France," Pastor Gagnier said. "I told him that Georges was a member of the French Boy Scouts."

Brunner interrupted him there. "I know," the German said, "the Jews have infiltrated everywhere."

The pastor left disappointed. "There was nothing I could do to budge him," he said.[11] Brunner had no patience with the distinction Vichy made between foreign Jews and Jews born in France. Brunner intended to arrest all Jews from the moment he set foot in Nice.

The next day Pastor Gagnier left by train for Arles, where Georges's parents were visiting his uncle. The minister wanted to inform the parents of their son's arrest. The train made several stops on the way. In Marseille, during a lengthy stop, Gagnier got called to the stationmaster's office, much to his surprise, to receive an urgent telegram from his wife. The wire said, "Baby is on your train." Baby was their code name for Georges Isserlis. Incredibly, Madame Gagnier had learned in Nice, Georges was on the same train as her husband.[12]

Georges had been put on the train along with other young Jews arrested by the Germans—one of the first groups of prisoners shipped out of Nice by Nazi forces still improvising at that early stage. Their prison car, attached to the end of a regular passenger train to Paris, was to be taken off at Drancy, the transit point for Auschwitz. But Georges and the other prisoners were not even handcuffed. Armed guards stood at the ends of the car, preventing them from leaving the train when it stopped at stations. Otherwise the prisoners could move around the car or go to the bathroom when they liked. Georges began to think about how he might escape when the train stopped at Arles.

Pastor Gagnier had no trouble finding Georges's car, guarded by the SS at the end of the train while it was stopped at the Marseille station. He was even able to speak to Georges through the window of his compartment. "I will inform your parents about your arrest," the clergyman promised.

"Tell them not to despair," Georges said. "All is not lost. I hope to see them very soon."

When the train left, Georges went to the toilet. The window there was fixed inside a wooden frame, covered in a thick varnish. Georges chipped away at the varnish to discover that ten copper screws held the frame in place. Breaking the glass window to jump from the train would have been heard by the guards and probably gotten him shot, Georges figured. But unscrewing the frame would let him remove the window quietly and sneak off. That would not be a problem. "There is a God," Georges thought. The Germans, expecting no resistance from the young Jews they had arrested, did not bother to search their prisoners before they boarded the train. "I had a nail file on me and began to unscrew the frame," Georges explained.[13]

He took more trips to the toilet, each time loosening more screws until there were only two left. Night fell as the train neared Arles. Georges decided to jump there, but first he needed to alert the five other prisoners, all in their twenties, who shared his compartment. "I will leave the widow open for you," he told them. "Take advantage of it and follow me."

"You're crazy," one of the other prisoners replied. "You'll hurt yourself or be shot. Besides, there is no need. It's all been a mistake. When we get to Drancy we will all be released." They were still under the illusion that only foreign-born Jews got arrested, not French Jews.

Georges knew there was no mistake. His French-born sister had already been deported to Drancy and on to Auschwitz. "Either you are Jewish or you're not," Georges told them. "That's all there is to it. If you are Jewish there is no error and you won't be liberated."

But he could not convince the others. Only Georges jumped. All the others died in the gas chambers.

Georges jumped as the train slowed down to enter Arles. He cut his shoe and tore a hole in his trousers but landed unhurt. Then he quickly made his way to the station, where he met Pastor Gagnier, who had just gotten off the same train. The two of them rode off together on bicycles borrowed from the pastor of Arles to tell Georges's parents that all was well.

The German guards had to lie to avoid blame for Georges's escape. They claimed they had shot him as he tried to flee. After the war, Georges saw a German document listing himself as having been shot dead while attempting to escape.

The narrow escape from death in wartime France motivated Georges Isserlis to do humanitarian work in later life. He became a surgeon, eventually for a French charity, Doctors of the World, traveling to French-speaking Africa, as well as to Mongolia, Sri Lanka, and other developing nations to perform operations. Well into his eighties, Georges decided "a retirement of doing crossword puzzles and watching television is not the answer." Although he could no longer operate, he continued the work for charities—teaching, consulting, and helping surgeons in Africa, a living testament to the enormous amount of good works made possible by the saving of only one life.

7

SAME CHILD, NEW IDENTITY

During the chaotic first weeks that the Germans occupied Nice, the Abadis operated on the run. Fearing the worst, they rushed children into Catholic institutions or Protestant families without adequately preparing them to assume the new identities that would save their lives. That was a mistake. Any child thoughtlessly mentioning his Jewish name at any moment risked alerting an informer and sealing his fate.

From the fourth week on, Moussa and Odette became more methodical, taking whatever time was needed to prepare the children, despite the dangers of any delay in the transfer to hiding places. Moussa called the process "depersonalization"—the training of the youngsters to forget who they were and become someone else. Before being hidden, they would have to learn new Christian names for themselves and their parents, new places of birth, and, hardest of all, they would have to say their parents were dead. Many feared just saying that could somehow make it so.

In the typical cover story, the child would have to learn that he or she was born into a Christian family in a French colony like Algeria or Morocco, places where the German occupiers could not check the birth records. The parents had supposedly died—perhaps in a bombing raid during the Allied landing in North Africa—the reason the child had been sent to France, to a convent or boarding school, or to live with a foster family.

Odette recounted one depersonalization session she conducted with a small boy, demonstrating how difficult the process could be.[1]

"Your name is no longer Smoilovich," she told the boy. "It is Dupont. That's what your papers say. So, repeat after me: Dupont."

"Dupont."

"Good. Again."

"Dupont."

"One more time. What is your name?"

"Dupont."

"Very good. You may leave."

The boy turned and walked away.

"Oh, Smoilovich," Odette called out.

Without thinking, the boy responded to his real name by turning back toward Odette. Odette sighed. They had to start again. "What is your name?"

"I can't do this," he told Odette. "How are my parents going to find me after the war if I have a new name?"

"They will. But for now you must answer to Dupont. Repeat. What is your name?"

"Dupont."

"Again."

"Dupont."

Depersonalization took place at the Convent of the Clarisses in Nice. Mother Antonia, the mother superior, turned over to the Abadis a pavilion outside the convent walls that had housed a summer camp for Catholic children. She authorized two nuns, Sister Andrea and Sister Emmanuelle, to help. When Moussa learned that Sister Andrea was seriously ill, and had only a few months at most to live, he urged her to return to the convent to rest, but she would have none of it. "Monsieur Marcel," she said, "give me the joy, the happiness, and the grace before dying to help you save these children."

Three months later, a priest arrived at the bishop's residence with a message for Moussa. "Sister Andrea has left us," the priest said. "I attended her during her last moments and she said to me, 'Tell Monsieur Marcel that I will pray for him and the children.'"[2]

The older children, aged twelve to sixteen, had the easiest time with depersonalization. They understood when Moussa told them their lives depended on it. Yet even for them, the experience could be traumatic. Jeannette Wolgust was fourteen when she went through the process. She became "Jeanne Moreau"—long before an actress made that name famous. For the rest of the war, Jeannette had to suppress her real name and say she was Jeanne Moreau. The effort became so ingrained in her that after the war she could hardly say her real name. Every time she tried, her voice would break. She noticed it only many years later, after her son asked her why she lowered her voice whenever she said her name.[3]

At age fifteen, Françoise Knopf had to take on a new identity and pretend she came from Morocco. Her visceral reaction: "I was so worried about disappearing from the surface of the earth that I put a testament of sorts into a bottle and buried it." At the time Françoise was hidden at a hospital, in an area under constant bombardment. "We didn't know if we were going to survive from one day to the next and I didn't want to be buried without anyone knowing my real name," she explained. So she planted her testament in the hospital garden. "I stated who I was, the names of my parents, why I was at the hospital, and where I came from. I revealed that I was never Moroccan but French. I gave my true identity."[4]

Not surprisingly, children under ten had the hardest time keeping to their new identities. "These children needed trust, friendship, and affection," Odette said. "They would tell secrets to each other."[5] At any time, a six-year-old might say to her new best friend, "My real name is not Cecile Leblanc; it's Rebecca Epstein. But don't tell anyone. It's a secret."

The new best friend would, of course, blab to other girls, and soon the mother superior of the convent school would inform Moussa that the Jewish name was generally known. Moussa had to urgently find another hiding place for Rebecca and lecture her on the importance of keeping her real name a real secret. He never knew when the Germans might raid in search of hidden children, so he could not leave a child at a convent if her Jewish identity were known. It was mortally dangerous for the child—and the convent.

For the younger ones, Moussa and Odette turned depersonalization into games. They would play teachers and students, calling on the children by their new names to act out classroom situations. They would sing songs with lyrics containing the new names. With children old enough to read, the Abadis would put the new names on scraps of paper to be held in little fists. Each child would then open the fist to see his new name. Closing and opening the hand over and over again would help register the new identity. The Abadis also had toys made out of bits of wood with the new names carved on them. Both Moussa's training as an actor and the university course he took in child psychology helped in the role-playing games.

It was far from all fun and games, however. Moussa had a temper. He would lose it when he grew impatient, and depersonalization sorely tried his patience. Children could not be released from the Clarisses convent to safe hiding places until they knew all their lessons perfectly—their new names and place of birth, the names and fate of their parents, where their father worked, and the rest of the cover stories. Sometimes the process took weeks. Moussa would start gently, telling the child, "This is very important. You must remember."[6] But as time wore on, he got testier. In bouts of temper, he would raise his voice, bark at the children to do better, and regret his behavior afterward.

"The whole depersonalization process," he said many years later, "was atrocious, odious, awful, for hour after hour."[7]

Jeannette Wolgust recalled it being worse than that. "For Moussa, the need to change the identity of a child was very difficult psychologically," she said. "He had the impression that he had stolen something from the children when he took away their real names. He felt that enormously, that he had wounded the children. And he was very much affected by all this."[8]

Jeannette spoke with authority. She probably knew Moussa better than anyone other than Odette. Among the former hidden children, Jeannette alone kept up a continuous relationship with the Abadis from the end of the war until the end of their lives. She became their closest friend, the executor of their estate, and the keeper of their personal archives. By some accounts, Moussa was depressed after the war from the effects of depersonalization and other torment in his clandestine work. The most Jeannette would say, however, was that "After the war, it took him years to overcome this trauma. He was a very sensitive man."[9]

After the chaotic first three weeks of the German occupation, most of the children taken in by the Abadis went through depersonalization. The relatively few who did not were either foreign refugees who spoke little or no French or were deeply religious youngsters who refused to eat anything but kosher food. As such, they could hardly pass for French Christians, so there was little point in hiding them in France. Instead they joined the groups smuggled out to Switzerland or Spain.[10]

Every child, however, had what the Abadis called a *fiche*, a file card with vital information. The cards listed the child's real name, date and place of birth, nationality, and last known address. They also contained the name, profession, and whereabouts of the parents. If the parents were known to have been deported, the fiche listed some other relative or contact, where possible. The child's photograph, fingerprints, and false name were also included. After the war, these cards would be crucial in the effort to reunite children with loved ones.

Moussa said he had three copies made of each card. One set got buried in the garden of the bishop's residence in Nice. A second, Moussa said, went out with the groups that traveled to Switzerland, with requests to the guides to hand them over to the International Red Cross in Geneva. The third set was the active one. While under preparation, these cards would be hidden between books in the bishop's library. Once finished, Moussa and Odette kept them.

"The fiches were a serious problem of conscience," Moussa said. "If the Gestapo got hold of one, they would know the real name and that could lead to arrest. But if we did not make these cards, who would know the real name of the child or how to reunite him with his family?"

Deciding that the risks had to be taken, Moussa made a card for every one of the hidden children.[11]

8

THREE GIRLS

The children taken in by the Abadis ranged from toddlers to adolescents. Often, though at tender ages, they had already survived enough traumas to fill a lifetime, all before undergoing the rigors of depersonalization. Françoise Knopf's nightmare, for example, began years before her family narrowly escaped arrest in a Nazi raid because they left the door of their Nice hotel room partly open, and the Germans thought their room had already been searched.

Françoise was eleven years old in 1939 when Hitler invaded Poland. The entire population of her hometown, Sarreguemines, in the Lorraine region of France, had to be evacuated the day the war began because it was right on the German border. As it turned out, the Germans did not invade France until the next year, but by then Françoise and her family were already veteran refugees. From 1939 to 1943, she struggled through four difficult years before getting to Moussa and Odette. While children between the ages of eleven and fifteen normally face nothing worse than the pangs of adolescence, Françoise spent those years running for her life.

Her childhood began happily enough. Her father, Jacques Knopf, owned a men's clothing store and managed to put aside considerable savings. Her mother, Sara, kept an orthodox Jewish home for Françoise and her younger sister, Paulette. Then war broke out.

On leaving the family home for what turned out to be the last time, they went by car to Nancy in northeast France to stay with friends for a few months. Then for three years, they slowly moved south, always refugees, always on the run, hiding a few months here, a few months there, before finally crossing the Line of Demarcation in the spring of 1942. They were arrested as soon as they crossed into the Free Zone. "My father was put in one camp, and my mother, Paulette, and I in another," Françoise said.[1]

Jacques Knopf had been wounded serving France in World War I. Regardless, French police working for Vichy arrested him and sent him to a labor camp.

Sarah and her two daughters were released first. Paulette, three years younger than Françoise, suffered from leukemia. They applied for relocation so Paulette could be treated outside the camp. A sympathetic French official signed the papers to get them out. Sarah and the two girls made their way to a village near Lyon. Then Françoise, fourteen years old, went back for her father.

The commandant of Jacques's labor camp gave him a pass to leave for dental treatment. "Take all the time you want," the commandant said, hinting that Jacques could disappear. The commandant, a Frenchman, "was a good man," Françoise said. "He gave passes to anyone who asked for one, because he hated his job. He knew the fate awaiting Jews who stayed in the camp and he wanted to get as many out as he could."

On leaving the camp, Jacques met up with Françoise. Together they took a train across the Free Zone to Lyon, even though they had no proper papers and risked arrest at any moment. "Throughout the train trip I walked ahead of my father looking for trouble," Françoise said. "We were checked twice. Each time I talked to the guards while he hid in the bathroom. I was fourteen years old, but I looked eighteen."

A cousin in Lyon, Madame Jeaune, had managed to stay in the city, working as a concierge and as a seamstress, because she had false identity papers. She had a two-room flat. Françoise and Jacques stayed in one of her rooms. For food Françoise went off to the nearby village where Sarah and Paulette lived, carrying an empty suitcase. She filled the suitcase with cheeses, hard-boiled eggs, and chicken for the trip back. "There was nothing kosher," Françoise went on. "I took whatever I could back to my father, always worried that someone would smell the cheese and that I would have to open the suitcase."

The clandestine life in Lyon did not last long. As soon as they could, Françoise and her family joined up and moved into the Savoy region, then in Italian hands, above Nice in the French Alps. It was a good solution—for a while. The Knopfs were together again, Françoise could return to school, Paulette could get medical treatment. "The Italians were nice and kind," Françoise remembered. "They serenaded us. We didn't even know a war was going on until one night they bombed a Resistance unit. It was horrible—bodies on stretchers everywhere."

With the fighting coming closer, and the possibility that the Germans might replace the Italians, the family decided it was time to cross the Alpine border into Switzerland. Françoise and her father went first. They hired a guide for the difficult trip over icy ground in the winter weather of late 1942. Snow often covered the trail. Françoise carried a knapsack with one change of clothing. "I was cold, tired, thirsty, and scared," she recalled. "The worst thing was the silence. I always kept my ears open listening for the barking of dogs. Armed German guards patrolled the region with the help of tracker dogs. If the dogs picked up your scent, you were finished."

Somehow, they made it across late at night, expecting a warm welcome from the Swiss. Instead, they got a nasty one from officials at the border. "To the Swiss we were refugees," Françoise explained. "We were nothing, and they were very rude. 'Go there, do this,' they said, full of self-importance. They could decide if you could stay or not. Your life depended on them. They were wary of taking in too many refugees."

The Swiss wanted to send Françoise and her father back, until Jacques reminded them that their own law required them to admit adults accompanied by minor children. Reluctantly, the Swiss let them stay.

But in the end, they could not. Sarah and Paulette were supposed to have followed with another guide. Jacques and Françoise waited for them, all nerves, and in vain. Finally the second guide arrived to say that Paulette had a fever and could not risk the trip in the cold winter weather. Devastated, Jacques decided there was no other choice than to go back to France and try the harrowing trip to Switzerland again, when Paulette would be stronger. Next time all four members of their family—father, mother, and two sisters—would go together. They would take turns carrying Paulette. That, anyway, was the plan. Françoise and her father did indeed go back to France. But there was never a second trip out. Although Jacques Knopf gave up his freedom in Switzerland to go back and rescue his youngest daughter, tragically, neither he nor his wife would survive the Nazi occupation of France.

Françoise, aged fifteen, lived out the next few months with her family in a Savoy mountain village under Italian control. By then Jacques's savings had nearly run out, in part because of the money paid to guides for the failed trip to Switzerland. The Knopfs resorted to selling the family silver, piece by piece, in order to get by. They remained in the village until the Germans arrived in Nice in September 1943. At that point Italian soldiers on their way home trucked Françoise and her family, along with other refugees, out of the Savoy region. "I was sick all the way down the mountains," she said. "When we got to Nice they gave us our papers and told us, 'Run because we cannot do anything more for you.'

"I looked at Nice, awed by the blue Mediterranean Sea. Such a beautiful place, I thought, and we have to run and hide or we will be killed here."

The family checked into a small hotel, waiting for a rescue from Donati's ships that never sailed. After the Nazis raided their hotel, only missing them by a hair, many other dangers awaited. The family had to leave the hotel. "We were homeless," Françoise said, "going around the streets, not knowing anyone."

Without ration cards they had trouble finding food. Paulette needed medicine and a doctor's care. When night fell, and an 8 P.M. curfew took effect, they had to be off the streets. So they found a door to an empty courtyard, sat down on the stones, and fell asleep. At dawn the next morning, Françoise noticed a church across the street. "Let's go there," she said. "At least Paulette will be able to lie on the benches." She thought the church would be like a synagogue, but there were no benches inside, only chairs.

On her own, Françoise decided to talk to the priest. "I was fifteen, not a baby." She went right up to the priest and told him, "Father, we spent the night out on the street. I have a very sick sister. We are Jews and need your help."

"What have you done, my child?" the priest asked.

"Nothing."

"You must have done something bad if the authorities are after you," the priest said. "My advice to you is to go to the authorities and turn yourself in."

Françoise walked away. "We won't find help from the church," she told her parents. "We have to find it somewhere else."

Again they wandered the streets. Françoise became the family provider. Because her parents had national identity cards stamped with the word "Jew," they had to keep to the shadows. But children under the age of sixteen, like Françoise, did not have to carry such cards. They could move around the city more easily without fear of being stopped, especially if they did not look Jewish, and Françoise did not. Her dark hair, tanned complexion, and straight nose helped her blend in with the Mediterranean look of the Nice population. So Françoise went for the food. She would buy a kilo of sugar on the black market, trade that for cigarettes, and that in turn for something for the family to eat. All the while, as they barely survived, the Knopfs had to keep away from German patrols. They knew they needed to do something else.

In their meandering, the Knopfs ran into family friends, the Kleins, also refugees surviving on the streets of Nice. The Kleins had heard about Moussa and Odette Abadi, but they were determined to keep their daughter, Madeleine, with them as long as they could. The Kleins, however, did tell the Knopfs about the Abadis. The next morning Françoise and Paulette each packed a little case and went with their parents to meet Odette at a small office. "It was the place where I saw my parents for the last time," Françoise recalled.

The Knopfs spoke with Odette, addressing her as Sylvie. At the end of the conversation, Sarah Knopf told her daughters, "You are going with Sylvie." Then Jacques took the girls in his arms. He blessed them and said, "We will see each other again."

"I was angry and hurt," Françoise remembered, "because my parents had not discussed this with me. I felt that I was already an adult. I had done grown-up things for them because being on the streets was a danger for them. They should have discussed important things with me, and they didn't. My father knew I was angry, but he knew how to convince me they were right."

"You are the only one who can help Paulette," Jacques said.

"And that was that. We left with Sylvie."

"Sylvie" took the sisters with four other girls to a boarding school for their depersonalization. The Abadis had not yet set up the system at the Clarisses. At the school, the Jewish girls had to stay hidden in a small room that the other students and most of the staff thought was empty, and they had to sleep two to a bed. After 5 P.M. they were told not to make any noise and not to go to the bathroom for the rest of the night to avoid discovery.

According to Françoise's recounting of the story, a man in a trench coat came in on the second day. "I am Monsieur Marcel," he said. He told the girls that they would be hidden in convents under new names and would have to pretend to be Catholics. He also explained, as gently as possible, why they could have no further contact with their parents until the end of the war. "I am going to teach you your new names," he said. "The next time I come, I will call you by those names, so I want you to remember them."

For Françoise Knopf, the oldest girl in the room, depersonalization was easy. She understood her life depended on changing her name. Her first name sounded French, so she could keep that. But because her family name could be taken as Jewish, she became Françoise Brun. Paulette too became a Brun. They had to learn that they were born in Mogador, Morocco, and that their parents, caught in the war in North Africa, had sent them to a convent in France for safety.

The younger girls in the room, seven years old or less, didn't understand the business about new names and began to cry. "You cannot cry any more," Monsieur Marcel told them.

The children looked at him, uncomprehending. "It was pathetic," Françoise said, referring to his stern, unsympathetic reaction. Monsieur Marcel was still himself learning the ropes in those first few days of the German occupation. He would get better at the human side of depersonalization.

Moussa Abadi was no saint. His temper, his impatience, his barking at innocent little children learning their new names too slowly for him, all revealed ordinary human frailities. Like other mortals, his character had its good and bad sides. Above all it was his stubborn, uncompromising determination to save lives—despite the temper tantrums and other defects—that enabled the Marcel Network to succeed.

When Monsieur Marcel left, Françoise tried to explain to the younger girls why they had to learn the new names. The next day, Sylvie took Françoise to the Joan of Arc convent in Grasse to begin a new life. Paulette went to a children's hospital.

✦

Marthe Artzstein traveled a very different road to Moussa, but one that was in its own way just as complex and harrowing as the road Françoise had been forced to follow. Françoise, at least, stayed with her parents until she was handed over to Odette. Marthe, at the age of eight, found herself without parents and had to save herself. "I was completely alone in the world," she said.[2]

Her father, Herco Artzstein, a Polish-born Jew living in France as a tailor since 1929, was arrested in 1941 and sent to a labor camp south of Paris. In the summer of 1942, Herco volunteered to harvest corn, managed to escape, and made his way to the Free Zone to hide. The family was preparing to join him, but they never had the time to carry out their plans.

For Bastille Day, the French National Holiday on July 14, 1942, Marthe left her mother, Havasura, and her brother, Noel, in Paris and went off to the country house of the family nanny to play in the fresh air. Three days later her mother and brother were deported in a massive Nazi roundup of Paris Jews. When Marthe returned to the family apartment, no one was there.

The nanny left Marthe with her parents' friends who lived on the ground floor of the building, the Weiss family. The Weisses were Hungarian Jews. At the time, in deference to Hitler's Hungarian allies, the Nazis were not arresting Hungarian Jews, but that restraint did not last long. Months later, Marthe awoke to find that the Weisses had been arrested during the night. She climbed out a ground-floor window, letting herself down onto a Paris street. "At first I didn't know where to go," Marthe said, "but I think maturity comes very quickly to children in times of war."

The Weisses had friends they used to visit in the evening. Often they brought Marthe along. She remembered the address and how to get there. "But when I arrived they said they could not keep me because they themselves were hiding." They put her in a home for war orphans.

Marthe kept her head. She remembered the secret address her father had given the family to contact him, and sent him a letter there. "It was like the bottle you throw into the sea," she said, "but he received it."

As an escaped prisoner hunted by the police, Herco Artzstein could not go to Paris to collect his daughter. So he turned over the job of retrieving Marthe to an aunt who lived in a small town in central France, Borg-les-Orgues. The aunt sent a friend, the mayor of her town, to Paris to make the arrangements with the director of the children's home. It was a tough assignment. "The director did not want to give me to just anybody," Marthe said. "He made me hide in a garbage can that was empty but smelled terrible."

Eventually the mayor convinced the director to part with Marthe. The girl was afraid, not knowing the mayor, but went with him to her aunt's house, where her father reclaimed her. Together they hid in the Savoy region under Italian control until September 1943 when the Italians left. Like Françoise, Marthe and her father were trucked down the mountains to Nice by Italians on their way home. Marthe called her hair-raising ride "Dante-esque" because "when we got to Nice the Germans were practically on our heels."

Nice was too dangerous for Marthe's father. He spoke good French but with the heavy foreign accent typical of a Jewish refugee. He could not risk encountering the city's constant patrols and searches. Better to hide in the countryside, if he could find a safe home for Marthe. "I was a burden for my father," she said. "To save himself he had to find a place to put me so he could move freely." Father and daughter stayed briefly with a cousin in Nice until arrangements could be made. Eventually, through contacts in the Jewish community, Herco Artzstein found Moussa and Odette Abadi.

"Parting with my father was rather dramatic because I didn't know if I would ever see him again," Marthe said. "I had already been taken from this one to that one, very difficult for a child. Now it was good-bye and I didn't know where he was going. I can't even remember what we said."

Marthe was taken to the Clarisses convent where Moussa replaced her family name of Artsztein with the Christian name of Arthieu. By then she was nine, old enough for the depersonalization to be relatively easy for her.

As Marthe remembered it, Moussa never had to tell the older children they risked their lives if they didn't learn their new names and cover stories perfectly. "We knew the climate," Marthe said. "We felt it. He didn't have to say it."

She too recalled Moussa getting angry with the younger children when they couldn't get their new names right, but, under the circumstances, she thought such bursts of temper understandable. "He was impatient because there was so little time and it was urgent to place us," Marthe said. "Certainly he was a very good human being, a great man. He did his best to put the youngsters at ease."

"Your parents will find you," Moussa kept saying to all the children.

"He was trying to reassure us," Marthe explained, "but we were not reassured just like that."

Marthe went off to the Joan of Arc convent in Grasse, where she would soon meet Françoise Knopf and Jeannette Wolgust. The three of them would become lifelong friends.

✦

Jeannette Wolgust was born in Warsaw as Jeannette Swita, her maiden name, and moved to Paris as a two-year-old. She arrived in Nice with her parents and her younger brother, Jean, in July 1943. Jeannette, then nearly fourteen, remembers the summer months of 1943 in Nice as "a vacation of sun and sea."[3] She also remembers going to a children's clinic where Odette gave her mother a slip of paper containing the address of a pharmacy where the Abadis could be contacted.

When the Germans arrived, the family tried to hide, but soon the parents realized their children would be safer in other hands. They still had the address from Odette. With a heavy heart, her father took Jeannette and Jean, then five, to the pharmacy to say good-bye. "I don't remember any screaming, shouting, or crying," Jeannette said. "It was the most extraordinary thing. My little brother and I didn't understand anything. We were anesthetized. I must have said good-bye in a rather cold, indifferent fashion. All I knew was that we had to stay there. And a little while later, Moussa appeared."

Jeannette would have recognized Odette. She didn't know Moussa at all, but she liked him from the start. Unlike Françoise and Marthe, whose first impressions of Moussa recalled his sterner side—a man under pressure to get them renamed and safely hidden as quickly as possible—Jeannette recalled most of all his kinder, softer side. "He had a warm voice and knew how to make a child feel comfortable," Jeannette said.

She had no trouble undergoing depersonalization and becoming Jeanne Moreau. The hardest part was the separation from her little brother. Moussa explained, gently she recalled, that the Catholics had no co-ed boarding schools. "Automatically, I was going to the nuns and my brother was going to the priests." In the end, Jean actually went to live with a Protestant family.

Jeannette was taken to the Joan of Arc convent in Grasse, one of four Jewish girls hidden there by the Abadis. Jeannette was fourteen, Françoise, fifteen, and Marthe, nine; Denise Touchard, the fourth girl, was ten. For them, life at the convent, cut off from all family ties, trying to learn how to pass for Catholics, would be full of new traumas. Only their friendship for each other, and the tender loving care Odette provided on monthly visits, got them through the ordeal.

9
The Convent

Take a young Jewish girl, give her a new name, put her in a convent, and tell her to pass for a Catholic. This was easier said than done, Jeannette Wolgust quickly realized at the Joan of Arc convent in Grasse. Only the mother superior and an abbot who came to teach there knew her real identity. Jeannette was supposed to keep it secret from the other nuns and all the students, a tall order since she arrived not knowing the first thing about how Catholics practice their religion.

In one early test, Jeannette heard the girls in her class whispering about confession. Jeannette had no idea what that meant. Worse, the word she heard them use was "confess." At age fourteen Jeannette knew enough French jargon to break the sound of "confess" into two words—"con" and "fess," slang referring to body parts covered by underwear. Jeannette knew that kind of talk was not used in polite society, and certainly not in a Catholic schoolroom. "But I couldn't ask the girls what it meant, because they seemed to understand and I didn't," she said. Confused, she asked to go to the bathroom to compose her thoughts, "And when I came back there was nobody in the class. I didn't know what to do."

Jeannette ran down the hall, heading toward the mother superior's office, worried that she had made some terrible mistake. The abbot who taught at the school stopped her.

"What happened to you?" the abbot asked.

"I lost the other girls," Jeannette replied. "They started talking about 'confess' and then, suddenly, they all disappeared."

Jeannette began to cry. The abbot burst out laughing. He understood that the girls had left the class and gone to confession while Jeannette was out of the room. They had used a second door she never noticed.

"He calmed me down," Jeannette said, "escorted me back to the class, and said, 'See that door?' Then he opened the door that led to the chapel and the confessional." The abbot showed her the confessional, and how to behave in one.

"It sounds funny now," Jeannette recalled decades later, "but it was not funny then. I was frightened because I understood there were many things I was supposed to know but didn't. It was all so natural for the other girls, and I didn't understand."[1]

Nights at the Joan of Arc convent, a boarding school, raised other fears. Jeannette and Françoise Knopf slept in beds next to each other in the dormitory. Both feared they might reveal their Jewish identities while talking in their sleep. So they decided that they would take turns sleeping. The girl still awake was supposed to rouse her sleeping friend from any dangerous talk. "Of course, she fell asleep and so did I," Jeannette said. "The next morning we understood that this was not going to work."

Nighttime also brought reminders of the war around them. The girls could hear the Allied bombing attacks near Nice, some twenty miles away. American and British aircraft targeted bridges and other strategic assets in German hands. When the bombs got closer to Grasse, the students had to sleep in the catacombs under the cathedral to be safe at night. Jeannette was frightened by the bombs, but more scared by the thought of revealing her true identity.

As time went on, other problems arose. The nuns told Jeannette that when she grew up she would take her vows and become a nun in Indochina. "That was not exactly the way I saw my life," she said.

Still, all the Catholic training had an effect on her. One day in chapel Jeannette began to question her own religion. She felt ashamed and decided to write a letter to her parents saying that she would remain true to their Jewish teachings. Jeannette did not know where to reach her parents, but she did know the address of an uncle. So she sent the letter to him, hoping that he could pass it on. Although Moussa insisted on strict security rules against writing to relatives, Jeannette decided this letter was so important that she had to defy the rules, sneak out of the convent, and mail it. Fortunately for her, the letter caused no trouble. The Nazis opened French mail, but clearly not all of it. Later Jeannette would receive an answer by safer means—a secret message passed through agents of the Jewish Resistance—saying both her parents were alive and well in hiding.

✦

When Françoise Knopf arrived at the convent, she was fifteen. The mother superior, Mère Marie-Thérèse, pulled her aside and told her that she would be the leader, responsible for the three younger Jewish girls. Françoise felt up to the task, already mature for her age. Long before the war, her father began taking Jewish refugees from Germany into the family home in Sarreguemines on the German border. Often Françoise slept in the attic with the maid to free up her bedroom for newcomers. She learned about hardship, resistance, and sacrifice. Another child might have cried when told that she would be responsible for the other girls. Françoise just listened quietly and nodded.

The mother superior also told Françoise that because of wartime shortages there would be very little food. "Then later I heard from another nun that this was because the Jews had sold all the food on the black market," Françoise said. "That did not go down too well with me, but I couldn't do or say anything. I had to take care of the other children."

Françoise remembered Jeannette as a blonde with light blue eyes and a sunny disposition. "I liked her the minute I met her." The two younger girls, Denise and Marthe, she described as "morose." Poor Marthe's head was shaved because she had lice. She put on a little hat and never took it off. "From the day I met her to the end of the war, I never saw her without the hat," Françoise recalled. "She let me wash her but she would not let me remove the hat." For the three other Jewish girls, Marthe became "Martoune," an affectionate nickname. They would call her nothing else at the convent.

Denise, a timid, introverted girl with brown hair, rarely said much. She already suspected that the Germans had killed both her parents. Little Denise wore her sorrow on her face. By then Françoise feared that she had also lost her parents, and Martoune her mother. Only Jeannette knew for sure that both of her parents were still alive. Not surprisingly, she was the liveliest and the happiest of the four Jewish girls at the convent.

Françoise decided it was her duty to protect the other three. "I watched them like my little sisters," she remembered. "One night Martoune did something silly and was punished by the young nun who slept in our dorm. She made Martoune get out of bed, kneel down, and recite prayers. Martoune recited them all right, and then fell asleep on the very cold tile floor. I waited for the nun to come back and say 'that's enough,' but she never came. So I picked up Martoune, and put her in my bed and we both fell asleep. You can imagine what happened the next morning, two girls in one bed.

"The mother superior wanted to punish Martoune and me. I said, 'You cannot do that without hearing me out.' And I threatened to call the bishop if she didn't listen to me."

Needless to say, the mother superior was not used to such back talk, least of all from a young girl. But she listened. Françoise had been trained by her father to stand up for her rights in the face of anti-Semitism or bullying in the schools of her hometown. "That's why I said what I did to the mother superior."

Françoise explained that Martoune had done as she was told, recited the prayers, and then fallen asleep on the cold tile floor. "I picked her up and put her in my bed because I didn't want her to catch pneumonia. And that's how we fell asleep."[2] Mère Marie-Thérèse believed Françoise and punished the nun instead.

Jeannette, Françoise, Martoune, and Denise were all good students. They rapidly learned their prayers and the other elements of Catholic lore because their lives depended on it. They also excelled because they had nothing else to do but to stay at the convent and study when the Catholic girls went home for the weekend. Coming to the convent from French secular schools was another advantage for the Jewish girls. Their prior education had been superior.

"The teachers at the convent were poor," Françoise explained. "They taught things like manners." Some of the Catholic girls at the convent came from the wealthy families that had made Grasse the perfume center of France. As Françoise put it, "The parents didn't really want their daughters to be educated. They only wanted them trained for lives as good wives, good mothers, and good Christians." Among the other Catholic students, she said, "were ignorant peasant girls who wanted to become nuns and be married to Jesus."

Jeannette despaired of ever getting her high school diploma because she needed a foreign language for that and none was taught at the convent. "I'll teach you," Françoise offered. "I speak German." Nearly everyone in Françoise's hometown on the French-German border was bilingual.

Bishop Rémond occasionally visited the convents and boarding schools where Jewish children were hidden. If he met a child he knew to be Jewish, he tried to reassure him or her that their deception in pretending to be good Catholics was no sin. Lisette Levy was nine when the bishop came to visit the convent where she had been hidden. Like all the other girls who met the bishop, she had to kneel before him and kiss his hand. The bishop knew her true identity. Rémond winked at Lisette, pointed to the sky, and told her, "He will forgive you up there just as we forgive you down here."[3]

When the bishop visited the Joan of Arc convent in Grasse, he asked to see the best students in the school. The nuns chose the four Jewish girls to come forward. It was one of the proudest moments of their stay.

That moment paled, however, when compared to the monthly visits by Odette. For Jeannette, Françoise, and Martoune, the strongest memory of their life at the convent was of spending precious time with her. She came to pay their school fees, bring their ration cards, and check on their studies and their health. But she stayed to give the girls much more than that. She hugged them, squeezed their hands, and took them on her lap in the closest thing they would know to a mother's love while in hiding. She brought them little presents—a bar of chocolate, or a small toy. Just the look of her was a breath of fresh air for the girls—a pretty blonde not yet thirty with a smiling face, full of warmth and tenderness, all in sharp contrast to the humorless nuns. "Odette was our big love," Jeannette said. "She was joyful, bubbly like champagne, with a singing voice. She would laugh and make us laugh." Odette would stay for an hour or an hour and a half. Their time with Odette was the big event in the girls' lives. According to Martoune, "We looked forward to her visits as if the Messiah was coming."

They called her "Mademoiselle." Jeannette had first known her as Odette Rosenstock, the doctor at a clinic in Nice, and was terrified of blurting out that name by accident, thereby blowing Odette's cover as Sylvie Delattre. So Jeannette persuaded the other girls to call Odette simply Mademoiselle. Soon everyone joined in. One of the nuns, or one of the eighty Catholic students at the convent school, would announce Odette's arrival by telling the Jewish girls, "Your Mademoiselle is here."

They would meet in a reception room, with Odette awaiting them in an armchair, her arms outstretched. Martoune, the youngest at nine, would be the first to jump into her lap. Denise, ten, stood at one side of the chair leaning in, to be the second closest. The older girls, Françoise and Jeannette, closed in where they could. Occasionally they got some lap time too. Odette had caresses and kind words for each of them in turn. Inevitably there were little jealousies when she left. "Mademoiselle took you in her arms longer than me," one of the girls would say. Or, "You're lucky. She took you in her lap."

Odette was far more than a mother figure. For Jeannette, she was also the only link to life before the war. Sometimes Odette brought Jeannette a letter from her parents or took one back, carried by trusted members of the Resistance.

For all the Jewish girls at the convent in Grasse, Odette was the only continuing link to the outside world, the only human being they saw regularly who came from beyond the convent walls. "I needed contact with someone from the outside," Jeannette emphasized, "because in the convent we knew absolutely nothing about the real world."

The Jewish girls exercised by walking inside the convent grounds with the nuns. But they could not leave without the special permission of the mother superior, something that was almost never granted. German soldiers patrolled Grasse. They or the French police stopped and questioned children on the streets. Indeed the girls always feared the Germans would enter the convent to check their papers. "The Germans had boots with iron tips and heels that made a lot of noise," Martoune explained. "We could hear a squadron marching outside the convent. The sound of the boots always scared us. And when the noise decreased, we would say to each other, 'Whew, it's not for us.'"[4]

Just once, Odette managed to get permission from the mother superior to take Jeannette and Françoise, the two older girls, out for the afternoon. She took them to have their hair done, and topped off the outing with ice cream at a café. "Finally, we lived like two normal girls," Jeannette said. "It was fabulous."

Odette could also be strict. She insisted that all the girls study hard, but warned them when their convent studies seemed to be leading them away from their Jewish roots toward Catholicism. "When you are living in a religious boarding school," Martoune recalled, "all those prayers in the morning—before entering class, before leaving class, before and after eating—all those prayers all the time begin to mark you, and after a while you begin to think that maybe it's true that the Jews killed Jesus."

One day near Christmas, Martoune took Odette into the convent chapel to show her a manger scene marking the birth of Christ. Martoune knelt down and crossed herself. Suddenly, Odette smacked her on her hand.

"What's the matter with you?" Odette said. "You are Jewish. When you are with me you don't have to do that."

"I was flabbergasted," Martoune said. "I had not realized what I was doing, and she made me take a step backwards. If the war had lasted a few more months, who knows, maybe I would have become a Catholic."

When she left the convent, Odette would visit other girls hidden in the Grasse area on the same day, among them Françoise's younger sister Paulette, who was under treatment for leukemia at a children's hospital, using a Christian name. Every day Odette made another round of visits in another part of the Nice region, most of the time in public buses, unheated against the cold winter air on the way to mountain villages. The buses traveled curvy, dangerous roads, often in the fog, sometimes skidding on ice. There were many accidents, though none involving her. Odette bunched the visits by area to include as many girls as she could in a single day.

Moussa meanwhile undertook a multitude of tasks. Among other things, he visited the boys under the Abadis' care, crisscrossing the same area as Odette. One of his regular stops, the Grasse area, included a call on Jeannette's younger brother, Jean, hidden with a Protestant family. Sometimes Moussa wrote letters to the younger boys in the names of the parents they desperately missed. He forged several letters to a boy of seven who became increasingly suspicious. "One day the boy sprang on me," Moussa recalled, "because he finally understood that I had been faking the letters. He told me: 'I will never trust you again.'"[5]

Moussa also met regularly with Maurice Brener for the money that financed the Marcel Network and with representatives of the American Friends Service Committee, a Quaker organization that supplied him with clothing, chocolates, and other gifts for the children. During the war, pacifists in the Quaker organization ran aid programs in several European countries. With the help of the Quakers, Moussa set up a clandestine storage room for the clothing. Within a month, however, the Gestapo discovered it, and confiscated the entire stock in a raid. Moussa had to start all over again, collecting more clothes and finding a safer place to store them.

Once Moussa received from the Quakers a large tin of strawberry jam, a rare treat in wartime Nice. He decided to bring it to a convent that hid

Jewish girls. At the gates, he met the mother superior, a stout woman with big red cheeks.

"What news are you bringing me?" the nun asked.

"No news this time. But I brought you some strawberry jam."

Moussa watched the nun slap her thigh in joy. "Why did you do that?" he inquired.

"Because I have just prayed to the Virgin for some jam," she replied. "And here it is."[6]

Apparent miracles like that were exceedingly rare. Most of the surprises Moussa encountered were no fun. As but one example, a little girl hidden by the Abadis died in a hospital under her false Christian name. The nuns at the Catholic hospital insisted on a religious burial conducted by a priest. Within twenty-four hours, Moussa arranged for a young rabbi to attend the Catholic ceremony, standing discreetly in the background. In a hushed voice, the rabbi recited the Kaddish, the Jewish prayer for the dead, using the girl's real name.

On another occasion, a mother superior in a Nice suburb summoned Moussa to tell him she could no longer hide the seven Jewish girls at her convent. "You have to take them back because I am risking too much," she said. Moussa reported her demand to Bishop Rémond. "We'll have to find new places for the girls," Moussa told him, "but it will take time. What do we do?"

The bishop knew exactly what to do. He called in the nun for a talk in his office, with Moussa in attendance. She repeated her demand to take the girls back, this time more respectfully, as a request. "It was the first time I saw the bishop angry," Moussa recalled.

Rémond told her: "Ever since you were ordained you have asked Christ every morning and every night to be put to the test. Now that God is putting you to the test, is giving you the opportunity to do what you asked for, you are reneging. Well, go back and take care of those girls."

She knelt, kissed his hand, and left to do his bidding. "We had to deal with unexpected situations every day," Moussa said.[7]

At night, Moussa prepared false papers at his office in the bishop's residence. He worked by candlelight, with heavy curtains drawn across the only window in the room. From the outside, the office appeared dark, as if no one was there. To the left of Moussa's desk was a wall panel about three feet high and ten feet long. The panel looked no different from the rest of the wall. Most visitors would not notice the latch that could slide the panel back, opening up a discreet storage space. Sometimes Moussa hid children in the space behind the panel, until their papers were ready and he could take them to safer havens.

On several occasions during the day, when Moussa worked in the office alone, there were false alarms of impending raids by German patrols or French police nearby. He would then jump out of the ground-floor window into the garden, get on his bicycle, and ride off.

Even by working day and night, there was no way that Moussa and Odette could visit 527 children every month. Fortunately, they never had to. "We tried never to hide more than 140 children at any one time," Moussa explained, "although we never turned any child away."[8]

The Abadis managed to keep the number to about 140 by operating a revolving-door system. They often placed children in hiding for only a short time—as little as a few days—while the parents secured safe havens for their entire families. That done, the children rejoined parents, freeing up their former hiding places in Catholic institutions and Protestant families for other children to move in. Other youngsters saved by the Abadis went off to Switzerland or Spain and no longer required hiding places or visits in France. They, too, would be replaced by new arrivals. Still others were never hidden at all by the Abadis. They were saved while still in the care of their parents, or in the care of Christian friends of the parents, with the false papers, ration cards, and funds that Moussa and Odette provided. No visits to these children were necessary. All these factors helped the Abadis keep the number of children they visited at any one time down to a manageable level.

Between them, Moussa and Odette could visit as many as 140 hidden children at least once a month, as groups of six or more in the same town, or even the same school, could be seen in a single day.

All told, the Abadis saved 527 children between September 1943 and August 1944—some 300 in Catholic institutions, about 100 in Protestant families, and the rest by sending them to Switzerland or Spain or by providing crucial aid to parents or family friends.

Incredibly, with all the problems they faced every day, and all the children who depended on them, the Abadis often managed to make a special effort to meet the needs of just one boy or girl. Jeannette Wolgust recalled one telling example of this. She had been awarded the title role of Joan of Arc in a play to be put on by her convent school at the municipal theater in Grasse. The other girls in the cast would have their proud parents, other relatives, and friends in the audience applauding them. But Jeannette would have no one. "It's not fair," she told Françoise.

Jeannette had a telephone number from Odette to call only in case of an emergency. "If one of the girls needs a doctor," Odette had explained. Jeannette called that number from a phone in the convent chapel. It rang at the bishop's residence in Nice, where a priest on the staff answered.

"I want to speak to Mademoiselle Sylvie Delattre," Jeannette said.

"What do you want from her?"

Jeannette mumbled something unintelligible.

"Where are you?" the priest asked.

"The Joan of Arc convent in Grasse."

"What is your name?"

Jeannette told him.

"All right," the priest said. "I'm coming." Then he hung up.

"Oh dear," Jeannette said to herself, fearing trouble ahead. "What do I do now?"

The priest arrived an hour and a half later. "What's the problem?" he asked.

"We are putting on a play on Saturday night and I want Mademoiselle Delattre to come see me," Jeannette replied sheepishly.

The priest laughed and said he would see what he could do.

Saturday was only three days away when Jeannette called. She knew Odette was very busy and unlikely to come on short notice. But, on

Saturday night, Odette was in the audience, applauding, and backstage afterward to congratulate Jeannette. "You cannot imagine my happiness," Jeannette said.[9]

In fact, Odette was not alone at the play. She had brought Jeannette's little brother, Jean, with her. And not only that, but because Jean would be out too late to go back to the family that was hiding him, Odette had gotten special permission from the mother superior for Jean to spend the night in the convent, no small feat. Here was a boy—only five years old, but still a boy—with permission to spend the night in a girls' dormitory inside a nunnery. They put Jean at the end of the dorm and drew curtains around him. Such was the extra mile Odette Abadi went for just one of her girls.

10

Boys

While Odette took care of the girls, Moussa looked after the boys. As with the girls, the struggle of the boys to survive was often hair-raising, and sometimes miraculous, perhaps in no case more so than the story of Armand Morgensztern. At age ten, Armand found himself in Drancy, destined for the gas chambers at Auschwitz. Despite his tender age, he managed to save his own life—by talking his way out of the death trap.

Armand was born in Paris, the son of Polish immigrants, Charles and Zisla Morgensztern. When war broke out in 1939, his father, a ladies' tailor, volunteered to serve in the French Foreign Legion. Armand, then seven, remained in Paris with his mother. A year later, mother and son watched German tanks roll through the city at the Place de la Bastille. The French crowded the sidewalks of that major square, not to cheer, but only because no one could cross the street.

Later that day, as Armand and his mother shopped for food, two German soldiers entered the store and offered the little boy a bar of chocolate. "I refused," Armand recalled, "but they insisted. What could I do? I accepted. It made me feel like a traitor, but people in the neighborhood said I was lucky because I had gotten a piece of chocolate. That's how bizarre things were then."

In 1941, Armand, then nine, was playing in the street when he saw his father coming home after being demobilized. "You cannot imagine the joy," he said. "Life started anew." Charles turned from tailoring to making gloves, but any sort of joy under the German occupation was short-lived. French police checking on all foreign-born Jews demanded that Armand's father report to them with his identity papers.

"Don't go," friends said. "It's a trap." But Charles Morgensztern would not listen. "There is no danger," he said. "I served France as a soldier. They won't harm me."

Wrong! Charles was arrested, interned at a camp in the Loire region for several months, and then deported to Auschwitz. Before leaving the camp, he managed to send his son, his only child, a last letter and a gift—a model boat carved in wood. More than sixty years later that boat still holds the place of honor on the mantelpiece in Armand's living room. Even as a boy, Armand understood when he received the boat that he might never see his father again. "I ran out of the house to cry," he said.[1]

Paris was too dangerous, Zisla Morgensztern decided, after her husband's arrest. So she and Armand moved to the home of friends in the countryside at Vigneux, some twenty miles south of the capital. Although Jewish, the friends considered themselves safe. The husband had been a prisoner of war, and neither the Germans nor the French police were then arresting former POWs. Zisla made the move to Vigneux just days before the Nazis conducted a major roundup of Jews in Paris on July 17, 1942, infamous in France as the "*rafle du Vel'd'Hiv.*"[2] The narrow escape rattled her. She was still too close to Paris for comfort, she realized. So Zisla left Armand behind and traveled south into the Free Zone to look for a safer haven around Lyon. She planned to send a guide to bring her son to her, before school started in the fall. But she waited too long. Police arrested Armand in October during a roundup of Jews in Vigneux, and took him to Drancy.

Armand was ten years old and alone. No matter, even ten-year-olds got interrogated at Drancy. "Where are your parents?" the police at Drancy asked.

"My father was arrested," Armand replied. "I don't know where my mother is." He did not want to say she was in the south, because he knew it was forbidden to cross into the Free Zone.

The interrogators didn't know what to make of his story. They said they would call him back another day for more questions.

Others waiting at the reception center in Drancy told Armand he would probably be deported. Scared, he began to cry. A French official walked by and asked what was wrong, Armand told him he was afraid of being deported, a banal answer he realized years later, because just about everyone at Drancy would be deported, but the official took pity on this one small boy. "Come see me tomorrow and I will tell you what to do," the man said. Armand remembered his name only as "something like Arboeuf."

Detainees at Drancy had to be present for roll calls, but in the intervals between them during the day, they could wander about the prison camp and call on various offices. Thus, the next day, Armand accidentally ran into "Arboeuf" in a hallway. "Don't say your parents have been deported and you should be all right," the French official advised him.

Armand did as he was told. Through several more interrogation sessions he repeatedly said his parents had not been deported. The fact that he could not pinpoint their actual whereabouts turned out to be irrelevant. Only the claim of no deportation mattered. Armand did not know it then but the bureaucratic rule followed by the police at Drancy at the time was simple: if the parents had been deported, the child should be deported as well; if the parents had not been deported, then the child could not be deported either. On Armand's eighth day at Drancy, the interrogator told him, "You are free. Take your things and go." He was the only one of his childhood playmates in Paris to survive the Holocaust.

Armand went to live with an aunt in the suburbs. The aunt's son, Armand's cousin, worked for a furrier. German officers wanted furs for their lady friends in Paris so they tended to leave furriers alone. Armand had escaped Drancy, and was safe for a while with his aunt, but he faced more dangers ahead.

Zisla sent a guide to the aunt's house to collect Armand and take him across the Line of Demarcation to join her in Lyon. On the way to the train station in Paris, the guide told Armand, "If anyone asks, you must say you are my nephew." Then he tore off the yellow star that Armand, like all Jews, was required to wear, and put it in his jacket pocket. "You won't need this anymore," he said. The guide had false papers with Christian names for the two of them so they could travel safely to Lyon.

They took an overnight train. Armand soon fell asleep, leaning against the guide. When the police came to check the identities of the people in Armand's compartment they saw the boy sleeping peacefully on the guide's shoulder. They would have to wake him and move him away so the guide could take out his papers. Instead, they just let the boy sleep, and never asked for the papers.

Zisla met them at the train station in Lyon. Overcome with gratitude, she kissed the guide. "I had never seen my mother kiss anyone except my father," Armand said.

"Then the guide put his hand in his jacket pocket and discovered that my yellow star was still there. He had forgotten to throw it away. Had he been searched on the train, you can imagine what would have happened."

Armand and his mother stayed in Lyon for nearly a year. Then one day, the director of the school came into Armand's classroom and said: "All Jews should get out of the city because roundups are about to take place. You must go and hide."

"It was extraordinary," Armand said. "France was collaborating with the Germans, but not all Frenchmen were bastards. There were all kinds."

Zisla decided to move with Armand to the Savoy region of the Alps, then in Italian hands. Again they needed false papers to get there, and false ration cards to live. This time Armand, now eleven, did the forging himself. "I had a very nice handwriting and could imitate the official script of functionaries," he said. "When we passed into the Italian Zone, a German official with a lamp checked our papers. I was shaking. But he said, 'It's okay. You can go.'"

They went to a Savoy village called St. Gervais les Bains, and shared a house there with a father and daughter, also Jewish refugees. The little girl was none other than Marthe Artsztein—Martoune. "I know that's hard to believe," Armand said. "These things are only supposed to happen in novels or in the movies, but it was true." Two children, on very separate roads to the Abadis, were thrown together for a few months.

Martoune was then nine, two years younger than Armand. They became friends. Herco Artsztein, Martoune's father, and Zisla Morgensztern, Armand's mother, became more than friends. The two single parents never lived together in the same room. They lived in separate rooms with their children in the same house. But they were both about thirty years old, both lonely, and did not know if their spouses were still alive. They became lovers. "I knew it a long time ago," Armand said, "but I only admitted it to myself recently."

During the Italian retreat from Savoy, a military convoy trucked Martoune, Armand, and their parents to Nice, where Martoune's father found out how to contact Moussa Abadi. Then they split up, with Martoune headed to the convent in Grasse, and Armand to the College Sasserno, a Catholic boarding school for boys in Nice. After the children left, Marthe's father and Armand's mother were arrested in Nice and deported together to Auschwitz. On arrival, Zisla Morgenzstern went straight to the gas chambers. Martoune's father survived because tailors were needed. At the time, their children knew none of that.

Zisla left Armand in Nice with a man in a beret called Monsieur Marcel. He took Armand's little suitcase, put him in a horse and buggy, and drove him to the boarding school. Depersonalization came easily, given Armand's age. He became Armand Morini, from Corsica. The Allies had just liberated the French island and the Germans could no longer check records there.

Armand spent two academic years at the boarding school. At first there was one other Jewish boy hidden there, then the other boy left with his mother, and Armand became the only Jew remaining in this Catholic world. For him it was a lonely, hungry world of severe food shortages. When the other boys left for weekends or holidays, Armand stayed and studied, all alone, benefiting only from the extra bread rations the departing boys left him.

As Armand remembered it, Moussa brought him to the school but never visited after that. He was an exception, one of the relatively few Abadi children never seen regularly by Moussa or Odette. Apparently because he was in school in Nice, and had no serious problems there, they left the money for his school fees at the bishop's office and relied on the school to monitor his health. Odette did manage to visit Armand twice. The first time she asked him what he wanted most—a favorite toothpaste—and the second time she brought it to him. But unlike the girls at the convent in Grasse, Armand never enjoyed the kind of substitute mothering that Odette could provide. He was truly alone.

Once, during a vacation period, a priest at the school had a birthday party with cakes and other goodies. Armand, the only student left at the school, was not invited. "I didn't complain," he said. Instead, he chose to focus on the more positive side of his time as a Catholic student. "They never drilled me on the New Testament in Catechism class, only the Old Testament. It was a delicate connivance, but much appreciated." One weekend, another priest at the school invited Armand to a Sunday lunch at his family home, where the priest's warm, affectionate parents gave the lonesome boy a brief taste of normal life. "To me that priest was a saint," Armand said. "He made me understand what Christian charity and goodness were all about."

✦

Armand's story, like those of Françoise Knopf, Jeannette Wolgust, and hundreds of others, helps prove the falsity of three myths about the Holocaust years in France. The first is that because of the attitude of the Pope, the Catholic Church in France did nothing to help the Jews. On the contrary, thanks to rare prelates like Bishop Rémond, Archbishop Saliièges of Toulouse, and Cardinal Pierre Gerlier, the Archbishop of Lyon, the Church made a difference by opening at least some of its boarding schools and other institutions, at considerable risk, to hide Jewish children. The care they gave was hardly perfect, but cannot be faulted as they accomplished the essential—they saved Jewish lives. Of course, the Catholic

Church could have done far more. But it is wrong to say the Church did nothing to help. Perhaps no other French bishop risked as much, or accomplished as much, as Paul Rémond.

The second myth was that Jews in France marched like lemmings to the gas chambers, offering no resistance. Thanks to people like the Abadis, Maurice Brener, and Georges Garel, sophisticated Jewish Resistance networks were established, financed, and successfully run to ensure the survival of the Jews in France, both children and adults. In no other European country did Jews save as many of their own people.

The third myth is that the French people, with their long tradition of anti-Semitism, collaborated with the Germans to make matters worse for the Jews. That is partly right. But the whole truth presents a different picture. The fact is that some 73,000 men, women, and children—about a quarter of France's total Jewish population of 300,000 in 1940—perished in the Holocaust, a colossal, tragic loss. But nearly three-quarters survived.[3] That large majority lived because French Christians, as well as the Jewish Resistance, supplied crucial help.

Overall, despite the appalling collaboration of Vichy in the deportation of Jews, the French record is outstanding when compared to the rest of Nazi-occupied Europe. The Nazis killed about two-thirds of the Jews of Europe, compared to about one-quarter in France. Today there are some 600,000 Jews living in France, according to the World Jewish Congress, the largest Jewish population in Europe. None of that would have been possible if thousands of French Christians had not aided Jews during the Nazi occupation.[4]

In Armand's case, a French official told him how to talk his way out of Drancy before the Nazis could put him on a train to Auschwitz. Another Frenchman, the director of his school in Lyon, provided the timely warning to leave the city. In Françoise's case, the Frenchman in charge of a labor camp let her father leave for dental treatment and told him to take as much time as he liked, literally inviting him to escape. In the case of Jeanette Wolgust's younger brother Jean, a French Protestant couple hid him to save his life. French non-Jews also provided essential help for the children smuggled out to Switzerland or Spain. In addition to those who helped actively, there were other non-Jewish French who contributed passively by refusing to cooperate with the German occupiers.

✦

Armand narrowly escaped the death camps on his own, before getting to the Abadis. Other boys had equally harrowing near misses after being hidden by Moussa. In the most spectacular case, thirteen Jewish boys housed at the same Catholic school fled together unharmed in the middle of a Nazi raid.

The boys were all boarding students at the Dom Bosco vocational school in Nice when Gestapo agents, backed by a truckload of German soldiers armed to the teeth, rushed into the school and demanded that the director hand over the Jews. The intruders, acting on tips from informers, had reason to believe that the school sheltered at least a dozen Jewish boys. The soldiers, some carrying machine guns, looked menacing enough, but were too few in numbers to surround the sprawling complex that included a church, classroom buildings, and workshops.

The director, Father Vincent Simioni, denied there were any Jews at the school.

"Never mind," said a Gestapo agent known in Nice only as "Alice la Blonde." "There's no point in lying. I can tell Jews by their noses."[5]

Alice la Blonde demanded to be shown into the classrooms, one by one. Every time she spotted a suspected Jew she commanded, "Get out!" eventually selecting a dozen boys for Semitic looks. She ordered their trousers to be pulled down for inspection, but none of them were circumcised. In fact, none were Jewish. Still, Alice ordered the boys held until they could produce baptismal certificates from parents and both sets of grandparents.

While Alice inspected the classrooms, the thirteen real Jews were quietly led to safety outside her view. Marcel Dallo, a sixteen-year-old altar boy at the time studying at the school, watched them escape. According to him the Jewish boys crossed the schoolyard in groups of three or four and went into the church on the school grounds. Inside the church they walked under scaffolding to a side door and then down the stairs to the crypt under the church. The scaffolding had been put up as the first defense against a German raid. Any search party was supposed to be told, "Don't go near the scaffolding because it might fall on your head," Dallo said.[6] It was only a delaying tactic. As expected, the Germans brushed aside the warning and searched the crypt. But by then all the boys had escaped through a window on the left side of the crypt that opened to the ground level outside. Visitors to the crypt today can still see the escape route, now the only window in clear glass at the end of a line of stained-glass windows. Once outside the back of the church, unseen by the German soldiers at the front of the school, the boys were rushed to temporary shelters and then to new safe havens arranged by Monsieur Marcel. As Moussa often said, yet another crisis, such as urgently finding new hiding places for thirteen boys, "was our daily bread."

✦

During the war, and long after it, almost all of the children hidden by the Abadis had no idea who had saved them. Jeannette Wolgust and Françoise Knopf were rare exceptions. The others knew at most only the cover names—Monsieur Marcel and Sylvie Delattre—but not the real identities of either Moussa or Odette. Julien and George Engel and their parents were a case in point. The survival of the Engel brothers was perhaps the most remarkable of any of the Abadi children, and yet the identity of the people who ultimately saved them remained unknown to Julien and George for most of their adult lives.

Their parents, David and Rosa Engel, never even learned the Abadis' cover names. They didn't live long enough. David and Rosa had tried to build normal lives, but too often they found themselves in harm's way, in the wrong place at the wrong time. Their story was all too common in the Europe of their day, a world gone mad.

Both came from Poland. They went to Germany to be educated, met and married, only to flee in 1933, the year Hitler took power. They settled in Antwerp, Belgium, where Julien and George were born, and they acquired a furniture store. Then they fled again after Nazi troops swept through Belgium in 1940 on their way to France.

In 1941, the Engel family took refuge in Nice, when the Free Zone still looked safe. But, a year later, French police there, under orders from Vichy, began massive arrests of foreign-born Jews. So the Engels fled yet again. They paid a guide to smuggle them into neighboring Switzerland. Instead, the guide pocketed their money and betrayed them, leading the Engels to their arrest at a frontier police station. The family then went by regular passenger train, the parents in handcuffs guarded by a French policeman, to Perpignan, in southwest France, and internment behind the barbed-wire fence at nearby Rivesaltes.

At the time, September 1942, Jews in France did not yet know about the Nazi death camps. Those held at Rivesaltes thought they would be sent to do forced labor in Germany, leaving their children behind. Nonetheless, as parents lined up along the fence for farewells with their young, fear of the future mixed with the grief of separation. Some parents stretched bloodied arms through the barbed wire to hold their children one more time, shrieking the names of sons and daughters. David and Rosa Engel controlled their emotions as best they could, determined to leave their boys with the impression that the parting would be only temporary. In the meantime, they told nine-year-old Julien to take care of four-year-old George. "We went away dry-eyed," Julien said, "believing we would see our parents again before too long." The last image David and Rosa Engel had of their young sons was of their backs as the boys were led away to buses and an unknown fate. Julien had put his arm around the shoulder of his little brother.

The buses took the children released from the internment camp to shelters run by social welfare agencies. They did not know it then, but Julien and George left with one of the last groups of detained youngsters to be freed anywhere in France. In fact, they were not supposed to survive. In July 1942, the Vichy government abandoned its policy of releasing Jewish children under sixteen and instead ordered internment camps in the Free Zone to deport them with their parents. Incredibly, despite that order, Rivesaltes continued to spare the children. The reason is another remarkable example of a French Christian risking his life to save Jews. Paul Corazzi, the local French official in Perpignan responsible for enforcing Vichy policy at the Rivesaltes camp, was horrified by the new order to deport children as well. So he sat on it, withholding it from camp authorities for nearly four months, including September, when his bureaucratic delaying tactics saved the lives of Julien and George Engel.[7] Only two months later, in November 1942, when the Germans occupied Rivesaltes—and most of the rest of the Free Zone as well—they finally put a stop to any such exceptions. From then on, whole families, including children, were deported to Auschwitz, from everywhere in the South of France, as had long been the case in the north. By sheer luck, Julien and George lived.

Liozia Fachette, their mother's cousin, collected the boys after their release from Rivesaltes and took them to live at her villa in Nice. More luck. The area was still in Italian hands, the one part of the south still outside German occupation. Liozia, the widow of a Frenchman, was a French citizen. And so far, the Vichy police in Nice were arresting only Jewish refugees from abroad, not French Jews like her. But Liozia remained prudent. She told the boys that if anything happened to her, they should jump over the low brick wall at the bottom of her garden and stay with a neighbor, Monsieur Neybourg.

Julien and George felt comforted in the Fachette family villa near the sea. Whenever Julien asked Liozia about his parents, she said, "They have been put to work somewhere in Germany." She wanted the boys to think their parents would be coming back after the war.

In September 1943, nine months after the Engel boys arrived at the villa, German troops marched into Nice to replace the Italians and complete their occupation of the Free Zone. No longer was there any pretense of Vichy acting independently. No longer were further repressions slowed by the Italians. French police and the Gestapo could now operate as ruthlessly anywhere in the south as they had all along in the north. In Nice,

Vichy began arresting not only Jewish refugees from abroad, but French Jews as well. Liozia went out shopping one day and never returned home. A French friend who had been with her rushed back to tell the Engel boys, "Your cousin has been arrested. Leave now!"

Julien and George jumped the brick wall with just the clothes on their backs, dirt-smudged from playing in the garden. Within the hour the Gestapo arrived at Liozia's villa, looked in vain for relatives, then sealed off the place as confiscated property. Had the boys not run in the nick of time, they too would have been arrested and deported to the death camps.

Monsieur Neybourg, the neighbor on the other side of the wall, happened to be the Honorary Consul of Sweden in Nice. He knew people who could safely hide the boys.

Julien remembered only that "a nice lady named Sylvie who worked for the Catholic Church" came on the third day to take him and George to a home for abandoned children in the hills above Cannes, called the "Le Rayon de Soleil" (The Ray of Sunshine), where they hid until the end of the war. Still more luck.

Alban and Germaine Fort, who created and ran the home, were ahead of their time. Orphanages in Europe then often warehoused children, neglecting and mistreating them. Many young people left these institutions in worse shape than when they entered. The Forts, in sharp contrast, created a family atmosphere for the seventy children they housed, including the Jews hidden among them. "They were wonderful people," Julien said. "They were full of love and warmth, however many kids were there." The children lived in a large mansion surrounded by eight acres of gardens. The rich Americans who owned the property went home after the Germans invaded France and let the Forts use their idyllic setting for the rest of the war. According to Julien, "It was a marvelous place to be. If you had to spend time during the war in the circumstances we did, you couldn't have made out better."

The Engel boys stayed with the Forts for nearly three years, until 1946. All the while Julien did his best to look after his little brother. One day Julien found a bicycle hoop—the metal rim from an old bicycle wheel that could be rolled along by a little stick—and gave it to George. The rim became a prized toy. It enabled George to join in hoop games with the other kids. "I still remember the fun I had and the joy that hoop gave me," George said.[8]

Julien also began to follow the war news. With time, his fears that his parents would never return grew. At the end of the war, after the Soviet Army liberated Auschwitz and other death camps in the east, and the Western Allies freed those in Germany itself, there was still no trace of David or Rosa Engel. By 1946 "our last hopes vanished," Julien said. "I resigned myself to being an orphan."[9]

The war was over but Julien and George Engel had still never heard of Moussa and Odette Abadi, the people who saved their lives by arranging to hide them with the Forts. It would take the Engel boys decades to learn the truth, for one simple reason. Moussa and Odette refused to talk about their wartime clandestine work for nearly fifty years afterward.

11

SWITZERLAND

During the war, Moussa and Odette took help wherever they could find it, sometimes from unsavory sources.

Smugglers on the border between Switzerland and France thrived during World War II. On one side, neutral Switzerland enjoyed a bounty of supply. On the other, war-torn France, plagued by shortages, seethed with demand. Supply here, demand there, what could be better for the cross-border smuggling trade? Gold watches and gold coins, two Swiss specialties, made particularly heady profits for the smugglers. The French used them to bribe German officers or to trade on the black market. Ladies' underwear and other small items that were easy to smuggle also sold well.

Of course, the wartime profits came with added risk for the smugglers. In peacetime, all they needed to worry about were customs police at fixed checkpoints—relative child's play to avoid on unwatched mountain trails. During the war, patrols of armed German soldiers aided by sniffer dogs moved along the border region, complicating the smugglers' task. So, naturally enough, the smugglers became the experts on the German patrols, with precise schedules on how many soldiers could be expected, when, and where. Their information proved vital to Moussa Abadi and the guides he used to sneak Jewish children out of France and over the border to safety in Switzerland. After all, they were in much the same business, smuggling children rather than goods past the same German patrols.

The smugglers, Swiss and French, were the last link in the chain that made the Marcel Network's operations successful. The Catholic institutions, the Protestant families, and the help of other individual Frenchmen, all played essential roles in saving Jewish children hidden in France. The cooperation of the Jewish Resistance, and the information supplied by smugglers, became the keys to sending Jewish children safely out of the country to Switzerland, and, to a lesser extent, to Spain.

Smugglers working the Swiss frontier charged the Jews money for the details on German patrols, a small profit sideline. According to one knowledgeable source, Georges Loinger, smugglers supplied an update on patrols to guides leading Jewish children out of France, and got paid about one dollar for each child in the guide's group. Loinger ran the Swiss connection for the OSE, the same charity that had employed Odette at the clinic in Nice. He took some children out himself and hired guides to take out others. Among the hundreds he saved were dozens handed over by Moussa Abadi.

Loinger, a tough, strong survivor, escaped from a prisoner-of-war camp in 1941 and served the Resistance after that. He was ninety-eight years old, still clearheaded and going strong in 2008 when interviewed for this book. In setting up the operation to smuggle out children, Loinger studied the Swiss-French border, much of it along snowcapped Alps. He chose Annemasse, a French town barely a mile from the frontier, down from the mountains in an area of low hills, southeast of Geneva. "The mayor of Annemasse put us in touch with smugglers we could trust," Loinger said. They in turn showed him the way out, past the German patrols.

With Loinger, the children made the trek at night, a short, dangerous walk of about half an hour to the nearby border, in violation of the nighttime curfew. At the frontier, Loinger lifted barbed wire on the French side so the children could crawl under, led them across a wooded no-man's-land, and then got them through the barbed wire on the Swiss side. He stayed behind, leaving the children to walk into the hands of Swiss border officials. Loinger told the children to tell the Swiss they had been taken to the frontier by the French Red Cross. Other guides, at other locations nearby, made the trip during the day, but followed much the same pattern as Loigner.

"The Swiss were like a boat," Loinger said. "Take too many passengers, and the boat sinks."[1] What he meant was that the Swiss sympathized with the plight of the Jews, but as a place where the Nazis banked, and as an exporter of goods to Germany, neutral Switzerland had a strong interest in maintaining good relations with Hitler's Reich. The Swiss tried to strike a balance by limiting the number of Jewish refugees they took in, turning some back at the border. But they accepted the children, and placed them in the care of the Swiss Red Cross.

Max Poch made the trip to Switzerland at age twelve, along with his brother, Maurice, then thirteen. Moussa arranged their escape from France through contacts at the OSE. Their younger sister, Andrée, then three, stayed at the family apartment in Nice with their parents. Soon after the brothers left home, their parents were arrested in the apartment and deported to Auschwitz. Andrée was spared because she just happened to be playing with a friend her age at a neighbor's when the Gestapo picked up her parents. The neighbors looked after Andrée until Moussa placed her at a Catholic home for girls in Grasse, the third Abadi child from the same family. It would be nearly two years before Max and Maurice learned of their parents' fate.

Max and Maurice started their journey on a train to Lyon, with a guide Max remembers only as Monsieur Fizler. "If questioned on the train," Max recalled, "we were supposed to say we were orphans from Calais, victims of bombardments on the channel ports that killed our parents, and we were being moved to safer ground near Lyon." From Lyon they went to a town near the Swiss border. Max could not remember the name of the town, only that he and Maurice spent the night in a monastery there, joining into a group of fifteen Jewish children between the ages of eight and fourteen. "They welcomed us at the monastery and gave us something to eat," Max said. "While we were eating, a priest stood behind each child, as if he was responsible for that child. We went to sleep in the monks' cells. Again, at each cell, a priest slept across the threshold, continuing to protect us."

Early the next morning, the children left for Switzerland, Fizler on a bicycle at the front of the line and the children walking in single file behind him. Max remembered Fizler as a man of about thirty, short and squat, looking much like the peasants who lived in the border area. "He knew what he was doing and where he was going," Max said. "He must have taken children out on that route many times."

The children walked for about four miles, over foothills with soft ups and downs. It was early October, not yet cold.

Each child carried a bag with a change of clothing and some bread and fruit, trying to look like kids from the region out on a school hike. "Stay in line," Fizler told the children. "No noise and no horsing around." He wanted the children to be quiet and alert, ready to act the minute he saw trouble ahead, and to listen for orders from him to lie down or to run and hide.

But they never saw a German patrol, probably because Fizler had learned from smugglers when and where to avoid them. The only people the children met along the way were local peasants going about their business. "These people were not stupid," Max explained. "They probably knew what was going on, because we weren't the first children they saw heading for the border. But as long as we were only children they apparently decided not to do anything about it."[2]

Max was neither hungry nor thirsty nor even scared. "My older brother was with me," he said, "and as long as Maurice was there I was not afraid."

In the early afternoon they found themselves at the border, in front of a high barbed-wire fence. Fizler lifted the barbed wire for the children to crawl under. "Over there is Switzerland," he said, pointing ahead. "Go! Go! Go!!"

They saw only fields and trees, no roads. Max and Maurice began to run, not knowing where they were heading, and often looking back, bewildered that Fizler was no longer coming with them. Then suddenly,

Max saw a man dressed in a gray-green uniform. "I thought he was a German," Max said. "He made a sign for us to come closer and I saw that he had the Swiss cross on the buttons of his uniform. We had been told in advance to look for that. Only then did I understand. We really were in Switzerland."

Heaven it was not. The Swiss military took in Max and Maurice as French refugees who had crossed the border illegally. First came the interrogations. Name? Place of birth? How did you come to Switzerland? Where are your parents? Do you have relatives in Switzerland? And on and on. Then they took the boys to a place that Max called "the camp at the end of the world."

The camp consisted of barracks. In each barrack there were rooms with no beds. The boys slept on straw, spread on the floor. "We stayed there like that for forty days," Max said, "forty days in the same underwear.

"They fed us fairly well," Max remembered. "We didn't starve, but it was nothing like a family meal." During the day the boys were not bothered. They could play, write letters, or pretty much do what they liked. Still, Max and Maurice thought only of one thing—escape. "My brother and I wanted to rebel, to go back to France and find our parents," Max explained. "We didn't want to stay there. We planned to run away, but before we could go I fell while playing in the camp and broke my arm. I was taken to Geneva, where my arm was put in a cast, and from then on it became impossible to leave."

When they did leave, representatives of the Swiss Red Cross collected them and took them to a children's home. "It was more like a boot camp," Max said. "They began by shaving our heads to avoid lice." But at least the boys finally got a change of clothing, in military terms a new uniform. Discipline was strict. Boys who misbehaved got punished by being stuck in solitary confinement for a week. According to Max, "It was a dark hole."

Here the rooms at least had beds, but no blankets. Instead the boys covered themselves with potato sacks stuffed with newspapers. They had left France in early October. Now it was late November, well into the

Swiss winter, and bloody cold in their room with no blankets. Max said a friend at the children's home died because snow got into his room and he had nothing to cover himself with against the cold.

"And we were badly fed," Max recalled. "We had to steal apples to get by."

Eventually, Jewish organizations in Switzerland took an interest in the Poch brothers. They offered to take them out of the Red Cross children's home and place them with adoptive parents. "We refused," Max said. "In our heads we had to find our parents first. We didn't want to be adopted."

Max did, however, accept offers from a local Jewish charity to be taken out of the home from time to time for an afternoon's change of scenery and a special treat, like a bar of chocolate. Max had more contact with the Jews than Maurice did. "I guess because I wanted the chocolate they offered more than he did." When he was thirteen, the charity arranged a Bar Mitzvah for Max. "I did it for the presents," Max said.

The boys stayed at the children's home from November 1943 to July 1945, two months after the war ended in May. Then the French Red Cross repatriated them to France. At that stage they still did not know that shortly after they had left Nice for Switzerland, their parents had died in Auschwitz. Max's aunt, his father's sister, signed the papers to bring the boys back to France. But before agreeing to grant the aunt custody of the boys, the French authorities had to confirm her claim that their parents had indeed been deported to the gas chambers. Once they had the confirmation, they gave Max the shock of his young life.

It came at the border as Max and Maurice returned to France. A French official told the brothers, "Your parents have been deported." Only at that moment did the Poch brothers discover that their parents were dead. "It was rather brutal," Max remembered. "It was said coldly, the way only civil servants can say things."

Several of the Abadi children interviewed for this book said it took them decades before they could speak about the traumas they suffered during the war, even to their families and closest friends. The deaths of parents and siblings, the fears, the hunger, and the suffering were all too painful to recall. They shut out the childhood memories in trying to get on with their lives after the war. Some never spoke about their wartime ordeals until they were grandparents. Max Poch built a new life for himself. He married, had children and grandchildren, and enjoyed a career representing French banks in Africa before retiring with his wife to Guadeloupe in the Caribbean. In an interview during a visit to Paris, Max spoke calmly, without emotion, giving the impression he had come to terms with his past. His brother, Maurice, however, turned down a request for an interview. For Maurice, more than sixty years later, recalling the traumas of the war years was still too much to bear.

12

Close Calls

"You could not do the work we did with impunity," Moussa Abadi said. "We knew perfectly well the risks we were taking. Every morning when I drank my coffee with Odette, I didn't know whether I would find her safe that evening, or even whether I would be alive."[1]

Moussa was not being overdramatic. He knew the Nazis employed a small army of informers in Nice. On any day any one of them could stumble on yet another desperate parent handing over yet another child to Monsieur Marcel, exposing his rescue efforts. Moussa also suspected that the Germans tapped the phones at the bishop's office and had the residence under surveillance. He feared that any time he left the residence to visit a hidden child he could be followed and watched. In sum, Moussa knew the odds were against him, but that he had to carry on, for the sake of the children.

One day at the residence in early 1944, Father Auguste Rostan, the bishop's chief of staff, took Moussa aside and told him, "You are a wanted man. Be careful because there is a price on your head." The Germans had offered money for information leading to the arrest of a Jew, a certain Monsieur Marcel said to be hiding children. They didn't yet know Moussa's real name, but they were on to him.

"How do you know this?" Moussa asked.

"A priest learned about it from his parishioners," Rostan explained. "Our parishioners take Communion every day. They think they are good Christians but some of them are doing bad things." Among them was a parishioner who worked with the Germans and told his priest about the hunt for Monsieur Marcel. Moussa needed no further convincing. "From that moment on," he said, "I knew they were looking for me and that they were looking for Odette."[2]

True enough, the Germans had heard about Monsieur Marcel, but they had not yet tied him to Bishop Rémond. Indeed, at the time, the bishop himself was in far more danger. The Germans had a mole at the residence, the doctor who came occasionally to treat Rémond. According to documents found after the war, the doctor recommended the immediate incarceration of the bishop for his role in helping Jews, and not only children. The bishop, like Pastors Evrard and Gagnier, did what he could to hide Jewish adults as well.

Rather than following the doctor's suggestion immediately, the Germans hesitated. Paul Rémond was a popular figure in Nice, a strong moral authority. His arrest could have provoked a public outcry, and certainly would have led to less cooperation with the occupying forces. So the Germans decided to move slowly and carefully, determined to collect conclusive evidence against Rémond before arresting him. According to both René Rémond, the bishop's nephew, and Ralph Schor, his biographer, the Germans did indeed tap the bishop's telephones.[3]

Rémond suspected as much. To cope, he avoided using the phone for clandestine work or spoke in code when he needed to risk making a call. He would say, for example, to a priest: "I have some friends with me who are looking for a nice place to stay in the countryside. Can you help?" That meant "I have some Jews in my office who need a place to hide."[4] The wording may not have fooled the Germans, but it didn't give them the evidence they wanted either.

So they turned to provocations. The Gestapo agent known as Alice la Blonde showed up at the residence on a rainy winter night with two

Jewish-looking children in tow, demanding to see the bishop. “Please hide them,” she begged Rémond, “as you have hidden so many others.”

The bishop had been warned about Alice, known as a Gestapo agent ever since she burst into the Dom Bosco vocational school in a hunt for Jewish boys. Alice had a reputation in Nice as a particularly nasty piece of work and could be easily recognized by her dyed hair, said to be “too blond” to be believed. Perhaps it was the hair that gave her away, or maybe the overacting, as Alice became increasingly agitated and started to shout in pleading to help the children. Through it all, Rémond calmly repeated that he had no facilities at the residence to take in children. He politely showed Alice and the children in her charge to the door.

The Germans tried two other provocations, hoping to trap the bishop in a compromising situation. They sent a false British aviator to the residence with a story about parachuting into Nice when his plane was shot down. He asked for a place to hide. Another Nazi agent presented himself as a professor from Germany, an anti-Nazi activist seeking political asylum. Both agents were told that the bishop could not help them.

Rémond had every reason to reject any such provocation that would have shown him to be defying the German occupiers. The Vatican, after all, had recognized Vichy as the legitimate government of France. That put the Catholic hierarchy under papal orders to cooperate with Vichy and its collaboration with the Germans. Any act by the bishop against the Germans would have been seen by the Vatican as an act against Vichy, in defiance of the Pope’s instructions.

As a result, Bishop Rémond developed a dual personality. In public he appeared to be cooperating with the regime. He refrained from speaking out against Vichy’s anti-Jewish measures and maintained cordial relations with Vichy officials in Nice. Visitors to his office saw a signed photograph of Marshal Pétain, the Vichy government’s head of state, on the bishop’s desk. At the same time, in secret, Rémond did all he could to help Moussa Abadi save Jewish children. Indeed, the public image of cooperating with the regime created an excellent cover for the bishop’s clandestine work.

Even the photograph of Pétain was misleading. Rémond, as a former combat officer himself, had great respect for Pétain as a military figure, the hero of the French victory over the Germans at Verdun in World War I. To Rémond, Pétain also embodied the effort to maintain a French national identity under German occupation. Furthermore, Rémond and Pétain maintained a personal friendship. Pétain had a vacation home on the Riviera at Villeneuve-Loubet, not far from Nice, and often invited Rémond there. None of this implied Rémond's support for Vichy's anti-Jewish measures, which in fact were drafted and carried out by other officials under the leadership of Prime Minister Pierre Laval. For Rémond, Pétain was the best of the Vichy regime, and Laval the worst.

In meeting German officers at the residence, Rémond always seated them in such a way that they would be sure to see the momentos of his war service in a display case on the wall. The display included photographs of Commandant Rémond in uniform, with his saber and the pennant of his company of machine gunners. All this, together with the picture of Pétain on Rémond's desk, projected the image of a French patriot with friends in high places, reinforcing the notion that any move against him for illegal activity would have to be backed by incontrovertible evidence. In the end, the Germans made no move to arrest the bishop.

Moussa and Odette, in contrast, appeared to be increasingly in danger. One day, as they were sitting in a sidewalk café, Moussa saw a Frenchwoman known to be a German informer moving toward a telephone booth. "This is bad," he said to Odette. "Let's go." They left money on the table along with their unfinished cups of tea, then got up and ran. They had gone only about a hundred yards when they looked back to see a car full of Gestapo agents pull up at the café. "After the war," Moussa said, "the woman admitted to me what she had done. She said, 'You avoided arrest by thirty seconds.'"[5]

There were other near misses, none more harrowing than one involving Odette alone. She had spent the day of April 22, 1944, visiting girls in Grasse, and found a seat in the public bus back to Nice, dead tired. As the bus got under way, Odette noted with surprise—and some anger—

that two boys the Abadis had hidden, thirteen-year-old Joseph Gartner and his younger brother Theodore, age four, were seated nearby. At first she thought the boys had run away from Seranon, the mountain village where the local priest, Father Goens, hid them in his home. Odette rose to scold them, but retreated to her seat after Joseph Gartner signaled her with his hand to back off. Only then did Odette realize that plain-clothed police surrounded the boys. They were under arrest.

Father Goens had bragged to villagers about the children he sheltered. The talk got around and someone informed the Germans. The plain-clothesmen arrested the boys in the village and escorted them by bus to Nice, their first stop on the road to Drancy and their deaths in Auschwitz. After their arrests, Bishop Rémond removed Father Goens from his post and exiled him to Italy.

Moussa Abadi named only two children hidden by the Marcel Network who he knew had lost their lives to the Germans—Joseph and Theodore Gartner. Moussa took comfort in the 527 children saved, but the loss of the Gartner boys pained him for the rest of his days. He could never forget his meeting with the boys' father shortly after the end of the war, which he recorded in his diary.

Alfred Gartner, then forty years old, survived the Nazi death camp at Birkenau. His wife died at Auschwitz. He returned to Nice with the joyful aim of recovering his sons. "I endured the camps, the forced labor, the beatings," he told Moussa. "I endured illness, injuries, starvation, and cold. I endured all that because I wanted to live, so that I could take back my two boys."

Moussa stared back blankly, unable to speak.

After a long silence, Alfred Gartner understood. He asked what happened to his sons. With great regret, Moussa told him. Another long pause ensued.

Finally, Moussa broke the silence. "Do you have a family, Monsieur Gartner?" he asked.

"A brother, somewhere in Belgium," Gartner said. "But a brother can never replace a wife and children."

"For an hour and a half I was the impotent witness to his pain and despair," Moussa wrote in the diary. Then the mood changed.

"Somehow Monsieur Gartner found the strength to ask if we had succeeded in saving many children," Moussa noted. "I gave him several details about our clandestine work and a small miracle occurred. He began to smile, yes, smile."

"Thank you," Gartner said. "Thank you for having tried to save my children and for succeeding in saving hundreds of others." Then he left, bent over like an old man.

"Monsieur Gartner," Moussa wrote in his diary, "in the name of all the children who live, who laugh, and who play, I ask you to forgive me."[6]

✦

If anything, the arrest of Joseph and Theodore Gartner may have had a greater effect on Odette. When she stood up in the bus and moved toward the Gartner boys, the police escorting them must have noticed her. It is even possible that one of the police followed her back to her apartment in Nice. No one knows for sure. Odette's illegal work could also have become known to the Germans in many other ways, perhaps through some anonymous French informer. But clearly there is a strong possibility of a sinister link with the incident of the boys on the bus. In any event, on April 25, 1944, only three days after she saw the Gartner boys for the last time, the French Milice arrested Odette.

Odette Rosenstock pre-war

Moussa Abadi

Moussa (top) as Knock on New York stage, 1937

Moussa and Odette Abadi in Nice, 1943

Moussa and Odette Abadi in Nice, 1946

Odette and Moussa fifty years later

Religious wedding of Moussa and Odette, Paris, 1989

Moussa at his desk in the Bishop's residence

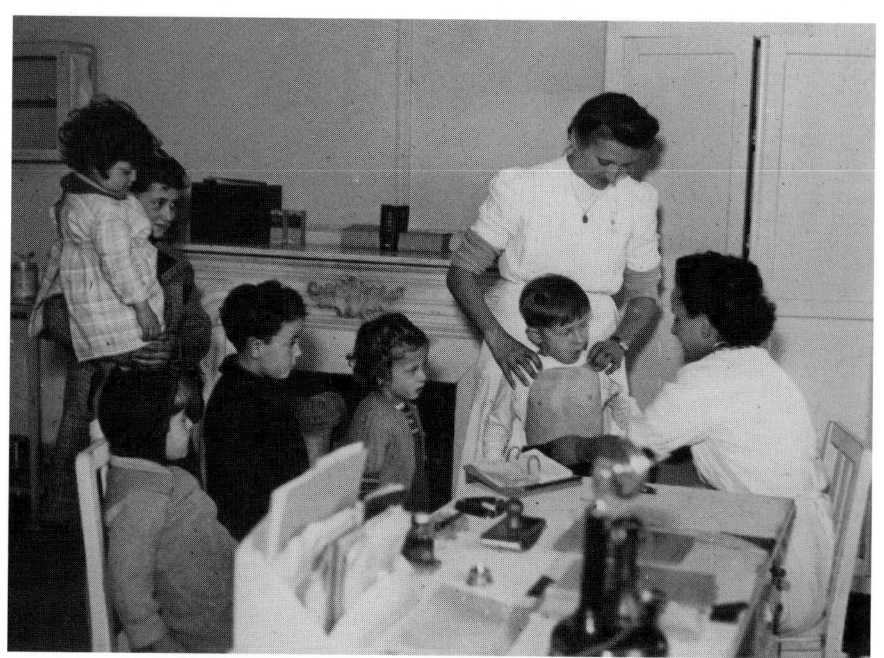

Odette (right) at OSE clinic

Moussa with Bishop Paul Rémond

Paul Rémond, Bishop of Nice

Moussa and Bishop Rémond hide fiches between books

Julien Engel with arm around younger brother, George, 1942

Julien Engel (2nd from right) and brother George (right) at a reunion with Abadis fifty years later

Left to right: Denise Trichard, Jeannette Wolgust, Françoise Knopf, and Marthe Artsztein at Joan of Arc Convent, Grasse, 1944

Left to right: Marthe Artsztein, Françoise Knopf, Jeannette Wolgust, and Camille Gustave (Catholic classmate from Joan of Arc Convent) in Paris, 2000

Martoune, age 9, 1943

Martoune and Odette fifty years later

Max Poch (left), age 9 and his brother, Maurice, with their baby sister, Andrée, and their father

Correspondant (nom, date et lieu de naissance) Mme Germaine Ranson
16 Av. St Lambert
Nice.

Adresses successives de l'enfant en France :

Parents en France et à l'étranger (noms et adresses) :
Dora Poch dite Henriquez
50 Ramon de la Cruz
(Madrid.)

Histoire de l'enfant et de la famille (date d'entrée en France, profession des parents, conditions de dislocation de la famille, etc...) :

POCHE ANDREE

EMPREINTES

Index gauche	Index droit

Fiche for Andrée Poch

No 72

NOM (en majuscules) : POCH

PRÉNOMS : Andrée

Née le 25-9-1940, à Nice.

Nationalité : Française

ADRESSES
- au pays d'origine : 7 rue des Fêtes Paris
- dernière connue en France :

Nom du père : Jules Nationalité : Franç.

Résidences successives (à l'étranger et en France) :

Nom de la mère : Rose Taubenblatt Nationalité : Fra.

Résidences successives (à l'étranger et en France) :

Frères (prénoms, dates et lieux de naissance, adresses) :

Maurice 13 ans } en Suisse.
Max 12 ans }

Sœurs (prénoms, dates et lieux de naissance, adresses) :

Reverse side of same fiche

Pavillion at the Clarisses convent in Nice where children learned their new Christian names in "depersonalization"

Pastor Pierre Gagnier

Pastor Pierre Gagnier

Pastor Edmond Evrard

The street sign on the Paris square named for the Abadis says their Marcel Network saved the lives of 527 Jewish children

13

Odette Arrested

The knock on the door of Odette's apartment in Nice came at 6 A.M. When she opened it, Odette was already dressed, ready to leave for work. An agent of the French Milice pushed his way in. "We have information on you," he told Odette. "I have to bring you to the Germans right away."[1]

"He began to search me," Odette said. "I didn't try to resist." Then he began to search her apartment in a move that could have doomed the Marcel Network. Moussa used Odette's place as a mail drop and had hidden some incriminating papers there. Had they been found, he too would have ended up in Nazi hands. Fortunately for Moussa, the Milice agent paid little attention to Odette while looking around.

"I told him that I had to take care of something, and he let me leave the room," Odette explained. "He was very stupid." Two other members of the Milice stood guard outside the door, eliminating any chance that she could flee. But Odette had some room to maneuver, a few moments alone in the bathroom during the search, and managed to destroy the papers that Moussa had left behind. The police found no trace of Moussa, away at the time collecting funds from Maurice Brener in Paris. For the moment, anyway, Moussa remained in the clear.

Odette, however, had to worry about much more than her own fate. The one document the Milice did find in their search was a potential time bomb—the letter identifying Sylvie Delattre as a social worker employed by the bishop of Nice. Odette knew the Germans would certainly question her on any link to Paul Rémond. If they forced her to talk, she might endanger the bishop and the hidden children.

The Milice turned Odette over to the Germans at the Hotel Excelsior, which the Gestapo had converted into a makeshift prison. "Of course, I was slapped and pushed around a bit," Odette said. "But there was no torture."

The next stop was the basement in the Hotel Hermitage, for what Odette called "a much more muscular interrogation." In later years, she never described what "muscular" meant, not in any interview, not to any friend, not even in the book she wrote. She did say, however, that, "They threatened to shoot me."

Odette was ready for torture, ready to die before implicating Moussa and the bishop and endangering the children. She fully expected torture, perhaps to her death, as friends of hers had died at the Hermitage. The friends had been interrogated in the basement, and then locked in hotel rooms on the upper floors between questioning sessions. "They threw themselves out of windows in order not to talk, or perhaps because they were suffering too much," Odette said. Above all she feared the Germans would inject her with truth serum and force her to talk when she would be too drugged to resist.[2]

Almost certainly the Germans beat her, but apparently never applied either extreme measures of torture or truth serum. Her interrogators simply did not know who they had at their mercy. They thought Odette was just another Jewish woman in hiding. They never asked about the Marcel Network because they didn't know her role in it. Odette herself helped keep them in the dark by telling a story that limited the damage.

Under the "muscular" interrogation, Odette volunteered that she was not Sylvie Delattre. She gave them her real name of Odette Rosenstock, admitting she was Jewish, thereby raising her credibility in German eyes.

Then she simply lied. Odette said she had given Bishop Rémond the false name of Sylvie Delattre so she could get the job as a social worker. No one would have employed her with a Jewish name. The Germans bought her explanation. They did not pursue further Odette's link with Rémond.[3]

The Germans also tried the good cop/bad cop tactic with her. They took her from the basement interrogation, shivering with cold, and delivered her upstairs to a higher-ranking woman officer. The officer gave Odette a cigarette and said, "I admire you," referring to the way she had withstood the beatings. "I could not have done what you have done." Then she added: "I promise that if you give us a few names of other Jews we will let you go, take you to Switzerland, and that will be the end of your nightmare."

"If you were in my place," Odette replied, "would you talk?"[4] The woman turned her head aside, mumbling something about "damned intellectuals" before she had Odette taken away. On May 2, 1944, a week after her arrest, Odette was shipped off to Drancy, en route to Auschwitz.

In the end, what saved her from extreme torture was essentially German bureaucratic incompetence. Two Gestapo agents had been on Odette's trail, deliberately not arresting her, hoping that she would lead them to the network that they heard was sheltering Jews. But they had not yet briefed others in the Gestapo office in Nice on their tracking operation. In short, the right hand of the Gestapo didn't know what the left hand was doing. The two agents tracking Odette just happened to be on a mission to Paris when Odette was arrested in Nice and could not participate in her interrogation at the Hotel Hermitage. The Germans who did question Odette never knew what to ask.

When the two tracking agents returned to Nice, the Gestapo finally pieced together the truth. They discovered the mistake of having let Odette go on to Drancy without a maximum interrogation. Belatedly they tried to put things right. On May 16, two weeks after Odette's departure from Nice, according to documents uncovered after the war, the Gestapo chief in Nice, a certain Dr. Keil, sent a telegram to the commandant of the internment camp at Drancy demanding that "the Jewess

Rosenstock" be held there for further questioning. Drancy replied that Odette "was evacuated to the East before your telegram arrived" and could not be interrogated further.[5] For the time being, anyway, Moussa, the bishop, and the children they hid were all safe. Odette, however, was on her way to hell.

Odette's last night at Drancy ended at 5 A.M. when she and others were ordered to assemble in the large central courtyard. There were 1,200 men, women, and children in her group, all chosen to be deported. "None of us really knew then what deportation meant," Odette recalled. But by her arrest in 1944 Jews knew enough to fear the worst. "We had heard on English radio the horror stories of two or three escapees from death camps," Odette said. "They spoke of entire trainloads gassed on arrival. Reason made it hard to admit that such things were possible, but at the same time we knew that there had to be some truth in all that."[6]

By 7 A.M. the deportees were seated in buses on the way to the nearby train station at Bobigny. They passed a working-class district where ordinary people went about their usual early morning business, buying milk and bread or heading for their jobs. Odette watched them through the window of the bus, thinking she might never again enjoy such simple, everyday pleasures. Nobody on the street, she noted, paid any attention to the poor creatures in the buses. Odette thought about the deportees trying to be courageous, and compared them to the people outside not wanting to know. She could no longer hold back her tears.

At the railroad station Odette was herded onto a cattle car with sixty other people. Hay covered the floor. A single bucket served as the only toilet. The Germans ordered Odette, as a medical doctor, to supervise the sanitary arrangements and the organization of the people in the car, an almost impossible task in such crowded and primitive conditions. She arranged for a blanket to be hung around the bucket for a modicum of privacy, had the suitcases piled in one place, tried to comfort the children, and attempted to allot everyone a minimum of space to lie on the hay. "You had to be diplomatic," she remembered. "People used to being free didn't take kindly to orders from a stranger." Then the doors clanged shut, producing total night inside the cattle car, and little air. The train lurched forward. "The cards were dealt," Odette said. "There was no more hope."

The trip to Auschwitz took three days and three nights. A second bucket provided drinking water for everyone in the car. It was refilled once a day at station stops, when the toilet bucket got emptied at the same time. There was no food, no medicine for those who fell ill. People sitting or lying down fought over floor space for their legs. When the train moved, the car shook badly, throwing deportees against each other. Heading to the makeshift toilet meant bumping against other people, setting off more shouting matches and sometimes fights. The stench in the train became unbearable.

Odette's car included fifteen children, already orphans. Their parents had been deported earlier to Auschwitz and now they were making the same journey. No one could shield the children from the constant talk in the train about gas chambers. But two young women in their twenties, Fanny and Renée, helped Odette to distract the little ones, leading them in singing songs and playing games, laughing and smiling. At night though, Renée huddled against Odette, sobbing.[7]

On the third night, the train finally arrived at Birkenau, the end of the rail line at Auschwitz. The sprawling extermination camp, which took its name from the Polish town nearby, was divided into three parts. Auschwitz I, the original site, served as the administrative center. It was designed to look like a labor camp. A sign over the entrance, still there, read "*Arbeit Mach Frei*"—German for "Work Makes One Free." Most arrivals never got to walk under that sign and into Auschwitz. Instead the vast majority of inmates got herded into Birkenau, also known as Auschwitz II, which contained most of the barracks, and the gas chambers. It was the largest of all the Nazi extermination camps. Some 960,000 Jews perished there. Auschwitz III was the actual labor camp, where inmates worked in an arms factory, in a chemical plant, in mines, or in farm fields.

The barracks at Birkenau were only a short walk from the railhead. Still, deportees arriving with Odette had to wait several hours until dawn in their putrid railway cars before the doors at last opened and German soldiers barking orders threw them off the train. The soldiers moved the prisoners into lines, shouting, blowing whistles, beating the laggards with batons. "*Schneller, schneller, los, los,*" the Germans screamed. "Faster, faster, go, go!" Everyone was terrified, the children most of all.

German guards quickly confiscated the miserable little suitcases the prisoners had taken on the train. They tossed out the bodies of deportees who had died on the trip. Then they prodded those prisoners too sick or too feeble to walk to get into the back of trucks, with no kindness intended. Those trucks went straight to the gas chambers.

All the other prisoners continued the forced march to the camp; cold, hungry, thirsty, exhausted, and filthy from the long ordeal on the train, and now more frightened than ever. Jewish detainees from the camp, armed with canes to beat the new arrivals, helped the Germans keep them in line. Detainees did all sorts of appalling jobs at the camp—from beating new arrivals to removing dead bodies from the gas chambers and harvesting their gold teeth—as a way to survive themselves. While forced into jobs they hated, some of them tried to do what they could to help the new arrivals. Others became more brutal than the German guards themselves.

As Odette walked along with two children, one at each hand, a detainee pulled her forward, with the curve of his cane wrapped around her neck. "I'm a Greek, a Jew like you," he told her, speaking rapidly and in a hushed voice. "You must let go of the children if you want to live." Odette ignored him, tugged tighter on the little hands, and walked on. Other detainees then tore the two children away from her. Odette tried to go back, looking for them, only to be pushed by the detainees toward the front of the line at the entrance to the camp.

Four German officers stood at the large gate leading into the camp, pretending not to have seen the scuffle over Odette as they calmly sorted out the arrivals. "*Links*" or "*Rechts*" they would say—left for the women, right for the men—ordering selected prisoners to enter the camp.

A large group of newcomers remained outside the gate. They included children, the elderly, those judged too weak to work, pregnant women, and women who would not let go of children. Had the two children not been pried away from Odette, she too would have joined that group, all of whose members were destined for the gas chambers. Instead she moved unwillingly to the left and entered the camp. She tried to maintain her dignity, walking in as slowly as possible with her head held high, refusing to be intimidated by the Germans. "I am the one who is judging them," Odette told herself.

About three hundred women from the train, including Odette, filed into the camp, greeted by woman guards armed with leather belts who beat them and shouted "*Fünf zu fünf*!" Those among the prisoners who understood German told the others they were to form ranks of five by five and march on. The new arrivals were led into a large stone hangar and told to wait.

In the next few minutes an unusual-looking group of women prisoners from the camp entered the building. They appeared vigorous, comfortably dressed, almost elegant. Odette guessed that these women, all young and attractive, had been allowed to live only if they served as whores for the pleasure of the German soldiers running the camp. The whores threw themselves on the new arrivals, demanding in a mixture of Yiddish, German, and bad French that they be given a skirt, or a pair of shoes, a scarf or a ring. They said the newcomers wouldn't need their clothing or jewelry anymore, and that refusals to hand them over would lead to cruel punishments. But they left as soon as the German women guards entered the hangar.

Each of the new prisoners received a number, recorded on a list next to her name. The number was tattooed on her forearm. Odette became A-5598. Next they were stripped naked and shaved—heads, armpits, and pubic hair. Someone approached Odette to say "tell them you are a doctor and you won't be shaved." She did, and as a result, they left an inch of hair on her head. Anyone resisting the shaving got beaten. Women denounced by the whores to the guards for refusing to give away clothing on arrival also got beaten. After the shaving, the new prisoners no longer recognized each other. Odette had trouble finding her friends from the train.

The showers came next. Four women stood under each showerhead. They were ordered to sit down. Then they heard the noise of the ventilation system in the building cranking up. "We all thought the gas was coming," Odette said. "There was utter panic. But it wasn't gas, not this time." The water came on—ice-cold showers.

From the showers, the guards took the women to a room with a long table piled with prison clothes. An inmate would be handed a shapeless dress, spotted and torn; a pair of men's underpants, more or less patched up; and shoes of haphazard size that never fit—sometimes even two left shoes or two right ones—often without shoelaces.

By then night had fallen, and it had turned cold. They had spent the whole day without food or drink. Now they were pushed into a barn-like building and told to sleep on wide bunks made of wooden planks—ten women to a bunk—with no bedding and no blankets. They lay down as best they could. All ten had to lie on the same side. It was impossible for any one of them to turn over unless the nine others also did so at the same time. But they were all so exhausted that they fell asleep almost immediately. They had survived their first day at Auschwitz, feeling lucky to be alive.[8]

Odette awoke to sounds of leather belts smacking flesh, cries of pain, and orders to get outside. It was 3 A.M. Stars filled the sky, and, with them, flames from high chimneys seen behind rows of barracks. The crematoria worked at night, burning off the remains of the unfortunates taken to the gas chambers. "Look, over there," one of the guards said. "That's the old people and the children from your train."

Icy wind tore through light clothing. Odette's teeth chattered. She and the others stood at attention in rows of five by five for over an hour, through an interminable roll call. The guards counted, got the numbers wrong, and counted again. Some prisoners fainted. The guards blamed them for the confused count, beat other prisoners in frustration, and counted yet again.

When the guards were finally satisfied with the count, teams of two women detainees arrived, each carrying a stretcher between them. A large vat sat on the stretcher, filled with a steaming liquid. The detainees nearest

Odette poured the liquid into a billy can covered with mud and handed it to the first prisoner in the first rank. "Drink that and pass it on," the detainee said. "It's for five." By the time the tin can got to Odette the so-called coffee was cold and tasted awful. But it was the first "meal" in the five days since the train left Drancy.

After that, they marched five by five to the toilets, a long rectangular building with an entry door on one of the short sides and an exit door on the other. Guards ordered the women into the building one hundred at a time. The smell was overpowering, the noise from chattering women like a huge birdcage gone crazy.

A wooden bench-like structure ran down each long side of the building, each with fifty toilet holes in it. Prisoners had to sit on the holes, barely separated from the woman on the left and the woman on the right, facing the parallel row of women opposite. It is hard to imagine a more demeaning way to answer the call of nature, but here was one of the few places at Auschwitz where prisoners could, however briefly, talk freely before guards ordered them out again. The prisoners dubbed the toilettes "Radio Shithouse," the place where they could exchange news, real and false. Odette remembered hearing there at least a dozen times that Paris had been liberated and Hitler assassinated.

Later that second day, they finally ate, a greasy soup and a hunk of bread shared by five prisoners. Then they went back to the barn-like building where they had slept the first night, this time for interrogations, questions that would determine the barracks and the job assigned to each new inmate. It was Odette's turn.

"Last name?"

"Rosenstock."

"First name?"

"Odette." The Belgian woman detainee who interrogated Odette in French wrote down "Odette Sarah."

"But my name is not Sarah," Odette protested.

"Here all Jews are called Sarah," she was told. "Besides, your name no longer has any importance. Only your number counts now. Profession?"

"Doctor."

The interrogator paused, looking interested. "Maybe you have a chance here," she said. "But don't get your hopes up."[9]

14

MOUSSA ALONE

When Moussa left for Paris to see Maurice Brener, he thought his biggest problem was money. "The knife was not yet at our throat," he said, "but the money had nearly run out."[1] They were behind by a month or two in the payments to some of the Catholic institutions for school fees, and food for the children. Although no one had yet threatened to throw the children out, the Catholics appeared increasingly nervous over the shortage of funds. Moussa had also fallen behind in payments to some of the Protestant families. None of the families made threats or begged for more money, but the hardships for them could not go on forever either. Everything depended on Brener raising more funds from the Joint Committee, or so Moussa thought when he left for Paris. He had no idea that the worries over money, bad as they were, would be overshadowed by a far graver crisis when he got back.

The trip to Paris and back took four days. Moussa went by overnight train, concealing compromising papers in his bedding. Brener had his own problems as a wanted man, hiding from the police, and facing ever more complications in getting money smuggled in from Switzerland. But when Moussa explained the gravity of the situation for the Marcel Network, Brener replied, "I will do the impossible to help you out."

According to Moussa's financial accounts, he was spending about 200,000 francs ($2,000) a month to hide, feed, clothe, and educate an average of 140 children, an enormous sum in the France of 1943. Moussa waited twenty-four hours in Paris while Brener came up with the needed funds. When Moussa took the overnight train back to Nice, he felt relieved over his replenished budget, without the faintest notion of how Brener had managed.

On arrival at Nice, Moussa dropped off his suitcase at the modest hotel where he lived, a short distance from Odette's apartment. He got on his bicycle to join her and was only a few yards from the building when he saw Odette's concierge standing outside, looking at him and shaking her head no. Moussa understood and kept on pedaling.

He spent an anguished day, waiting until it would be safe to go back. "I was going mad," he said. Finally, under the cover of night, he returned to Odette's building. The concierge let him in. "They arrested Mademoiselle Delattre this morning," she told Moussa. "They were still here when you came by. If you had stopped they would have taken you too."[2]

Moussa's first reaction was pure folly: "I must rescue her," he thought. He knew the Gestapo would take Odette to Drancy, so he decided to go there to help her escape. Moussa turned to contacts in the Resistance, asking them how to do it. Impossible, they replied, persuading him to drop the idea.

Although crazed with concern for Odette, Moussa also agonized over the threat to the bishop, the children, and himself if she was forced under torture to talk about them. He knew she would resist, as long as she could, but, as he told Rémond, "No one can be sure they won't talk under torture."

Moussa had gone to see Monseigneur Rémond, to tell him of Odette's arrest, and to warn him to be careful. The bishop, clearly troubled, looked Moussa in the eye and said: "The noose is tightening around us. Sylvie has been arrested. You are a wanted man with a price on your head. I think you should go into the back country and lay low for a while because it's just too dangerous for you now. It doesn't have to be for long, perhaps two or three weeks. Let the storm pass, and then you can come back."

For the first time since he had met Paul Rémond, Moussa angrily raised his voice in reply. "Monseigneur," he said, "you a combat veteran of World War One, you are asking me to be a deserter. You are protecting me. But what about the children? Have you thought about them? Who is going to protect the children?"[3]

The bishop's chin trembled. Then, as he pondered a reply, he squeezed his eyeglasses so hard that they cracked in his hand.

The brutal truth was that the Marcel Network had no backup plan, should both Odette and Moussa be unable to continue. They had considered letting the Church take over all the placements of children, all the visits as far as Catholic institutions were concerned. In short, priests operating out of the bishop's office would try to do everything that Moussa and Odette had done. But the idea was rejected as too risky, presenting too many chances of a priest being followed, or of being a double agent, or saying something indiscreet, or otherwise making errors leading to a search of the bishop's office, the discovery of the fiches hidden there, and the arrests of the children. As Moussa said, "All it would take would be for one link in the chain to break and the rest would crumble."[4]

And even if the priests could have taken on the job, there would still be no one covering the children hidden with Protestant families. The pastors, unlike the bishop, worked almost alone, with virtually no staff. They were simply unable to drop everything and work full time, as Moussa and Odette had done, looking after hidden Jewish children.

The bishop understood. Moussa would have to carry on, whatever the risk. Rémond rose with difficulty by putting both hands on his desk. He took Moussa by the arm and escorted him to the door. "The only thing left to do is to pray for you," the bishop said.[5] Moussa's grandfather had come to much the same conclusion years before. Moussa was nineteen years old then, determined to leave Damascus forever, and saying good-bye to his grandfather for what would be the last time. The two were extremely close, with the grandfather especially important in seeing to the boy's religious education.[6] The old man put his hands on Moussa's head and gave him a farewell blessing. At the door to the bishop's office, Rémond made the same gesture, hands on Moussa's head for another blessing at another of life's turning points. "It was extremely touching," Moussa said.

The bishop added, "If you can, pray for me as well."

Moussa left the residence deep in thought. "The bishop was right," he told himself. "I have to hide somewhere around here. But where?" He knew he couldn't go back to the hotel where he lived. Fortunately, by the end of the day, he had a solution of sorts. Moussa went to see the headmistress of a boarding school where he had hidden some girls, and this time she came to his rescue. The headmistress offered to let him sleep in one of the classrooms, on the floor. "I have to ask you not to undress," she said apologetically, "because you need to be able to leave very early." The most she could do in the way of bedding was to put a carpet on the floor for him.[7]

That Spartan arrangement was fine with Moussa, even though it meant he had to leave the school before dawn. Otherwise the women who came to clean the classrooms at 6 A.M. would discover him. Moussa slept in his clothes, with the carpet folded around him like a sleeping bag. In the morning, he managed to make himself a hot drink and take a biscuit from the school kitchen before leaving for the day.

Wandering around the nearly deserted streets of Nice at that early hour was too dangerous for a wanted man. So Moussa went to Father Rostan with an idea. "I need a list of all the times for morning Masses at all the churches in Nice," he said.

"That's curious," Rostan responded. "Whatever for?"

"I want to go to Mass every morning at a different church between six and nine A.M."

Rostan understood. Moussa needed to lose himself in any ordinary crowd of people.

Moussa got the list and began a pattern that would last for months. "Every day at six thirty A.M., I was first in one chapel, then another, then a church," he said. "No practicing Catholic ever attended so many Masses in so short a time."[8]

With Odette gone, Moussa was now alone. He realized there was no way he could do all her work—and all of his—by himself. He would have to cut back their operation, or hire someone else to share the load. Neither option looked attractive. Cutting back was out of the question if that meant putting children at risk. But no one he hired to share the workload could ever replace Odette. "She enabled the children to live," Moussa explained. "She nourished them with kindness, tenderness, and hope. Children talked to her like a mother. She was everything to those girls and they couldn't wait for her next visit."[9]

Moussa found himself overwhelmed while trying to figure out what to do next. The Germans were still arresting Jews in the spring of 1944. New children kept arriving from concierges and others, needing to be placed. There was hardly any time to visit the others already sheltered. Desperate, he turned to the bishop.

"In principle, I am against bringing in someone from the outside," Moussa told Rémond. "But if you know of someone absolutely sure, I won't refuse the help."

"There is a Belgian social worker," the bishop replied. "I can guarantee her honesty."

Moussa gave her a try, but she lasted little more than a week. "I found out that she was trying to convert the children to Catholicism," Moussa said. "She betrayed the bishop, who had been very specific in warning her against doing any such thing. She had a moral contract with us and she broke it."

So Moussa fired her. It was a terrible scene, he recalled, with such anger that he could never bring himself to mention her name.

"You betrayed the bishop's trust and mine," Moussa told her. "Those children are Jews. Their parents were arrested because they were Jews. We are hiding those children because they are Jews and their families want them to remain Jewish."

The woman accused Moussa of brutalizing her, and he agreed that he did. "I brutalized her in words," Moussa admitted.[10]

After that, Moussa decided that on balance he would be better off trying to cope alone than to take on another new and untried partner.

He called on the Catholic institutions and the Protestant families to tell them that Odette had been arrested. Then he added what he hoped was true—that she hadn't talked, and that there was no risk. They would continue as before, with Moussa visiting when he could. There would be far fewer visits without Odette, but they would manage. To those who were uneasy, Moussa would say, "If you don't trust me, I will take the children back." No one asked him to do that.

As far as the children were concerned, they somehow accepted that things would be all right even though Odette would no longer visit. "They had incredible maturity," Moussa said.

Not everyone was so easily convinced. At the Joan of Arc convent in Grasse, the mother superior, Mère Marie-Thérèse, learned of Odette's arrest and began to panic. She feared Odette would talk under torture about the convent's role in illegally hiding Jews, and the Germans would arrest her and the young nuns in her care. Before that happened, she wanted the Jewish girls to leave. If the Germans found no Jews there, maybe the convent would be all right. Still, that course of action troubled her conscience. She could not bring herself to expel the younger girls, Martoune, nine, and Denise, ten. They could stay and she would try to keep their Jewish identity secret, she decided. But the older girls, fourteen-year-old Jeannette and fifteen-year-old Françoise, would have to go. That way Mère Marie-Thérèse hoped she could limit the dangers and still live with herself.[11]

She called in Françoise, to tell her about Odette's arrest and to say that only the two younger girls would be allowed to stay. Françoise understood perfectly well the atmosphere of fear at the convent, and not only because of Odette's arrest. A German officer had recently brought a little French girl to live and study at the convent. The girl's mother, the German's mistress in Cannes, did not want her daughter at home while she entertained her officer. So she sent the girl to the nunnery, with the German as escort. "When the mother superior saw the German officer enter the convent, she practically had a heart attack," Françoise said. "That and the arrest of Odette made her tremble."[12]

Moussa knocked at the door while Françoise was talking with Mère Marie-Thérèse. "He arrived by bicycle from Nice twenty miles away, tired and unshaven. He looked terrible," Françoise said. But, despite his appearance, Moussa managed to calm the mother superior down, and assure her that Odette hadn't talked. In the end, Mère Marie-Thérèse relented. "All right," she told Françoise, "you can stay."

Françoise had another idea. She told Moussa she wanted to take over for Odette.

"I'm old enough," she said.

Moussa refused, of course. He could hardly agree to put a teenager in such a dangerous position. "I promised your parents that I would take care of you, and I will," Moussa told Françoise. "Just shut up about Odette and go back to your studies."

"He was rough," Françoise said. "But he had to be in order to do what he did."

Françoise never knew just how tough Moussa had to be. One day a French policeman stopped Moussa on a narrow street in the old town of Nice and searched him. In Moussa's jacket pocket the policeman found dozens of blank ration cards.

"What's this?" he asked.

"I stole them," Moussa said, "to sell on the black market." Better a small lie than the big truth about using the cards to save Jewish children, he thought.

"You swine," the policeman said, beating Moussa with a baton until he fell to the ground. Then he kicked him in the ribs, before leaving Moussa moaning in the street.

No one passing by offered to help Moussa. He just lay there until he recovered sufficient strength to get up and move on. All he could think of was his luck to be the victim of a French policeman and to get away with only a beating. If a Gestapo agent had searched him and found the ration cards, Moussa would have been arrested, interrogated, and deported, dooming what remained of the Marcel Network.

There was one other close call while Moussa spent his nights sleeping in the classroom. Returning one day to his former hotel to pick up some clean clothes, he parked his bicycle outside and told the man at the reception desk, "I've been away for a while. I just need to pick up some laundry and then I'll be leaving again." He paid his bill and went up to his room to collect his things.

When he came downstairs to leave, Moussa saw Alice La Blonde and another Gestapo agent at the reception desk. They approached him.

"Your papers," Alice demanded.

He gave her a false ID card in the name of Fouad El Moussri (Fouad the Egyptian) which identified Moussa as an Egyptian born in Damascus. The papers also said Moussa was a naturalized French citizen working as a university professor.

Alice inspected the card, then asked the man at the hotel desk, "He lives here?"

"Yes, he's been living here for quite a while," the desk clerk replied.

Alice handed back the card. "You can go," she said.

"I got back on my bicycle with my little bundle of clothes and pedaled without knowing where I was going," Moussa said. "I had never been more frightened, not even during that narrow escape at the café."[13]

At least he was still free. Odette, he knew, might not be alive.

15

AUSCHWITZ

Odette's first weeks in Auschwitz were the hardest on her physically. Her group of arrivals remained in quarantine, assigned to brutal tasks. They dug stones out of the earth, wielded axes to break the stones, and hauled heavy pails filled with the broken stones, all to make cement for building new barracks or fixing old ones. The soup-and-bread diet left them near starvation. They shivered against the cold. When it rained they slid in the mud. The hard labor exhausted them. All the while the guards shouted, "*Schneller, schneller*"—faster, faster—and hit the laggards with their belts.

It all had a sinister purpose. The initial quarantine period filtered out the weaker women, those least able to resist, and sent them to be gassed. At the end of the quarantine, the survivors would be assigned to new barracks and new jobs. Some women worked in the camp, perhaps as secretaries, or in grimmer assignments such as disposing of bodies; others toiled as slave labor in the factories, mines, or farms where thousands died from beatings, illness, and starvation. For most inmates the choice was either the furnace or being worked to death.

Odette's profession as a doctor had been noted, but no one pulled her out of quarantine for medical duties. She later learned a bitter truth. The camp authorities thought they had a surplus of doctors among the inmates at Auschwitz, and felt no need to look for more, despite the fact that some of the so-called physicians had received inadequate or even no medical training. So Odette's file sat ignored, in limbo. Bizarrely, her prospects changed when a call went out for ten women to volunteer for an ethnic study. The Germans wanted to investigate various physical and racial characteristics of Jews. Curious about the notion of an ethnic study at Auschwitz, Odette volunteered. It was a decision that probably saved her life.

The study took place in a room at the camp hospital. Odette's examiner was a Polish woman, a prisoner who spoke French. As she stripped naked for the study, Odette said she was a doctor and that she hoped she would be able to work at the hospital herself. The examiner measured Odette's nose, her ears, and was proceeding down her body when they heard a screaming match from the office next door. It turned out that the camp's German doctor-in-chief, Edward Wirths, was firing an inmate doctor, a Jewish woman who had displeased him. When things quieted down, one of the chief doctor's assistants opened the door to the examining room and explained what had happened. They needed a new doctor as a replacement. "We have one right here," Odette's examiner said. "Try her out."

"Well, as long as you are here," the assistant told Odette, "get dressed and come on through."

"That's how I was hired as a doctor," Odette said.[1]

Odette entered a different world. As a doctor, she was assigned to Barrack 19, a smaller, better kept blockhouse near the camp hospital. There was still no running water inside, but to Odette, after sleeping on shared wooden planks with no protection against the cold during the long quarantine, the dormitory in Barrack 19 with its individual beds and heat from a fireplace seemed like comparative luxury. There was more bread, better soup with a bit of meat, sometimes a piece of cheese or a spoonful of jam, and once an apple. The building housed women doctors and nurses. Other prisoners kept the place clean.

Her first job was simple but tiring—health inspection. She awoke at 5 A.M. and spent each day, along with several other doctors, examining more than a thousand women from different barracks, looking at their eyes, their throats, their general comportment. She looked for any signs of fatigue, of lice, or contagious disease. Odette understood perfectly well that anyone found with a serious medical problem would be sent to the ovens. So she signed all her reports with a zero—meaning no problem found. She would return to her bed exhausted, crash, and start again the next day.

On her rounds Odette discovered a barrack of prisoners that housed only identical twins—female twins of all ages. "I had the feeling I was seeing double," she said. The twins still dressed in the clothes they brought with them. They received extra food, and they slept in proper beds. Like real princesses, they never had to work, but suddenly their charmed life ended. One day the twins were gone, replaced in the barrack by women dwarfs.

Odette learned later that the twins ended up on the dissection tables of Joseph Mengele, the second-ranking doctor at Auschwitz, who conducted grotesque experiments on the inmates. Mengele injected chloroform into the hearts of each pair of twins, killing them instantly. Then he dissected them to meticulously study the similarity of their body parts. With other inmates he injected chemicals into eyes in attempts to change their color, or amputated limbs without anesthesia. Eventually he used the dwarfs in still other experiments. After the war Mengele fled to South America and died in Brazil in 1979, drowning while swimming in the sea, possibly after suffering a stroke. He was sixty-eight and had escaped prosecution for war crimes by hiding under false identities for thirty-four years.

Most of the treatment at the camp hospital in Auschwitz had nothing to do with Mengele's experiments. The hospital was designed to get inmate patients back to work with minimal medical care, if possible, or to send them to the gas chambers if not. Odette spent only a month as a health inspector, then got reassigned to work inside the hospital, a series of barracks serving as wards. She found that patients there had no sheets or blankets and such a paltry diet that she often supplemented it with some of her own bread or soup rations. The supply of medicine was criminally short.

"I had tablets for coughs, some morphine, and very little else," she said. "I had about a fifth of what I needed."

Sometimes Odette obtained additional medicine for her patients from "Canada," a warehouse area a few hundred yards from the gas chambers. Inmates at Auschwitz called the area Canada because it was a place of abundance. Suitcases seized from arriving deportees got opened and sorted there. Valuables like jewelry found in the suitcases got shipped back to Germany. Valuables for the camp, such as cigarettes, clothing, or lipstick, often found their way into the pockets of the inmates doing the sorting. These items then got traded for extra food rations from the guards. Occasionally friends of Odette working at Canada arranged trades that resulted in extra medicine.

Despite the hellish conditions at the hospital, Odette was able to help patients from time to time. "I could listen to them, perhaps relieve their pain," she said. "I had the feeling of being a little bit useful."

Odette could never relieve her own emotional pain, however. The fate of Moussa and the hidden children obsessed her. Sometimes she could no longer control her anguish. Another woman prisoner once found Odette in tears.

"Why are you crying?" the woman asked.

"The children," Odette said.

"Are you married?"

"No."

"So how many children do you have then?"

"Hundreds," Odette said.

She never explained what she meant.

The inmate doctors at Auschwitz, Odette found, came from the best and the worst of humanity. The best stayed with their patients until the end, doing the most they could for them. The worst took medicine from their patients and sold it for food or cigarettes. Some of them were not even doctors. They were nurses, even doctors' wives, pretending to be doctors in order to survive. They got away with it because no one at Auschwitz could produce diplomas or other papers to prove their qualifications to camp authorities. The real doctors among the inmates knew each other, however, from conversations over medical questions. They did their best to keep the fake doctors from causing any damage to patients and tried not to expose them as frauds.

The phony doctors included a fortune-teller from Paris. She threatened to give patients the evil eye unless they handed her some soup or whatever else she wanted. After the war, Odette saw this same woman cross a street in Paris through slow traffic and throw herself in front of a car. The driver, thinking he might have killed someone, got out of his car to see if she was all right. The woman refused his offer to drive her to a hospital, and promised not to sue, but asked him for some money because she had none. The driver, grateful she wanted nothing more, emptied his wallet. Appalled, Odette walked on.

In the macabre world of Auschwitz, the Germans used an orchestra made up of woman inmates to soften the harsh realities of the death camp. The orchestra played when work details of prisoners marched out of the camp gates in the morning and returned exhausted at night, in an effort to put the minds of the detainees at ease.

Membership in the orchestra meant a chance to live, with better food rations. Violette Jacquet-Silberstein, a violinist in the orchestra, denied reports that it suffered a high rate of suicide from the trauma of being forced to play as victims were herded into the gas chambers. "We never played during death marches, and there were no suicides by the musicians," she said in an interview.[2] The orchestra did, however, give concerts for the SS tormentors. They played mostly Germanic music—German operas, Viennese operettas, and some modern melodies. Patients could hear the concerts from their hospital beds. Some of them covered their ears, trying to shut out the sound. Others somehow managed to enjoy the music, which reminded them of happier times in their previous lives.

Once while Odette was at Auschwitz—"an historic day," she said—prisoners were served macaroni cooked in milk. The exceptional treatment immediately touched off rumors. Prisoners said Allied troops must be coming close. But such hopes were quickly dashed. The reality turned out to be quite different—a masquerade for the benefit of inspectors from the Red Cross visiting the camp that day. Music and macaroni created a rather different impression for the inspectors.

Odette's mother and sister had arrived at Auschwitz a year before her, but Odette refused to believe they had perished. She sought out nurses in her barrack who had been there more than a year, may have known her relatives, and might give her some clues to their fate. At first, the nurses tried to avoid hurting Odette. Then one night, after yet another round of questions from Odette, a veteran nurse exploded in frustration. "You mean you haven't stopped looking for them?" she asked Odette. "You must be crazy. If they were still alive you would know it. You can count on the fingers of one hand the Frenchwomen who are still alive here from that time, and we know who all of them are."

The nurse went on to say that Odette's mother, Marthe Rosenstock, had been sent to the gas chambers on arrival. Her younger sister, Simone, who had wanted to work as a seamstress for a Paris fashion house, had been assigned at Auschwitz to a work detail repairing roads. After four months of bone-crunching labor, Simone ended up in the hospital flat on her back and hardly able to move. She could not get up for an inspection and was put on the list of those to be gassed. "There it was," Odette recalled later. "Finally, I knew with certainty that they had died. I had wanted to hope. But now I could no longer lie to myself."[3]

On Yom Kippur, the Jewish Day of Atonement and the holiest holiday of the year, the Germans celebrated at the hospital with a selection for another massacre. The selection process began with an order to the doctors: "By noon, you must supply a list of all patients who cannot be cured in the next two weeks." Odette knew what that meant. She refused to make up any such list. She had diagnosed all of her patients with minor ailments like the flu, even those with tuberculosis, malaria, or epilepsy. She stuck with those falsified reports, hoping they would not be put to closer scrutiny.

Later that day Mengele arrived, dressed in an immaculate white medical coat, followed by sycophantic assistants. Among them was a secretary with a nervous tic. "*Achtung*!" yelled the woman guard in charge of the hospital ward where Odette worked. Doctors and nurses in the ward stood at attention near their patients. The ailing prisoners remained in their beds. The secretary with the tic began to call out the numbers of prisoners one by one. When her number was called, the patient would have to get out of bed, stand up, and strip naked for a hurried, cursory examination by Mengele's team, as Odette and the other doctors in the ward hovered around them. Mengele would write something in his notebook. Then the next number would be called, and the next. "I would try to intervene," Odette remembered, "to say that this patient was about to leave the hospital or that one was improving. Sometimes I was listened to, sometimes not. I really couldn't do anything more than that."

Some prisoners could not stand on their own. A nurse would try to help. Mengele would note that, and laugh, or berate the nurse for being unable to make the patient stand. Another cry of "*Achtung*" signaled that the selection was over. Mengele left for the next barrack that served as another ward.

Odette never came anywhere near Mengele's experiments. The selection process was the closest she ever got to him, and that was bad enough. Odette retained a lifelong hatred of Mengele. Years later, she turned down a job with Amnesty International, the prisoners' advocacy group, because she could not bring herself to oppose capital punishment. "If I saw Mengele again, I would kill him," she said.[4]

After the selection was over, none of the prisoners in Odette's hospital ward knew what Mengele had marked in his notebook—whether she had been spared, or selected to be gassed, or destined for one of the experiments. A patient would ask another, "What do you think he put down for me? I thought I was looking better." Those who managed to stand up knew only that they were better off than those who stayed in bed. Those not able to stand already knew what would happen to them. Yet, that evening the soup was brought into the ward as if nothing had occurred.

A day passed, then a second. Still nothing happened. It was September 1944, some five months after Odette had arrived at Auschwitz, and darkness fell at 7 P.M. A single lamp lit the ward. Suddenly, on the third night, the guards entered and barked a sinister order: "Change the barracks."

The secretary with the tic announced, "Everyone I call will go to Barrack 22." Tears, screams, moans, and beatings followed, as the unfortunates on the list got forced out, or those too weak to walk were carried out. Pitifully, some of the women selected tried to hide, to no avail. Those who remained in the ward felt relieved, almost happy.

The women moved to Barrack 22 were locked in there. As a doctor, Odette managed to visit them. "There were those who didn't believe they would be going to the gas chambers, those who suspected, and those who knew for sure," Odette said. She knew for sure. She had seen other selections. But when some of the women asked her, "Is it true? Is it going to happen to us?" she couldn't admit it to them. Odette later said, "I was unable to tell them the truth."

Other women asked Odette to pass on messages to loved ones. She promised to do what she could. One woman had become deaf from the mumps and could not understand what was happening. Others were hysterical. "It was horrible," Odette said. "It is hard to believe that anything like that could happen. But it did."

That night the trucks came. Soldiers with pistols and batons forced the screaming women from Barrack 22 into the trucks for the ride to the gas chambers, then locked them in. The gas did not kill them all. Some were still alive when their bodies were thrown into the ovens and turned into dust.

Odette visited Barrack 22 again the next day. It was empty except a few traces of the departed left on the floor—a spoon, a toothbrush, a handkerchief, and everywhere pieces of bread. Terrified women forced out during the night had abandoned one of their most precious possessions, what was left of their bread rations.

Later that day the Germans disinfected Barrack 22, and the process started again.

As a doctor, Odette had a position of relative privilege among Auschwitz prisoners. Doctors could roam the camp and visit places that were off-limits to other prisoners. So Odette saw horrors that most of the relatively few prisoners to survive Auschwitz never witnessed firsthand themselves, including the various travesties of the so-called hospital, the barrack for the twins and then the dwarfs, Mengele's satanic selection process, and the despair of the doomed women Odette was able to visit in their locked barrack while they awaited execution. Other survivors may have seen one or more of these abominations. But as far as is known, no one other than Odette was an eyewitness to them all—and survived to write about them as she did.[5]

According to her book, Odette expected that sooner or later she too would be selected for the gas chambers. Fortunately, she was wrong. As Soviet troops advanced from the east into Poland, pushing back German forces, the Nazis understood that their days of running Auschwitz were numbered. They began to empty the camp by shipping able-bodied workers—and a few doctors with them—to the west, to the Bergen-Belsen death camp, thought to be safer because it was inside Germany itself. Odette joined a shipment of hundreds of Auschwitz prisoners to Bergen-Belsen. Once again, they traveled in filthy cattle cars on overcrowded trains—hungry, thirsty, cold, and often ill—fighting among themselves for leg room, breathing putrid air, this time for three days, to begin another life in yet another concentration camp.[6]

16

Bergen-Belsen

Moussa constantly agonized over Odette's fate. He knew she had been deported to Auschwitz, but nothing more than that. Was she alive? Tortured? Better off dead? His ignorance over her fate and his impotence to help her obsessed him. Still, for the sake of the children, he carried on in Nice as best he could, risking arrest at any moment. Nor was that all—sometimes even his friends added to his burdens.

Among these were Communists in the French Resistance. Although never a Communist himself, Moussa became their ally during the war for one simple reason—Communists played a major role in the armed struggle of the French Resistance to the Nazi occupation. The relatively small Resistance could never defeat the Germans by itself, but its sabotage operations hurt them and its intelligence-gathering aided the Allies during and after the invasion of Normandy. French Resistance forces blew up bridges and derailed trains along German supply lines. They guided Allied bombing raids, disrupted German communications, provided intelligence on German fortifications along the Normandy beaches, and helped Allied soldiers and airmen escape from behind enemy lines. Among the key contributors to these efforts were Communist units that had been battle-hardened during the Spanish Civil War of 1936–39.

Like all members of the Resistance, the Communists were hunted men, their families in grave danger. Moussa did what he could to help. Sometimes he supplied false ration cards to Communists' families, and he hid a handful of their children. The children of Communists in the Resistance were not counted among the 527 Jewish youngsters saved, but Moussa's same security rules also applied to them—such as never letting parents know where their children were sheltered. That's what got him in trouble with his Communist friends.

One day as Moussa walked down a quiet street in Nice, a man slid up to his side and whispered in his ear, "Tonight at nine." He mentioned an address.

"All right," Moussa said. "I'll be there."

At 9 P.M. Moussa found himself inside a dark, abandoned house. He opened one door, then another, found a staircase, and descended into a dimly lit cellar where four tough-looking men from the Communist Resistance awaited him.

"Do you recognize us?" their spokesman asked.

"Of course," Moussa said. "Good evening."

He'd met the spokesman, a heavyset unshaven man in his forties, on more than one occasion. The others, all younger, he'd also seen before.

"Good evening," the four replied. Then nothing. All looked to the spokesman as he searched for the right words to say next.

Moussa broke the awkward silence. "Well, what do you want from me?"

"We want to thank you for taking in the kids of our comrades," the spokesman said.

"You're welcome," Moussa told them. He paused, then asked, "What else?"

"We want to know the exact addresses of these kids."

"You can't be serious," Moussa said. "You know I can't tell you that."

"Why not? Don't you trust us?"

"Look, I have to be careful. Just like you don't tell anyone where you hide your arms, I don't tell anyone where I keep the kids."

The spokesman realized it was time to up the ante. "Listen," he said. "We appreciate what you've done for us. You're not really one of us, but who cares? You too are fighting the Krauts and that's good enough for us. But we cannot accept that you alone know the addresses of our kids. We insist—more than insist. Do you understand?"

"And if I refuse?"

"You'll end up giving us what we want. Be reasonable. Am I making myself clear?"

"Perfectly," Moussa replied. "You'll beat the hell out of me. Well, go ahead."

More silence. The four toughs looked at each other. Finally the spokesman caved.

"All right," he said. "You can go." He gave Moussa a shove. "What a bloody stubborn son of a bitch you are."

"*Adieu,*" Moussa said.[1]

He never saw the four Communists again. But from then on Moussa understood that even if the Germans or the French police didn't do him in, his so-called friends might save them the trouble.

✦

At roll call on her first day at Bergen-Belsen, Odette heard her name called out. At Auschwitz they had checked the prisoners present by their numbers. Odette was so used to being addressed by her number that when she heard "Doctor Odette Rosenstock" for the first time in months, she thought they were calling someone else.

She soon found out that the guards at Bergen-Belsen beat the inmates less. And the camp had no gas chambers. It shipped its prisoners farther east for execution. Apart from those differences, however, this was Auschwitz all over again, a killing machine of slave labor, illness, starvation, and selections of prisoners to be gassed. In some ways conditions were even worse than Auschwitz. The camp, named after two towns in northwest Germany and often called just Belsen, was riddled with more disease. Some 35,000 inmates at Belsen died of typhus alone, among them

Anne Frank, the Dutch girl who wrote the famous diary. The hospital at Belsen had no running water, sometimes no electricity. And unlike Auschwitz, there was no "Canada" for extra medicine.

Odette arrived at Belsen in November 1944, with winter under way, the ground covered in snow, and the icy wind bone-chilling. She stuffed rags into her outsized galoshes, but her feet still turned numb from the cold. Barracks were unheated, the hospital hopelessly short of medication to treat contagious disease.

The German chief doctor at Belsen, Alfred Schnabel, was an ear, nose, and throat specialist, hopeless at surgery. Odette once assisted him as the anesthetist for an emergency operation. Schnabel could not find the woman's appendix and searched for it through her intestines. Finally, in desperation, Schnabel summoned another doctor, a Jewish surgeon among the inmates, who immediately found the appendix, removed it, and sewed the woman up. Too late: the patient died on the operating table.

Odette spent Christmas Day 1944 at the hospital, receiving more patients than she could handle and getting less medicine to treat them. Christmas dinner was a rutabaga, cold and sliced. Odette closed her eyes and told herself it tasted like pineapple. A friend handed her a poem as a Christmas present. "Your smile is like a bouquet of roses for us," one line went. As she went to bed, Odette asked herself the same haunting, unanswered question that tormented her every night: What is happening in France? To Moussa? To the children?[2]

In early January 1945, Odette caught typhus. She lay in a coma, between life and death, for three weeks. As a doctor she got priority treatment, including medication denied to others. Injections saved her life. When she finally awoke, she could not move, but she recovered in another three weeks and was back at work by the end of February.[3]

In March, rumors grew about German retreats and Allied victories, with the Russians closing in from the east and the Americans and British from the west. The news from outside changed practically nothing inside Belsen, however. There the relentless killing churned on.

On April 15, 1945, a Sunday, Odette finished a morning round of consultations thoroughly exhausted. She retired for a nap, leaving orders not to wake her under any circumstances. But Michele, a patient at the hospital unable to control her excitement, roused Odette at 2 P.M. "The Germans have fled and the British are coming!" Michele said breathlessly. "They'll be here in three hours."

"You must be delirious," Odette told her. "Go back to bed, sleep it off, and dream of Santa Claus."

Then Odette herself went back to sleep. When she awoke again later that afternoon, the sound of tanks filled the air. A British voice announced in English over a loudspeaker, "Hello everyone. You are free."

"We went crazy in the hospital," Odette remembered. "We hugged and kissed each other. Those able to walk ran to the British tanks. We really were free."[4]

When British and Canadian troops entered the camp, they found that the departing Germans had cut the water supply, making it that much harder for the arriving Allies to care for the surviving inmates. The Allies found 13,000 unburied corpses in the camp and thousands of other inmates seriously ill or nearly starved, among them Odette Rosenstock. One year after her arrest in Nice the previous April—after Auschwitz and Belsen—Odette was still alive. Through it all, according to Jeannette Wolgust, "It was the hope of seeing Moussa again that kept her going and made her survive."[5]

The British tried to feed the prisoners with beef from army rations, but the inmates could not handle proper food. Their digestive systems were too weak from the long-term starvation diet. The British had more luck with skimmed milk and a rice-and-sugar-based mixture. With time and proper medical care, prisoners began to recover. Although some went home, Odette stayed behind in Belsen to help with former inmates who could not be moved. "I wanted to return to my life, to my companion," she said, "but I felt it was my duty to stay."

On May 21, Swiss doctors arrived to replace camp doctors like Odette. She would be leaving the next day with a transport of former prisoners returning to France. "I was drunk with happiness and anxiety at the same time," Odette remembered. The joy of going home mixed with fear over Moussa's fate. "I was dumbstruck," she said. "I couldn't speak."[6]

✦

It was Moussa Abadi's great good fortune that Nice had long since been freed. When the Allies liberated Nice in August 1944, Odette was still in Auschwitz. The war in Europe against Germany would continue for almost another year, until May 1945, while Odette languished in Belsen. But in Nice, Moussa's clandestine struggle was over.

He had run the network alone for four exhausting and dangerous months, from Odette's arrest in April 1944 to the liberation of Nice in August. All the time, the Germans were still arresting Jews, right up to the last days of their occupation. It is impossible to say whether Moussa by himself could have kept the network going for much longer. It was a blessing that he never had to try.

"We were liberated," Moussa said, "but I didn't know what had happened to Odette." Still, he knew he had to carry on with the next phase of the operation—the reuniting of hidden children with their families. Bishop Rémond had the same priorities. "My first thought is for Sylvie Delattre," he told Moussa. "I hope she is still alive." His second thought was to help reunite families. With the bishop's help, Moussa managed to rent an office in the building that, in a touch of bitter irony, had housed the Commissariat for Jewish Affairs, a center of repression during the Nazi occupation of Nice. From there, Moussa took out the fiches he had made for each child and began trying to contact their parents or other relatives. He was still working without help, but at least everything was now legal.

"When the parents came, I turned over the addresses of the children," Moussa said. "Sometimes they could not wait for them to be brought to my office and would go to collect the children themselves." That could be done with youngsters sheltered with Protestant families. The Catholic schools, however, insisted on proper paperwork before releasing their children, meaning that reunions with them took place in Moussa's office, where he could witness the joy.

"I remember one mother," Moussa said. "There were thirty people in the waiting room when I brought in this boy of five and pushed him toward his mother. She fell to her knees and crushed him to her bosom in front of everyone. Then she cried out, 'My husband was deported. My two daughters were deported. My other son was deported. All I had left was my youngest and I thought I would never find him.' She turned her eyes toward heaven. 'Thank God,' she said. 'Thank God.'"

"There was a total, indescribable joy in being able to return a child to his mother," Moussa said. "Although I knew Odette's life was in danger, I felt that what we had done for the children had to be done, and that we had not done it badly."[7]

In those cases when both parents died in the Holocaust, Moussa did his best to find other close relatives. If that failed, he had to place the hidden children in homes reopened by the OSE, the same homes that the Jewish charity had run before the war but had been forced to close during the Nazi occupation. For months the heartwarming work of reuniting families mixed with the heartbreaking task of providing for children left alone.

With the liberation came the settling of accounts. The French glorified activists in the Resistance and turned on the collaborators—beating informers or shaving the hair of women who slept with the Germans. It was not a time to forgive and forget treachery during the war years by neighbors or former friends. Moussa kept score, determined to shun those whose behavior had offended him during the Nazi occupation, no one more than Father Auguste Valensin, a Jesuit priest who had been a particularly close friend.

Before the German occupation, Moussa often met with the priest, a specialist on Dante, to discuss literature. "He was a great philosopher," Moussa said. "I was very attached to him." The two intellectuals—a Catholic and a Jew—enjoyed each other's company. Father Valensin traveled around Nice on a bicycle, his robe flowing. Whenever he saw Moussa on the street he would stop to say hello. After the Germans marched in, however, the priest's attitude changed. He passed Moussa without stopping his bicycle. "I figured that he had not recognized me," Moussa said. "Then it happened a second time. I raised my arm to say hello, but he passed without nodding. I was hurt. Here is a priest, a man of God, abandoning me, I thought, because I am a Jew, under threat, and it is dangerous for him to be seen with me. I found his attitude unacceptable. So after that, when he passed by me, I turned away and refused to look at him."

The day of the liberation, Father Valensin telephoned Moussa. "I need to see you urgently," he said.

"Really," Moussa replied coldly. "What for?"

"I want to confess."

"I don't have time for you."

"Please, I implore you," Valensin begged. "I have something very important to tell you."

"No. You abandoned me when I was in distress. I don't want to see you."

But the priest refused to give up. "Dear Moussa," he said, "let me see you for five minutes and I promise I will never bother you again."

Moussa relented. "How bizarre," he thought, "a priest wanting to confess to me."

"It's very simple," Father Valensin began when they met. "You noticed I was avoiding you. Yes, I am a coward. I was afraid I would be arrested and tortured because I knew about your clandestine activities."

"Why would you have been arrested?"

"Because I too am Jewish," the priest said. "There are two Jesuits here who were born Jewish. I am one of them. The Pope gave a dispensation for us to be accepted into the priesthood. Because I was born Jewish I was afraid to talk to you, afraid that I would be arrested and questioned about you. Will you forgive me?"[8]

Moussa did forgive. The two men embraced and resumed their friendship.

Nearly a year later Moussa enjoyed a far more welcome surprise. He opened an envelope to find a crumpled piece of paper inside. "Odette is alive, Bergen-Belsen," the paper said. It had been brought out by an inmate released from the camp after the British arrived. Moussa still did not know that Odette had chosen to stay to care for ill prisoners for a while. Nor did he know whether she was well or when she might leave, but, as he said, "She was alive and that was the most important thing."[9]

✦

Odette's train from Belsen arrived in Paris at the Gare de l'Est. Waiting there when she arrived was a medical student named Georges Isserlis, the former messenger boy for the Marcel Network who knew Moussa and Odette from Nice. Georges was helping the released prisoners off the train when, to his surprise, he recognized Odette.

"I don't know Moussa's address," he told her, "but I do know that he is alive and still in Nice."

"Although I don't cry easily," Odette said, "suddenly I was crying buckets."[10]

Georges Isserlis spent the whole night transferring former prisoners to buses at the train station, riding with them to the Hotel Lutetia in Paris, and then helping them settle in. The next day in class at medical school, he fell asleep, sitting in the front row. The professor said: "If you are not interested, you might as well leave." Georges went to see him later, apologized, and explained what he had been doing all night. He became the professor's favorite student.

The Hotel Lutetia, a Left Bank palace, had been the headquarters in Paris for the Abwehr, the German intelligence service. The French turned the luxury hotel into a reception center for former inmates returning from the death camps. Odette stayed there for three days of medical checks. French agents also investigated the arrivals to make sure no Nazis had infiltrated their ranks, posing as former prisoners in an attempt to save themselves. When they were satisfied, the French gave Odette a new ID card and let her go.

Odette remained in the French capital for a few days to find her father and confirm to him the deaths at Auschwitz of her mother and sister. It was a particularly difficult meeting because Odette blamed her father for leaving her mother and sister behind in Paris, vulnerable to arrest and deportation by the Nazis, while he went off alone in safety looking for a place for the family to hide in the south. According to Dr. Annick Alzoubi, a medical colleague and longtime friend, "Odette reproached her father and never had much further to do with him."[11]

While in Paris, Odette also contacted old friends. As soon as she learned Moussa's address from them, she took the first train to Nice. Moussa met her at the station with flowers. Against all odds, they were together again.

On her arrival in Nice, Odette was painfully thin, and still weak from her year in the camps. Her former employer, the OSE, soon decided to send her to Switzerland for a month, to recover and rest. "That was the worst thing for me to do," Odette said. "I shouldn't have been alone. I should have been with others."[12]

The time in Switzerland left Odette alone with all her terrible thoughts from Auschwitz and Belsen. She furiously wrote down her recollections from the camps, notes for an eventual book. The notes went into a bank vault where they would stay for decades. It would take that long for Odette to face the horrors of the past again, and write about them.

When the war ended all Odette wanted to do was forget. Moussa, she decided, was more marked by the Holocaust than she had been, possibly because his struggle to save the children had been harder on him psychologically than her struggle to survive the camps had been on her. Or perhaps she was just stronger. Or maybe he felt guilty that she had been deported rather than him. "Sometimes it was harder for those not arrested," Odette said.[13]

As usual, Odette was thinking more of Moussa than herself. In fact, she had suffered terribly in the camps. "The Odette who returned from Belsen was not the same," said her friend Marie Gatard. "She was like a dead person."

Slowly, Odette coped and improved. "She took intense pleasure in the simple things of life, smiling broadly over a cup of tea or the beauty of the countryside," Marie explained. "She devoted herself to others and to living in the present, both as ways to forget the past." But she could never completely forget. "Odette carried a kind of stone inside her after Auschwitz that weighed on her and pained her for the rest of her life," Marie said.[14]

On her return from Switzerland, Odette joined Moussa in the small apartment he rented in Nice after the war. She also worked in his office, helping to reunite families. They faced the future worn down physically and emotionally—Odette from the camps and Moussa from carrying on the clandestine struggle alone. But at last, they had each other.

17

LIBERATION

The clandestine work of the Marcel Network had ceased at the end of the war, but the unfinished business of reuniting hidden children with their families continued afterward. Although the peacetime work should have been easier, and often was, it also created some grave new difficulties that deeply affected Moussa.

On the operational level, the situation rapidly improved. Georges Garel reopened the Nice office of his Jewish charity, the OSE, now that it could operate legally again, and put Moussa in charge, with the title of regional director. Finally, Moussa was no longer relying only on himself. Since the time of the liberation of Nice in August 1944, Moussa's efforts to reunite families had been conducted on his own, as the war wound down elsewhere in Europe. But after the war, from 1945 on, as the head of the OSE office in Nice, he could tap into the nationwide resources of the Jewish charity for help—a considerable advantage. His OSE office provided both social services, including the effort to reunite families, and medical services at a clinic that again employed Odette.

The new problems arose on the emotional level. As before, the joy of reuniting families mingled with the pain of providing for children who had lost all known relatives in the Holocaust. But in the post-war years, as Moussa continued the effort to resettle children, a series of frustrations began to bother him, and eventually almost defeated him.

Moussa tried to stress the joy first. "The other morning in my office in just a few minutes I was largely repaid for all my efforts," he wrote Garel.[1] "A woman came in with an insane look on her face. She mentioned a name, her son. She thought he was dead. I looked in my files, pulled out a photograph of her son, and gave it to her. I told her he was alive—safe and sound. She looked at the photo, without saying a word. Then she covered it with kisses. Two days later her son was in her arms."

In the same letter, Moussa also revealed his pain. "The older children are beginning to question me seriously," he wrote. "Now that the Germans are no longer here they want to know why their parents are not yet coming back. I have to explain that their parents fell victim to the evils of mankind. I cannot tell you how little Samuel cried when he learned his father was dead."[2]

In the diary that Moussa wrote during the summer of 1945, there was much joy and much pain, but the frustration showed through more than anything else, beginning with his concern for Odette.

Odette was back, although not her old self. "She needs rest and calm," Moussa wrote in the diary. "She has to find herself again, to reassess the world and readapt. She is learning to live again."[3] Moussa wished he could do more to help Odette.

More frustration came from the fact that Moussa was no longer his own boss. He chafed under the bureaucratic command structure of a large organization like the OSE. "Why did you insist on that report?" he once asked Garel. "You know the answers as well as I do." Yet, for the time being anyway, Moussa swallowed such frustrations and soldiered on, reuniting former hidden children with their parents or other relatives when possible, or sending them to be cared for by charity if they were alone in the world.

Much of the frustration noted in the diary Moussa kept while at the OSE office came from dealing with the dregs of humanity, among them the ingrates, the people who never thanked the Abadis for what they had done. When faced with such behavior, Moussa could not help thinking about Odette, about all she had suffered at Auschwitz for saving children, and how these people could not even bother to say thank you.

Two such people, the Buras parents, particularly offended Moussa. The Abadis hid their two children for eighteen months. After the war, the parents did not come to Moussa's office to collect their youngsters. Instead, they arranged to have them taken to a bus station for the family reunion. "Monsieur and Madame Buras never thanked us for saving their children, never even sent us a letter saying the children had been returned in good health." Moussa wrote in the diary. "Not one word. Incredible."[4]

Another ingrate parent went further than neglecting to say thank you. He actually complained to Moussa about the family selected to save his son. The boy was the ugly, sickly baby that Odette had given to Madame Belliol, the peasant woman who had asked for the child no one else wanted. Madame Belliol had fed the baby, loved him, and nursed him back to life. He grew into a fine strong boy. His real mother died at Auschwitz but his father, Monsieur Lazarovich, survived. After the war, the father was appalled to learn that Odette had sheltered his son with a Christian family. "How is it possible that you put my son with these goyem [non-Jews]?" he complained to Moussa. "What you did was unthinkable. I demand that you give him back to me immediately." For once, Moussa was speechless.

Then there were the money-grubbers—the parents or other relatives who exploited the children returned to them in order to make money. A certain Monsieur S, who was reunited with his children by Moussa, submitted a bill to the OSE office in June for school supplies he said he bought for them. In July, Monsieur S submitted a similar bill for the same school supplies, although it was still summer vacation time. Moussa doubted the money was going for school expenses and doubted it was even needed. Monsieur S, he discovered, received enough money from two other Jewish charities to support his family. "I tried to put myself in his shoes," Moussa wrote in the diary, "and I decided he must have thought that since the OSE was there, he should profit from us too. The case of Monsieur S was not unique."[5]

Another case angered Moussa even more. This one involved the prim and proper headmistress of a snobbish school for girls in Nice. She hid a Jewish girl at her school during the war, then exploited her for money. At first the headmistress impressed Moussa as selfless and honorable. It took him a while to see through her hypocrisy. Her deception troubled him enough that he devoted several pages in his diary to it.

The headmistress took Sarah Krechman into her boarding school in 1942. Sarah's parents paid the school fees. A year later the Germans arrested the parents and deported them to Auschwitz. But the headmistress decided to keep Sarah at the school even with the loss of her fees. "I promised Monsieur and Madame Krechman that I would keep Sarah, raise her, and never abandon her," the headmistress told Moussa. "And I kept my promise."

Moussa said he found her attitude "commendable and touching."

After the liberation of Nice in 1944, Moussa called to ask if he should place Sarah at an OSE children's home. The headmistress told him that was not necessary, that Sarah could remain at the school. "And don't worry," she said. "I am not asking for anything from you." Moussa was impressed. Again, he thought the woman was selflessly paying for Sarah's upkeep out of her own pocket.

He learned the truth in August 1945, three years into Sarah's stay at the school. A cousin from a well-to-do family in Paris said she wanted to be responsible for raising Sarah. Moussa arranged a meeting in his office for the headmistress, Sarah, and the cousin. He explained that Sarah would be leaving the school to live with her cousin in Paris. "All that remains for me to do," he told the headmistress, "is to thank you for taking care of Sarah in an unselfish way that does you honor."

Then the cousin spoke up, timidly. "I would like to know," she said to Moussa, searching for the right words, "I don't want to be indiscreet, but I was given to understand that Monsieur and Madame Krechman entrusted to this woman a piece of jewelry of considerable value."

"That is correct," the headmistress said.

"All right," Moussa responded. "Then I would ask you to return this piece of jewelry to Sarah's cousin in the absence of her parents."

"But, but," the headmistress stammered. "It's . . . well, you see, the fees at our school are ten thousand francs a semester [about one hundred dollars then]. At a certain point I had to sell the jewelry for sixty thousand francs because, my God, I was falling behind."

"So then, Madame," Moussa said, "your unselfishness which I praised only a moment ago was fictitious."

"You don't think I could keep this poor child for nothing, do you?" the headmistress retorted. Then she turned over some papers to Moussa, showing her expenses for Sarah.

"Now I understand," Moussa said, "why you wanted to keep Sarah for so long. It helped you cover up the sale of the jewelry. And I suppose at this point you want to get rid of her because she is no longer profitable."

"Actually, Sarah's account is now in deficit," the headmistress said. "She owes us seven thousand francs."

"I'll pay all of Sarah's debts," the cousin assured the headmistress. "Just give Sarah to me."

It was all too much for Moussa. Brimming with sarcasm, he told the headmistress: "You won't forget, I hope, that when you have the occasion in the future to talk about what happened to the poor Jews during the war, you will manage to slip in a phrase like 'I personally took charge of an abandoned little girl for three years.'"

"I did everything I could for the welfare of this child," the headmistress insisted.

"For ten thousand francs a semester," Moussa said.

"That is our fee."

"No," Moussa said. "That is black-market charity."

He told the headmistress to turn Sarah over to her cousin as soon as possible.

"And what about her debt?" the headmistress asked.

"I'll pay you tomorrow," the cousin said.

"So everything is in order," Moussa declared, ending the meeting.[6]

Everything was not in order, of course. Far from it. Moussa had even more frustrating problems on his plate than Sarah's case, children so troubled by the loss of their parents that they wanted to kill virtually anyone in revenge. Moussa never wrote about these children in his diary. But in 1948, he told the journalist Morvan Lebesque the story of two of his former hidden children who no longer understood the difference between right and wrong, and were ready to kill.

Simone, aged fifteen, had stolen a gun. "I am going to stand in front of the house where my mother and father were arrested," she told Moussa, "and kill in cold blood the first man and woman who walk by."[7]

After the liberation of Nice, Moussa asked another former hidden child, fourteen-year-old Jacques, what he planned to do with his newfound freedom.

"I am going to take revenge," the boy said. Both his parents had been gassed at Auschwitz.

"How will you take revenge?" Moussa asked.

"I am going to kill."

"And who are you going to kill?"

"Anybody. It doesn't matter who."

"What about me?" Moussa said. "Would you kill me too?" Moussa had saved Jacques's life by hiding him.

"You or anyone else," Jacques said. "You, the liberators, the Germans, you are all responsible for my misery."[8]

Moussa said he "tried to reason" with Simone and Jacques. Lebesque's interview did not clarify what that meant, but it is likely that Moussa would have tried to get them to a child psychologist through his OSE clinic.

Still other frustrations for Moussa came from seeing the pain caused to couples who hid children, loved them, and did not want to give them up, but knew they had to return them to their parents or other relatives. Sometimes the child did not want to go back to parents he no longer recognized.

Moussa especially remembered the case of Jean, six years old, who was hidden with a family in Cannes. His father died at Auschwitz but his mother survived and came to claim him. "She threw herself on the boy like a she-wolf," Moussa recalled, "but he backed away."

"Jean, my baby," the woman cried. "Don't you recognize me? I'm your mother."

"My name is Bernard Dupont," the boy replied. "My mother died two years ago in Corsica." The cover story drummed into him at depersonalization had been learned so well that now he was repeating it to his own mother as if she were a Gestapo agent interrogating him.[9]

Moussa hoped that time together would repair the damage for both mother and son, but Jean's story, like so many others, began to get to him. His diary entries suggested he was fighting depression.

"I'm tired, weary, full of doubt," Moussa wrote in his diary on August 5, 1945.

> I keep asking myself, why? Why?
>
> I leaf through the voluminous correspondence of the OSE to find more misery, distress, illness, and recriminations.
>
> I keep looking for those parents who will never return to those children who have no family, nothing.
>
> I read through the files of our children: father deported, mother dead; mother deported, father dead; father and mother deported; father and mother dead. Mother deported, father shot; children ill, exposed to all infectious diseases; children tortured by uncertainty.
>
> Why? Why?
>
> Our clothing storehouse is empty. Our milk supply is running out and we are supposed to be the organization that rescues children.
>
> There is little Rafael who has no one anymore and he doesn't know it yet.
>
> There is the little Sternau, only four years old, who will not understand until much later . . .

Finally, Moussa answered his own question. "Why? Because we work for all those who are no longer here and for those not strong enough to suffer by themselves," he wrote in the diary. He had found his rationale to continue. But he was torturing himself with questions, while sliding downhill toward depression.

18

Reunions

For the children hidden by the Marcel Network, liberation was the moment of truth. Had their parents survived the war? Liberation separated those children whose prayers were answered from those whose prayers were not. For the most fortunate few, both parents remained alive. For others, one parent survived to love and care for them. For still others, an uncle or an aunt or a cousin did the best he or she could as a substitute parent. And for the rest, already matured by the experience of hiding out the war with strangers, there was no alternative to foster care.

None of them had it easy, not even the most fortunate reunited with both parents. All would be scarred for the rest of their lives by such wartime traumas as the forced separation from their parents, the slaughter of loved ones in the gas chambers, or the constant fear of arrest by the Nazis. Often for the hidden children, the reunion with their families after the war was almost as emotional in its own way as the separation had been under the German occupation.

Jeannette Wolgust considered herself among the most fortunate of the Abadi children. She knew that both her parents were alive, and she also knew exactly where they lived. "I had all the luck," she said.[1] Her parents had rented a small room in her uncle's house in Brunoy, fifteen miles southeast of Paris, and managed to hide there, waiting out the occupation. Jeannette had been kept informed about them throughout the war thanks to messages Odette brought to her at the convent in Grasse. When the Allies landed in Normandy in June of 1944, Jeannette figured Paris would probably be liberated before too long. But she could not wait to see her parents again, not until the liberation, whenever that might come, not one extra day if she could help it. She decided to collect her brother Jean, then six, and leave right away for Paris.

"I'm going to Paris," the fifteen-year-old Jeannette announced to the mother superior at the convent.

"No, you're not," Mother Superior Marie-Thérèse contradicted her. "You are not allowed to leave here yet."

So Jeannette telephoned Moussa.

"He was terribly hesitant," she said. He could not be sure she could travel in safety. The Allies still had to fight their way from the Normandy coast to Paris. (It was late June when Jeannette determined to go, and Paris would not be liberated until late August.) Of course Moussa hesitated. Here was an adolescent girl proposing to take her little brother and travel five hundred miles by train from Nice to Paris in wartime, unaccompanied by an adult.

But Jeannette insisted. "I know exactly where my parents are," she told Moussa. He began to analyze the various factors involved. The fighting was all to the north of Paris. Jeannette would be traveling to the city from the south, and would not have to go through the combat zone. Her train trip would be no riskier than others Moussa had approved when hiding children during the German occupation. Yes, she would need papers to travel, and yes, the police would check them on the train. But it was summer vacation time and her papers could say she and her brother were off on a holiday to Paris.

It was a plausible story. In fact, Jeannette had been planning to go on a vacation with the nuns. "I told Moussa that instead of going with the nuns, I was going to Paris. I had this crazy idea that if they refused, I would have taken my brother and run away. Moussa knew that, and in the end he let me go."

He did relent, but only when Jeannette agreed that two Boy Scouts in their late teens would escort her and Jean on the train. "Moussa preferred to let me go with the scouts than to risk my running away without them," Jeannette said.

The train trip proved uneventful. The police who came by didn't bother checking Jeannette and her brother. But in Paris, Jeannette admitted, "I did something stupid. I told the two Boy Scouts, 'Thank you very much, but I know how to get to my uncle from here by myself.'" She said good-bye and the two scouts left her and Jean at the station in Paris.

Jeannette soon regretted the decision. She had to change stations in Paris, still a city occupied by the Germans, to reach the suburban line train for Brunoy, where her uncle lived. Once there she realized, "I had completely forgotten that my uncle's house was on the edge of a forest about three miles from the station." It was already dark—and frightening—as Jeannette and Jean made the trek, with Jeannette holding a suitcase with one hand and Jean's hand with the other.

When they arrived at her uncle's house, Jeannette knocked on the door. "Maman and Papa were there," Jeannette said. "Maman let out a scream when she saw us—and fainted. We got down on all fours to revive her."

First it was kisses and tears. "Then Maman asked, 'What are you doing here?'"

"I wanted to see you," Jeannette replied.

"It's crazy," her mother said. "Don't you realize this was a very bad time to come? The Germans are retreating and there are gunshots everywhere."

Jeannette and Jean had to be hidden once again, this time nearby their parents for only a short while, until the Germans surrendered the Paris region. But the most important thing, as Jeannette said, was that "our family unit was re-formed."

Of the four Jewish girls at the Joan of Arc convent in Grasse, she stressed, "I was the only one to find my whole family again." Françoise and Denise lost both parents. Martoune lost her mother. "When I compared myself to the others," Jeannette said, "I always felt guilty. I had all the luck."

Nearly a year later, in May 1945, Jeannette received a letter saying Odette was back from Belsen, with Moussa in Nice. She further learned that Odette would soon be stopping in Paris on her way to Switzerland to rest. Jeannette decided to surprise Odette during that stopover at an apartment in Paris, and got the address. It was a Sunday morning when Jeannette arrived and Odette opened the door.

"Bonjour, Mademoiselle," Jeannette said.

"Unbelievable," Odette whispered, embracing her and inviting her in. They talked and talked. At long last Jeannette had re-established contact with the woman who had been her surrogate mother for more than a year, and who, happily, had survived the death camps.

"I don't want us ever to lose track of each other again," Jeannette told Odette. And they never did.

Her good luck continued after the war for another fifty years. Jeannette married Dr. Laurent Wolgust, a general practitioner, and lives in a pleasant house with a lovely garden in a Paris suburb. "I never had a career. I was a kept woman," she joked. "I've always been lucky. My parents really spoiled me. I had an adorable husband and a very comfortable life." Jeannette and Laurent had a long and devoted marriage, two sons, a daughter, and four grandchildren. Laurent died in 2012.

The Abadis became Jeannette's career. In their lifetime, she was their constant and closest friend. Over a period of twenty years she brought some of the former hidden children together again with each other and with the Abadis. At Odette's death, Jeannette became the executor of their estate and the caretaker of their archives. Into her eighties, she continued to keep track of them, still searching for new morsels of information about them, always seeking to promote the memory of what they accomplished. Moussa himself called Jeannette "the truest of true friends."[2]

Moussa and Odette made no attempt on their own after the war to locate former hidden children and resume relationships with them as adults. "We didn't want to remind them of a tragic moment in their lives," Moussa explained. "But when they sought us out, we welcomed them gladly."[3] Yet, this was only partly true.

Jeannette was the first example of a former hidden child who searched for the Abadis. In her case she was still a child. Françoise Knopf was the only other Abadi child besides Jeannette to keep up with Moussa and Odette from the end of the war onward. Françoise moved to the United States in 1953 at age twenty-six and from then on maintained a long-distance relationship with them by mail. Other former hidden children only managed to link up with the Abadis in the 1990s, a half century after the war, among them Julien Engel, Armand Morgensztern, Andrée Poch-Karsenti, and Martoune. But relatively few of the 527 children the Abadis saved ever saw them again.

They were so few, and it took so long for the reunions, Jeannette said, because Odette was protecting Moussa. Jeannette had wanted to bring the Abadis together with many more former hidden children years earlier. But Odette said no. According to Jeannette, "Odette would say that every time a former hidden child would appear, it would take Moussa forty-eight hours to recuperate because it was such an emotional strain for him to relive the past."

Odette said she was protecting Moussa by resisting reunions with former hidden children. But in fact, she was also protecting herself as well. According to her friend Marie Gatard, Odette had the same reaction as Moussa. For Odette too, the joy of the reunions was marred by the strain of reliving the past.

It wasn't just the traumatic memories coming back. Sometimes Odette found the meetings disconcerting. "I remembered holding little children in my arms," she told Marie, "and then I would see them again as grandmothers or grandparents. I didn't recognize anything about them."[4]

The whole truth is that Moussa and Odette always limited their reunions to a select few of the former hidden children. These exceptions were people with whom they established new relationships as adults, meaning those they could enjoy as friends in the present and focus on the here and now. Most of the former hidden children were in a different category for the Abadis—reminders of an era they wanted to forget. Yes, as Moussa said, by not seeing these children again, he and Odette were shielding them from revived memories of past suffering. But they were both also shielding themselves for the same reason.

✦

Martoune's story typified the ordeal of those hidden children who eventually reunited with one parent. Her mother died at Auschwitz. Her father survived the camps—ill, weak, barely alive. At the end of the war, Martoune did not yet know the fate of either of them. She only knew that once again she found herself alone in the world, as she had been that day in Paris when the Germans arrested the neighbors who housed her, but never looked in the bedroom where she slept. Then she was eight years old. Now she was ten, and again she had no contact with her family. "Despite liberation, nobody came to reclaim me," Martoune said.[5]

In fact, Martoune found herself alone even before the liberation. At the end of June the girls at the convent school went home for vacation. Only Martoune joined the nuns at their summer retreat, a residence in a small village between Nice and Grasse. By then, Jeannette had refused to follow the nuns and had gone off to find her parents near Paris. Françoise and Denise had been placed elsewhere. Martoune, still without family, no longer even had her friends with her.

After the liberation in August, she had no further contact with Moussa or Odette either. She found out later that her file had been turned over to the OSE, which placed her in another boarding school, Saint Marthe's in Grasse, after the war. On weekends, a Jewish family in Nice took her in. "They were adorable and would have adopted me in the end if no one claimed me," Martoune said. "The head of that family was a former commander in the Resistance, a wonderful man." During the week though, Martoune still had to soldier on through Catholic lessons and prayers. "I was still using my false name, Arthieu, still saying that with such a name my parents will never find me.

"Food was difficult to find after the war," Martoune said. "At Saint Marthe's there was so little food that you had to eat whatever they put on your plate, however bad. One day they served Jerusalem artichokes. I couldn't eat them because they made me nauseous. The nuns said that if I didn't eat them I couldn't leave for the weekend. So, under threat, I ate them. Then after the commander picked me up, I vomited my guts all over his beautiful car."

Martoune was never adopted because the OSE managed to locate a cousin of hers in Paris, and, through him, her father, Herco Artzstein. He was liberated from Auschwitz in May 1945, straining to walk on frozen feet. Martoune rejoined him and the cousin in Paris.

Herco had been a young and vigorous man of thirty-eight when he was arrested and deported to Auschwitz in 1943. He survived two years at the death camp by pursuing his trade as a tailor, a skill the Germans found useful. But when his daughter found him again he weighed only one hundred pounds. "You could see his skeleton through his skin," Martoune recalled decades later. "The man who came back was diminished, not the same man."

Herco learned at Auschwitz that his wife and their son had both died in the gas chambers. Eventually, he told Martoune their story. Herco himself lived for twelve years after the war, but never really recovered. He suffered several heart attacks and died at the age of fifty-two, leaving his daughter to take over his tailor's shop.

Martoune married at age twenty. Her husband, Victor Kuperminc, is a successful writer, perhaps best known for translating Leo Rosten's *The Joys of Yiddish* into French. They have a daughter, twin sons, and two grandchildren, and live in a comfortable Paris apartment on the right bank of the Seine. "Until about ten years ago," Martoune said in 2008, "I could not talk about what happened to me during the war, not even to my husband." Then she gave a brief interview for a television film about former hidden children. "The film unblocked me," she said. "I managed to get something out that had been obstructed in the past. Now I can talk about the war."

✦

Among the Abadi children who lost both parents, perhaps the most dramatic moment involved Lisette Levy. She was ten years old when she first started helping Moussa and Odette at the Clarisses with the depersonalization of the younger children. Lisette stayed there until the end of the war, the last Jewish child at the convent. By then she was twelve years old, still hoping to rejoin her parents and unaware that both had perished in the death camps.

According to Lisette's account, Moussa arranged for her to go to Israel after the war.[6] "I don't want to go to Israel," Lisette told him. "My parents know that I am in France and they will come for me here."

They argued and Moussa lost his temper. "If you don't agree to go to Israel, I will slap your face," Lisette quoted him as saying. She stood her ground. "And then," she said, "he slapped my face."

In the end, Lisette discovered her parents did not survive the war. She went to live with an aunt in Paris. "But I never forgot that slap," she said.

As far as is known, it was the only time that Moussa ever struck one of his hidden children. "I never saw him slap another child," Lisette said. She was with him through all the tensions of depersonalization, and often saw him lose patience with the little ones, but said he never did more than bark at them.

Moussa admitted slapping Lisette. His version of the incident, however, was quite different.[7] According to Moussa, Lisette refused to leave the convent because she was thinking of becoming a Catholic.

"But you are Jewish," he said he told her. "Your parents have suffered because they are Jewish.

"People have died for you because you are Jewish," he added, thinking of Nicole and Huguette, his two assistants who gave their lives helping him save Jewish children. "And now you are telling me you want to denounce your origins?"

Enough discussion, Moussa decided. "You are coming with me," he announced.

"No, I don't want to," Lisette answered back.

"And that was when I slapped her face," Moussa said.

Lisette never converted. Her aunt raised her as Jewish. Many years later Lisette indicated that the slap was forgiven, if not forgotten. She met

Moussa and Odette by chance on the Champs-Élysées in Paris, gave them a hug, and introduced them to her aunt.

✦

Armand Morgensztern, who lost both parents, remembers the liberation of Nice in 1944 as a rebirth for him.[8] At the time he was twelve years old, spending the summer at a camp run by his Catholic school. "When I saw that the Americans had landed, I said to one of the camp counselors, 'I am Jewish.' Finally, I could say it."

He also demanded to be called by his real name, Morgensztern, rather than the cover Christian name of Morini, given to him when hiding at the school. And, even though his parents had raised him totally outside of religion, Armand insisted on being allowed to go to a synagogue.

After the war Armand went to Paris to live with a cousin and study mathematics. He eventually became a leading expert in France on advertising and marketing theory.

✦

Julien and George Engel also lost both parents, but probably had more choices open to them after the war than any other children hidden by the Abadis. They had relatives in the United States, Britain, and in what was soon to become Israel. The boys could have gone to any of them. "I might have come out a Limey or a quasi Sabra," Julien said.[9] Instead, he and George went to an uncle and aunt, Jack and Bertha Finer, in Paterson, New Jersey, in 1946.

By then, Alban and Germaine Fort, who ran the home for abandoned children above Cannes, had become family for Julien. For three years the Forts had done far more than just hide the Engel boys. They provided a warm, affectionate family environment. The Forts set Julien on a path to a successful life, through French schools to Princeton, Oxford, and on to a career for nongovernmental organizations providing aid to countries in the developing world, many of them in French-speaking Africa. Julien specialized in programs helping emerging nations strengthen their capabilities in education, science, and technology. Like George Isserlis, the surgeon working for Doctors without Borders, his narrow escape from death in wartime France led to an adult life of humanitarian work. Julien settled in Washington, D.C., but often visited the Forts on trips abroad. George also prospered in America, selling computer systems.

The State of Israel later honored the Forts with the title of "Righteous Among Nations," a distinction awarded to non-Jews for saving lives during the Holocaust. A tree was planted in their honor at the Yad Vashem memorial in Jerusalem. That tree would lead Julien to a voyage of discovery.

Several years after Alban Fort died, Julien visited Yad Vashem. He wanted to bring Germaine Fort a photograph of the tree honoring her and her husband, but where was it among the thousands of trees planted there for the Righteous? Julien met with Lucien Lazare, an Israeli historian of French origin working at Yad Vashem, to help him find the right tree. He also told Lazare about the lady named Sylvie from the Catholic Diocese of Nice who saved his life—and George's—by taking them to the Forts at Cannes.

Lazare smiled. "That's not the full story," he said. "Let me tell you what really happened to you." And so in 1991, nearly fifty years after the war, Julien Engel finally learned the truth. Lazare told Julien that "Sylvie" was the wartime alias of Odette Rosenstock, and that she and Moussa Abadi had saved his life. Sylvie didn't work for the Catholic Church. It was the other way around. The Abadis had enlisted the bishop of Nice in their cause. In rescuing Jewish children, the Church in Nice worked for her and Moussa, the leaders of the Marcel Network.

"These are the people who saved you," Lazare told Julien.[10] He scribbled the phone number of the Abadis on a piece of paper. "They live in Paris. Give them a call."

When Julien phoned a week later, a halting, rather elderly voice answered. "I barely had time to mention my name," Julien recalled, "when he stopped me."[11]

"I remember you," Moussa Abadi said, thinking all the way back to the 1940s. "You had a brother. We placed you both in Cannes . . . "

Julien was stunned to be remembered like that after so long. To his great pleasure, Moussa invited him for a drink the next day at a Paris cafe, where he also met "Sylvie" again, this time as Odette Abadi. Julien arrived with a big bouquet of roses. "It embarrassed them no end. They were heading next to the theater and didn't know what the hell to do with the flowers," he said. But the reunion succeeded in establishing an immediate rapport.

"That people who played a vital role in my survival should still be around fifty years later really blew my mind," Julien said. "Then to have the opportunity to meet them was a very special kind of experience."[12] Over the next several years, Julien often called on the Abadis in Paris and learned more about them. Only in the last years of their lives did Moussa and Odette agree to tell their story, then mostly in private to trusted friends. But not even Julien, or any of the close friends, ever got more than a part of it, usually just the part that applied personally to them.

Julien Engel lives in a penthouse apartment overlooking the Potomac in Washington, D.C. with his French wife, Anne-Marie, a professor at Georgetown University. Most of the Abadi children remained in France after the war but a few settled in America, Israel, and other countries.

✦

Françoise Knopf felt distressed at the liberation. She was seventeen years old, hiding at St. Christopher's, a small Quaker hospital in Magagnosc, north of Grasse, and working as a trainee nurse. For her the war was over, but "I had no news of my parents," she said.[13]

Moussa invited her to Nice to discuss her future. "I kept wondering why," Françoise recalled. "I was waiting for my parents. I thought they would come back and I would discuss my future with them."

Although Moussa knew her parents had both died, he tried to spare her feelings and avoided telling her. Instead he took her to lunch, treated her as a grown-up, and said he had arranged for her to continue her studies in Lyon. She would live at an OSE orphanage there, waiting for news of her parents. Françoise agreed when Moussa told her that Paulette, her sister being treated for leukemia, would be going with her. Paulette wound up in a hospital in Lyon where doctors said they had no hope for her recovery.

While in Lyon, Françoise received a letter from a childless couple in Dijon, Andre Baruch Meyer and his wife, proposing to be her godparents. Meyer, a professor of chemistry at the University of Dijon, was prominent in the Jewish community there and had been told about Françoise by the OSE. "My godparents were absolutely wonderful," Françoise said. She spent summer vacations with them. And they arranged for Paulette to be treated at a leading hospital in Paris. Three years later, Paulette went into remission. Eventually, she would be well enough to marry and have children. In effect, the godparents saved Paulette's life.

No godparents, of course, could ever replace parents. When Françoise finally learned the fate of her mother and father, she was shattered. News of their deaths came in an official letter from the French government six weeks before Françoise was due to take her baccalaureate exams at the end of her high school years. She was too shaken to sit for the exams.

Later that same year, 1945, her father's friend, Joe Klein, returned from Auschwitz and gave Françoise the first detailed account of her parents' arrest, deportation, and final days. "Joe was desolate telling me all this," Françoise said. "But he had to so that I could start reciting the Kaddish for my parents"—the Jewish prayer for the dead.

Klein told this story: Once Françoise was safely hidden at the convent in Grasse, her parents, Rebecca and Jacques Knopf, stayed with the Klein family at a small hotel in Nice. The Vichy police came to arrest them there one day as they all sat down to lunch. The Kleins had a little girl, Madeleine, then eight years old. She started crying and the police left her alone. Madame Klein screamed, "Leave me too. I have to care for that child," but to no avail. The police took the Kleins and Knopfs away, leaving Madeleine alone and abandoned in the hotel.

The two couples were taken to a synagogue, a roundup point for Jews arrested in Nice, then put on a passenger train to Drancy. They were forced to pay for their tickets. "It was terrible," Françoise said, "people being sent to their death and made to pay for the trip."

From Drancy, the Kleins and the Knopfs were deported together to Auschwitz. The two wives went immediately to the gas chambers. Joe Klein and Jacques Knopf survived in the camp working as tailors, from their arrest in November 1943 to January 1944 when Jacques Knopf, near starvation and ill with diarrhea, died in Joe Klein's arms.

Françoise also learned that Madeleine Klein survived. An Italian maid who worked in the hotel found the abandoned little girl alone, bewildered and crying. The maid took Madeleine home with her and cared for her until the liberation. Then she called on Moussa, and showed him a picture of Madeleine with her parents, hoping that it would help Moussa find them. It was the last photograph that Jacques Knopf had taken of the Knopf and Klein families together. Somehow, Madeleine had the photo in her possession when the maid found her. Moussa contacted the OSE, which arranged to care for Madeleine until Joe Klein returned from Auschwitz. But first he showed the photograph to Françoise. She, Paulette, and their mother were in it too.

At eighteen, Françoise moved back to her hometown of Sarreguemines on the German border, working as a secretary for a cousin. With the help of a lawyer hired by her godfather, she sued in court and won back the ownership of her father's former clothing store. The money from the store helped her support Paulette. Françoise married, moved to the United States, and worked for fifteen years as a translator for the State Department. She and her second husband, Bert Bram, live in Chevy Chase, Maryland.

Françoise had a daughter, Sylvie, named after Odette's wartime alias. But for years, she could not bring herself to explain the connection. "I never talked to my daughter about the war," Françoise said. Her daughter was an adult before she learned that she had been named after Sylvie Delattre in a long overdue moment of truth with her mother. "Why don't you ever tell me about the war?" the daughter complained. "I want to know what happened to my grandparents, to my family."

"And so I told her," Françoise said, "mostly about the wonderful people who saved me—Sylvie Delattre and Monsieur Marcel"—Moussa and Odette Abadi.

Paulette also moved to the United States and married. She died of colon cancer at twenty-seven, leaving two sons. "The oldest, Joe, looks just like my father," Françoise said.

✦

The names of Françoise's parents, Jacques and Rebecca Knopf, are among those of 73,000 Holocaust victims in France carved in stone on the walls of the Shoah Memorial in Paris. Every year since the memorial opened in 2005 there has been a ceremony on Yom Hashoah, the Holocaust Remembrance Day, honoring the victims with prayers for the dead, commemorative speeches, and a roll call of names on the wall. There are too many names for all of them to be read in any one year. Instead, each year thousands of names are called out by convoys—the trainloads that took the deportees from Drancy to Auschwitz. Françoise, now confined to a wheelchair, was unable to come from Washington for the ceremony the year that her parents' names were read out. So Jeannette Wolgust and her husband went for her. "It was two thirty A.M. when they finally called my parents' names," Françoise said, "but Jeannette and her husband, Laurent, were still there. One could not ask for better friends."[14]

19

Depression

Moussa Abadi almost became famous in 1948. He granted an interview to Morvan Lebesque, a journalist with a left-wing weekly newspaper called *Carrefour*. In a three-part series of articles, Lebesque revealed that the Marcel Network saved more than five hundred Jewish children. There was little operational detail in Lebesque's series, not even any mention of Odette. But, for the first time, Moussa came out of the shadows, and the public learned some of his story. Soon afterward Moussa received offers to collaborate on a book or a film about the Marcel Network that could have made him a celebrity, possibly a rich one. He decided, however, to reject them all.

There were many reasons for saying no, Moussa explained to friends. He felt strongly that he had simply done his duty. Saving lives was reward enough. He sought no personal glory from a film or book. At the same time, he and Odette wanted to put behind them the horrors of the war. Doing a book or a film would have done the opposite—kept their minds in the anguish of the war years. As Moussa said, "The memories were still too painful, the stomach still hurt too much. We had seen too much."[1] So he and Odette said no to book and film offers in order to look to the future and get on with rebuilding their lives. "I wanted to hitch my wagon to the living," Moussa emphasized.

Apparently, other reasons played a role as well. The Lebesque interview showed Moussa that he could not control what went into a newspaper article, let alone a film or a book. He may have been annoyed by what the journalist chose to build up, such as the two murder-prone children after the war, and what Lebesque chose to play down, such as Odette's role. Moussa understood that if he could not control the end product, he could not rule out distortions designed to sell newspapers, books, or films, and he would have none of that. "We didn't want our story exploited for commercial reasons," Moussa emphasized. It would be better to say nothing at all.

Moussa did not give another interview about the Marcel Network for nearly fifty years. For decades, he and Odette never said a word about their clandestine activities to anyone but each other—not in public, not in private, not even to their closest friends. Moussa withdrew Monsieur Marcel to the shadows again. Lebesque's articles were quickly forgotten. The Abadis' friends in later years had never read them. When Moussa and Odette in the last years of their lives finally spoke about their wartime rescue of children, many of their most intimate friends learned about it for the first time.

In 1948, Moussa also withdrew from the OSE. As he wrote in his diary, he felt physically exhausted, and emotionally drained. The futile search for parents no longer alive, the pain of telling children they were orphans, the post-war shortages of essential supplies, and the bureaucratic frustrations of a large organization all wore him down.

An inspection by the OSE of Moussa's office proved to be the last straw. Teams of OSE inspectors routinely checked all branch offices. They audited the books, checked the sanitary conditions of the medical clinics, reviewed the health of the children being treated, and so on.

Moussa had nothing to hide. The previous year an official of the American Joint Committee, which still financed the OSE, visited Moussa's office and reported to the OSE: "If all of your clinics were managed as well as the one in Nice there would be no problems anywhere."[2]

But the idea of an inspection outraged Moussa. For him that meant his bosses didn't trust him, and if they didn't trust him then he wanted nothing to do with them. "For everyone else, the inspections were normal," said Betty Kaluski-Saville, a close friend, "but for Moussa they were unbearable. He took the attitude, 'You are not going to check on us. That's out of the question.'" Moussa and Odette gathered up their belongings, resigned on the spot, and left in late 1948.[3]

Katy Hazan, the archivist at the OSE, confirmed that Moussa resigned over the inspection issue, but she said it was only one of many reasons why he left. Among the others she cited his complaint that "the OSE demanded too many reports from him that took too much time away from the efforts to reunite families." She also said Moussa always preferred running his own independent operation and never adjusted to taking orders from others.[4]

Odette moved to Paris in 1948 and resumed her medical career in a series of administrative posts for the state health service. Moussa remained in Nice, working as a teacher of French. They were apart again—sort of—but only during the week. Almost every weekend, Odette came to Nice to be with him. According to Violette Jacquet-Silberstein, a friend of Odette's from Auschwitz, "Moussa and Odette wrote each other every day they were apart. They were long letters detailing everything that happened to each of them, from the time they got up in the morning to the time they went to bed at night."[5]

Andrée Poch-Karsenti, a former hidden child and later a personal friend, thought Odette turned to administrative work because she had such a horrendous time treating patients in the Nazi death camps that she could not bear to face patients again. Violette Jacquet-Silberstein agreed. "As a doctor at Auschwitz, Odette was traumatized to death," she said, "and afterwards withdrew completely from treating patients." But Jeannette Wolgust said Odette preferred administrative work because it allowed her to return to Nice every Friday night to Moussa. The truth may have been a bit of both.

In any case, during this period, something was wrong in the lives of the Abadis. Odette commuted like that for eight years, until 1956. She was the breadwinner; Moussa did not contribute much financially. With both Abadis discreet to a fault, neither ever said much to others about the years they lived apart during the week and together on weekends. But several of their close friends said in interviews that they heard enough to believe that Moussa suffered from depression. Moussa himself hinted as much at the time. "I had trouble getting back on my feet," he said.

Moussa had reached a low point in his life. He could not shake the traumas of the war years, and for a long time had little success in building a new career. The way he had left the OSE bothered him. "To put in doubt his honor, his word, his accounts could have been an element in depression," said his friend Betty Kaluski-Saville.

According to the historian Annette Wieviorka, who interviewed Moussa many years later, he was frustrated by his stalled career. "He was talented artistically," she said. "He could have been a writer or an actor. Instead, the war years pushed him in a different direction and afterwards it was hard to resume an artistic career. That could have depressed him."[6]

Olga Fink, the friend who introduced the Abadis, said Moussa took out his frustrations at the time by playing baccarat at the casino in Nice. Sometimes, she added, "he gambled away the rent money and Odette had to borrow from friends to keep them going." It was the only time in his life that Moussa gave in to a weakness for gambling, Madame Fink said. Depression may well have been the cause.[7]

Moussa nonetheless continued to function. He taught courses in French literature and the French language at the Centre Universitaire Méditerranéen in Nice, helping to prepare high school students for university entrance. Régine Zimmerman, who took a literature course from Moussa, remembers seeing him along the Promenade des Anglais in Nice in 1949, "walking slowly with his head bowed, looking like a tired old man." Moussa was only thirty-nine years old at the time. His hair was already graying. Still, she said, "He was a great teacher. You could tell that he really loved French literature."[8]

Only his love of the arts enabled Moussa to put his life back together again. He returned to Paris in 1956 to join Odette full time, determined at age forty-six to make his living in the world of the theater and by writing. He succeeded in both. For the first three years Moussa reacquainted himself with the Paris theater, attending plays and writing articles about them. Then, in 1959, he began a twenty-one-year run as an internationally known theater critic with a weekly radio program broadcast worldwide. Never again did Moussa Abadi show signs of depression.

20

Discreet

Late in life, Moussa Abadi wrote three books—one on the French theater and two on his youth in the Damascus ghetto. None of them said a word about the Marcel Network. All the other leading figures in the network were similarly discreet, steadfastly refusing for the rest of their lives to talk about their clandestine activities during the war.

Bishop Paul Rémond was named Archbishop of Nice in 1949. His participation in the Marcel Network had been known since the publication of Moussa's interview with Lebesque the year before, which mentioned him briefly. Rémond, however, devoted himself entirely to Church affairs in the post-war years and almost never said a word in public on his secret and perilous work during the German occupation. The one exception was a single line in a 1945 radio interview in which he said the Catholic Church in Nice had helped to save "about three hundred Jewish children" during the war.[1] He gave no details, refusing to elaborate further.

Paul Rémond died in 1963, silent to the end. According to his nephew, the historian René Rémond, he had burned all papers relating to the Marcel Network during the war to keep them from falling into the hands of the Gestapo. After the war, the archbishop declined to comment on the network, even in private, refusing to discuss it with bishops, priests, or his closest relative, his nephew. "My uncle never made the slightest allusion to his participation in the Marcel Network," René Rémond said.

Nonetheless, despite Paul Rémond's reluctance to take any personal credit, it is abundantly clear that his contribution to the Marcel Network was essential to its success. At grave risk to his life, Rémond provided hiding places for children and baptismal certificates to conceal their identities. He arranged an office for Moussa in his residence and contributed to forging papers there. He signed credentials to extend the protection of the church to Moussa and Odette in their clandestine work. Rémond could not prevent Odette's arrest, but only his support enabled Moussa to evade the Gestapo and soldier on without Odette until the end of the occupation. When nuns or priests buckled under the strain of hiding Jews, Rémond stiffened their spines and made them continue. It was an inspiring partnership—a high official of the Catholic Church with two young Jews. The Abadis created, organized, and ran the network, but without the support and protection of Paul Rémond, they probably would not have gotten started, or continued for very long.

Eventually, the State of Israel publicly paid tribute to the archbishop's contribution. René Rémond learned the details of his uncle's clandestine work for the first time in 1992, almost fifty years after the war, when Israel honored the archbishop with the title of "Righteous Among Nations" for saving Jewish children. "It was a revelation," the nephew said.[2]

In being named among the Righteous, Archbishop Rémond joined a group that included Oskar Schindler, the German industrialist who saved hundreds of workers on his list, made famous by the Steven Spielberg film, and Raoul Wallenburg, the Swedish diplomat who saved hundreds more Jews in Nazi-occupied Budapest. Israel awarded some two thousand French citizens, all non-Jews, the title of Righteous—10 percent of the 20,000 people honored as Righteous worldwide. The high French figure is a testament to the enormous role played by French Christians in saving Jewish lives. Among the French honored as Righteous were seven who played key roles in the work of the Marcel Network: Archbishop Rémond; Alban and Germaine Fort, who hid Jewish youngsters at their children's home in Cannes; Father Vincent Simeoni and Father Michel Blain, who saved Jewish children at the Dom Bosco vocational school in Nice; and Pastors Edmond Evrard and Pierre Gagnier, who helped Odette place Jewish children with Protestant families.[3] Trees are planted for them at the Yad Vashem memorial in Jerusalem.

In each case the awards were made after testimony to Israeli investigators by witnesses, people whose lives were saved by the honorees. In all cases except for Germaine Fort, the awards were made posthumously. Remarkably, there is no record of any of these honorees themselves speaking out publicly during their lifetime about their lifesaving work. Pastor Gagnier spoke for all of them, perhaps, in a declaration in Nice on May 18, 1945, when he said: "I believe that we Christians must not talk about what God has allowed us to accomplish for our fellow men in distress. It was a privilege for us to act, and to fight against the anti-Christian force that was German racism."

Maurice Brener died in 1978 and Georges Garel a year later. Like Archbishop Rémond and Pastors Evrard and Gagnier, both were instrumental in the success of the Marcel Network, and, again like the three clergymen, each of them went to his grave without saying a word in public about his clandestine work with the Abadis.

Thus Moussa and Odette Abadi were not alone in keeping silent for decades after the war. All of their key collaborators remained just as discreet. It was apparently a generational syndrome, with many factors involved, among them the desire to forget the pain of the past by refusing to talk about it, and the feeling that as they had done their duty, nothing more needed saying.

Only a half century later, in the 1990s, with the announcements naming the Righteous, did some light fall on the network, and then all of it on supporting players. Even then, the principal roles played by Monsieur Marcel and Sylvie Delattre remained in the shadows. As Jews, Moussa and Odette were not eligible to be included among the Righteous. Their story would be hidden until they decided to tell it themselves.

21

Drama

Moussa Abadi led a double life. He revealed in detail his secret mission to save children only a few years before he died. But his public life in the theater and as an author made him a well-known figure in French artistic circles decades earlier.

Well before the war, in 1937, Moussa enjoyed his first great success. When only twenty-seven years old he became a rising star. The one-time student actor was hired by a leading French director, Andre Barsacq, for a professional troupe called la Compagnie des Quatre Saisons (The Four Seasons Company), and played the lead role in New York in a classic French comedy, "Knock" by Jules Romains. The play, a satire on modern life, tells the story of a young doctor assigned to a mountain village where no one falls ill. Doctor Knock turns the village tavern into a clinic, introduces scientific methods, and ends up curing the population from illnesses they don't have. Knock grows rich and the locals regard him as a genius.

Moussa's troupe had been invited for a five-month engagement, from October 1937 to February 1938, by The French Theater of New York, an off-Broadway house at Fifty-eighth Street and Sixth Avenue. It was a different era. Nobody asked the audience to switch off cell phones. Instead, the program said: "Women are requested to remove their hats during the performance." "Knock," and the other plays performed in repertory by the troupe in New York, were all in French, with program notes in English but no modern simultaneous translation. No matter. As always, it was the reviews that counted, and Moussa received excellent notices.

The young Abadi was on his way. Theater would remain his lifeblood for the rest of his days, although his subsequent roles were in real life—as Monsieur Marcel saving lives during the war, and as a theater critic and broadcaster afterward.

One incident during the New York theater-run proved fundamental to Moussa's outlook on life. He met Antoine de Saint Exupéry, the famed French author and pilot, who inspired him to aim high, despite the risks. Saint Exupéry, author of *The Little Prince*, set time records as a pilot for long-distance flights such as Paris to Saigon. He died in a plane crash in 1944.

One winter night in early 1938, at loose ends in New York, Saint Exupéry decided to go to The French Theater. After the play he knocked at Moussa's dressing room door, introduced himself, and said: "I have just spent an enjoyable evening thanks to you. Would you join me for a drink?"[1]

Moussa readily agreed, fascinated to find himself in the company of a celebrated French hero. Saint Exupéry led Moussa along the Broadway sidewalk and into a bar where he ordered two whiskies followed by two more, and then another two. Moussa, unused to heavy drinking, found it difficult to finish the three whiskeys ordered for him. His head started to spin, but it gave him the courage to question the celebrity he admired both as a writer and a daredevil pilot. Saint-Exupéry had been talking in the bar about his coming attempt to set a new record time for a flight down the length of the Western Hemisphere from northern Canada to southern Argentina.

"You told me you want to break another record," Moussa said. "Why do you keep trying to break records when you have broken so many already?"

"Undoubtedly to try to surpass myself, to reach the absolute top of my potential," Saint-Exupéry replied.

"And how do you do that?"

"It's very simple. You must always try to go through the clouds."

Moussa never forgot that advice. For the rest of his life, he would aim high, despite the risks, and try to go through the clouds to do his best. When asked years later why he and Odette took the risks they did to save children from the Nazis, Moussa would reply like Saint-Exupéry: "Odette and I had to go through the clouds because we were where that had to be done when it had to be done."

He continued to aim high after the war. And again, he succeeded, this time as a well-known critic and broadcaster. From 1959 to 1980, Moussa hosted a weekly program on "The Theater of Today" broadcast by Radio France International, in France and around the world. Each of his eight hundred programs over those twenty-one years included an interview with a theater personality, among them the leading actors, directors, and playwrights in France, such as the actor-director Jean-Louis Barrault or the playwright Eugene Ionesco. His broadcasts also included his reviews of current plays.

"I always loved the theater passionately," Moussa wrote on his retirement as a broadcaster. "I served it to the best of my ability and consecrated a good portion of my life to it. I have perhaps contributed in a modest way to the influence of French culture abroad. Of everything that I did in my life it is perhaps this that I claim with the most pride." It should be noted that at the time Moussa and Odette had still not gone public with their account of saving 527 children during the war.

Moussa loved every minute of his theater life. He and Odette went to a play almost every night. They mixed socially with the stars of the theatrical world. He befriended younger playwrights, encouraged them, and helped them financially. They in turn adored him.

In interviews with three French playwrights, much the same portrait of Moussa's character emerges—a strong-willed, uncompromising charmer—all qualities that helped him succeed as Monsieur Marcel in saving the lives of hundreds of children against horrendous odds.

All three playwrights met Moussa as guests on his radio program and all three remained friends with him for decades afterward. Moussa was a perfectionist, they said, just one example of his strong will. He taped his radio interviews. "If he made the slightest mistake in diction, he would stop the tape and record the phrase again," Victor Haim, an actor-playwright and longtime friend, recalled.[2]

All three saw Moussa as an exceptional critic. He was honest, saying frankly what he loved about a performance, or what he hated about it, but he never got gratuitously nasty, never set out to destroy a career or a play as he felt some critics did. Moussa worried that critics had too much power. He wanted them to be fair, and tried to impose his own uncompromising standards on them. Once he was so angered by *Le Figaro*'s critic Pierre Marcabru, who mercilessly panned an actor in a review, that he telephoned Marcabru and berated him for going too far. "You yourself aren't good enough to play in an amateur theater," Moussa said, according to the playwright Robert Pouderou, a friend of the Abadis for decades.[3]

Moussa's strong will made him unbending in his convictions, and intolerant of those who disagreed with him. Once, Guy Foissy, a playwright and friend of thirty years, showed Moussa a script he had just completed called "The Wake," a farce about death. "He did not like it at all," Foissy said. "He did not want Odette to see it. He tore up the script and called it 'crap.'" A few years later Foissy returned to the subject. "You remember that play you tore up?" he asked Moussa. "You know, it is being performed quite often now." To which Moussa replied, "So what? That doesn't change anything. It's still crap."[4]

All three playwrights said Moussa had strong views on what ailed the modern theater. He refused to set foot in any theater that received subsidies from the state, arguing that such financing opened the way to government censorship of plays. He hated producers who put on classic plays for the umpteenth time, a safe bet to sell tickets, but a practice that denied opportunities to aspiring young playwrights with worthy new offerings—underdogs whom Moussa had long championed. Most of all he despised pompous theater directors. He felt they stole plays from the authors and, out of vanity, distorted them to enhance their own reputations.

Moussa himself stressed this point in *La Comédie du Theatre* (*The Comedy of the Theater*), published in 1985, the first of the three books he wrote. The passages in which he skewers directors are also good examples of his charm, his writing talents, and his impish humor. "The director is the child of our century," Moussa wrote. "He came to the world of the theater three thousand years after the author and the actor, and now it is he who reigns as the head of the family." Moussa called directors "omnipotent computers" and "absolute tyrants." Pity the poor author, Moussa wrote. The director proposes "a slight modification, only a suggestion, of course" to the author. By the fifteenth rehearsal, the slight modifications have transformed the meaning of the play. "The author permits himself to raise his little finger to remind the director that the play he wrote was a light comedy conceived only to amuse but has been turned into a heavy satire on daily bourgeois life." The original happy ending has been turned into a suicide. All that remains is the title, originally "Springtime for Martine." The director changes that to "The Machine."[5]

People who spent time in Moussa's company called him a great raconteur. He spoke beautiful French with a slight accent, rolling the letter *R* while recalling weird anecdotes from theater life such as this one told to Robert Pouderou:

> A man came to the box office of a Paris theater with a dog and asked for two tickets. "Are you expecting someone?" the cashier asked. "No, it's for my dog," the man said. "Wait a minute," said the cashier. "I have to ask the manager if you can bring in a dog." But the man would not be put off. "Don't worry," he told he cashier, "my dog is extremely well-behaved." The theater was far from full that night so the cashier relented and sold the man two tickets. During the first act the lead actress began a long tirade. The dog, on a seat near the stage, let out a long howl. "Shut up," the man said to his dog in a voice loud enough for everyone in the theater to hear. "Let the lady talk."

Moussa was generous to a fault. He had money in later life. Two incomes made Moussa and Odette comfortable. They lived in a modest apartment, had no children, and few expenses. They treated themselves to dinner in the best restaurants and vacations at luxury hotels. Moussa often invited younger playwrights to lunch and always picked up the check. "When we had financial problems, he lent us money," Victor Haim recalled. "He never asked when we were going to pay him back." The young authors would pay the debt eventually in cash, theater tickets, or gifts. "I must have had a dozen lunches with him per year," Robert Pouderou said. "I would tell him it's my turn, but he always insisted on paying. I would pay him back by inviting him and Odette to the theater."

Over lunch they would talk about the theater, about politics, but never about Moussa's clandestine past. Victor Haim once got close to the subject. "I had the feeling he wanted to say something," Victor remembered. "He started a sentence, but broke it off and all he said was 'someday I will tell you.' I never had the curiosity or the courage to ask him what would he tell me. I was younger. It was not considered polite to press an older person." (Moussa was already in his sixties at the time of that lunch, and Victor twenty-five years younger.) "I figured when he was ready to talk, he would tell me," Victor said. "But of course, he never said a word about the Marcel Network."

Guy Foissy got even closer to the truth, without ever knowing it. In the 1980s, Moussa and Odette came to visit Foissy in Grasse and took long walks with him around the city and outlying villages. They passed the convents, schools, and homes where they hid Jewish children during the war, often smiling but without saying a word. They didn't explain anything to Foissy about what these places meant to them. "It was very strange," Foissy said. "They were obviously getting pleasure reliving something, but I didn't understand what." In Grasse, they passed the theater where Jeannette Wolgust had played Joan of Arc. The building had become a bank. "That's where it was," Odette told Moussa, without elaboration. Only he could understand that she meant the former theater. Foissy, uncomprehending, walked on.

The three playwrights agreed that Moussa was a high-maintenance friend. They loved him, but admitted that it required work to keep the friendships going. He had a temper, demanded total loyalty, easily took offense, and often broke off friendships with people who told him something he did not want to hear. His broken relationships included both casual acquaintances and close friends like Victor Haim.

Victor was acting in a play at the Petit Odéon, a theater in Paris. Moussa phoned him after attending the dress rehearsal with other critics. "You started well," Moussa told him, "but then you were not so good. You got better later."

"I had the reaction of an actor," Victor said. "I am opening in the play tonight," he told Moussa in a raised voice. "You should not be giving an actor negative criticism on opening night. Give me a chance. The part I am playing is hard enough. If you start tearing me apart just before I go onstage that is not encouraging."

"One cannot tell you anything," Moussa replied. He said he had wanted to be helpful. Victor's reaction and tone of voice angered him. So Moussa broke off the relationship. Victor tried to repair the damage, to no avail. He phoned Moussa and apologized, as if it had been his reaction rather than Moussa's action that caused the problem. He wrote Moussa, and appealed to him through Odette. But Moussa refused to resume the friendship that had lasted twenty years. The same uncompromisingly stubborn willfulness that ruined his friendship with Victor and others was what had enabled Moussa to save children in his earlier clandestine life.

Even Victor, and the other friends Moussa broke with, never stopped adoring him. It pained them that he put them off. They were not blind to his faults. But in the end they still remembered him fondly. They, like all Moussa's friends, missed him and regretted his passing. To them, he remained an outsized character, a charmer, warm and generous, and, above all, an exceptional raconteur.

The stories he told usually came from one of the two worlds that shaped his life: the theater, the subject of his first book; and his youth in the Damascus ghetto, the basis for the other two. In his last two books, his storytelling skills reached their peak. The first, *La Reine et le Calligraphe* (*The Queen and the Calligrapher*) published in 1993, won the grand prize of the Académie Française, one of the most distinguished literary awards in France, roughly equivalent to the Pulitzer Prize or the National Book Award. Moussa won it in the category for short stories. The sequel, a further collection of short stories from the ghetto called *Shimon-le-parjure* (*Shimon the Perjurer*) was published in 1999. Both are subtitled *Mes Juifs de Damas* (*My Jews of Damascus*) and recount ghetto life in the 1920s.

Some seventy years separate the scenes in the ghetto from publication of the stories, a lapse of time allowing Moussa to exploit an imperfect memory with so many embellishments that the reader cannot tell the fact from the fiction. In all the stories Moussa lovingly re-creates the absurdities of ghetto life, with humor and a sharp eye for just the right detail to ring true. Examples follow, one from each of the Damascus books.

In *La Reine*, Moussa's uncle, a member of the ghetto's administrative council, visits a school that was supposed to be modernized with new equipment. He finds the new desks and benches just purchased piled up in a heap, unused, in a corner of the schoolroom. The children are on the floor memorizing Psalms.

> This was then the state of what we called a modern school. My uncle asked the children to go play in the courtyard without making too much noise. Then he addressed himself to the specialist on Psalms like one speaks to a delinquent caught in the act of shoplifting.
>
> "And now rabbi, you can perhaps explain why you are not using either the desks or the benches or even the chair that Mourade the carpenter made especially to measurements to accommodate the curve of your ample backside."
>
> "Desks. Benches. A blackboard. What would you want me to do with them?" the rabbi replied. "I taught for forty years in Aleppo. I have educated hundreds of Talmudists without ever resorting to such useless objects. One is far better off sitting on the floor. Our ancestors had no chairs or blackboards and that didn't stop them."[6]

In *Shimon*, the ghetto's Rabbinical Court convenes to hear a divorce case.

> The court, presided over by our Grand Rabbi, assisted by two notables and the rabbis Aboulafia and Khalfoune, had a peculiarity. Whatever the rigorists of Jerusalem might have thought, our court did nothing to enhance its own credibility. Its illustrious president spoke only Ladino, his mother tongue. And since no one else in the ghetto understood this "foreign" language, it was the wife of the Grand Rabbi—la Signora—who was given the task of interpreting, which she performed for better or worse, and usually for the worse as she came from Salonika and possessed only the vaguest rudiments of Arabic which she learned on weekly visits taking tea at the homes of the great ladies of our bourgeoisie.
>
> She had to attend all sessions of the court, next to her husband, and translate for him, word for word, everything that was said, and sometimes what was not said, by the litigants and witnesses, people who, let's face it, were only grudgingly tolerant of the presence of a woman in the tribunal, even if she was the wife of the Grand Rabbi.[7]

Moussa had a way with words. He was the talker. And Odette let him talk for both of them. But Odette was a formidable personality in her own right, something her many friends never let anyone forget. Together they were an extraordinary couple, as they proved in running the Marcel Network as a true joint venture. Neither could have done it without the other.

22

The Couple

As a student, Odette had a tragic love affair. "She had a lover in Paris," her friend Olga Fink said, "but he died of tuberculosis as a young man."[1] Two years later Odette met Moussa, and he became her life.

"He meant everything to her," Jacqueline Denechère said. "She idolized him. From her description, he sounded like a god."[2] Odette worried about him constantly. Several women friends spoke of lunches with Odette when she would leave the table to phone home and make sure Moussa was all right. She would come back beaming. All was still well in her world.

Moussa also worried about Odette. The ordeal at Auschwitz had damaged her lungs. Every winter she suffered from bronchitis, often coughing until it hurt, and then some. Jacqueline remembers Moussa putting a hand on her shoulder and saying during one of Odette's coughing spells, "I hope nothing happens to her." The thought of losing Odette terrified Moussa.

She was his essential support system. Moussa often said the Marcel Network could not have accomplished anything without her. He readily acknowledged that of the two of them, Odette was better organized, more practical, and stronger emotionally. After the war he continued an inordinate reliance on her.

Odette gave Moussa essential help in his work as a theater critic, prolonging a very long day for her. Her routine began with a full day as a doctor, then the theater in the evening, then typing up Moussa's review notes late into the night, as his handwriting was illegible and only Odette could read it. Odette enjoyed the theater, and, according to the playwright Guy Foissy, she became quite knowledgeable about French plays. But typing and sorting all of Moussa's papers was a labor of love.[3]

Odette firmly believed that Moussa had always remained faithful to her, especially while she struggled to survive at Auschwitz and Belsen for more than a year. That made her love him all the more. "She was very moved that Moussa had waited for her," said her friend Betty Kaluski-Saville. "He had no other love life while she was away. She spoke about that a lot."[4]

According to Dr. Annick Alzoubi, a colleague of Odette's at work and one of her closest friends, the highlight of Odette's day was coming home to Moussa. "Before entering their apartment she would powder her nose, put on some lipstick, and check herself in the mirror of her compact to make sure she looked her best," Annick said. "She did this every day, well into her seventies."[5]

Yet Moussa and Odette never showed their affection for one another in public—no hand-holding, caresses, or kisses. "But they were so together," Jacqueline Denechère said, "that when you saw them from behind walking ahead, you had the feeling they were only one person."

They were very different personalities who blended together perfectly. Moussa the talker, the great raconteur, held center stage. Odette, the good listener, encouraged his storytelling. She took pleasure in seeing how he amused other people. He was cerebral, an intellectual, the intelligence of the head. She was warm, soft, motherly, "the intelligence of the heart," said the playwright Robert Pouderou. "She smoothed off his rough edges."[6]

While Moussa thrived on writing, Odette loved to sing. According to Jacqueline Denechère, a professional singer and a friend of forty years, Odette had talent, but no confidence in her voice. "She would say, 'I sing off-key,' which wasn't true," Jacqueline recalled.[7] Odette never thought seriously of a career as a singer. She was too busy, first as a medical student and later as a doctor. But singing was a lifelong interest. Odette met Jacqueline through a voice coach and Auschwitz survivor whom they both knew. And when Odette retired as a doctor, her friends gave her an electric piano to encourage her singing.

✦

Some friends of the Abadis thought Odette lived under Moussa's thumb, always submissive to his domineering personality. Not so, said Julien Engel. "You have to remember that Frenchwomen of that generation deferred to their husbands," he explained. "But submissiveness was not part of her personality. She could not have functioned as a doctor if this were true."[8] Odette showed her toughness in her book about Auschwitz. And when Moussa tried to talk in public about her arrest or her time in the camps, she shut him up, and took over the conversation. The playwright Victor Haim agreed that Odette was no pushover. "When Moussa exaggerated," he said, "she would correct him and then tell him, 'Don't exaggerate.'"[9]

Still, Odette deferred to Moussa more often than not, even when he made her angry. Jacqueline Denechère recounted a story underscoring that point. Moussa and Odette were visiting Jacqueline and her companion, the journalist René Sicart, near Angers in the Loire Valley.[10] The Abadis came to look at Jacqueline's house. After the visit, Moussa wanted to return to their hotel for dinner. But first he said, "I must find my *biscottes*," a French version of melba toast.

Moussa did not eat bread, only a particular brand of *biscottes*, which he would wrap in tinfoil and open at the dining table whenever he ate out. This time he forgot the *biscottes*. "René will take me to look for some," he said, without asking René. All four of them drove off in search of Moussa's melba toast.

"I saw Odette very annoyed at Moussa," Jacqueline recalled. "She felt we were taking an unnecessary ride. It was a Sunday and most bread shops were closed. Odette was really angry but she did not say anything because

René and I were there and she did not want to spoil the pleasure of being together. But if her eyes had been revolvers, she would have shot him."

When her friends describe Odette, their first word is usually "elegant." She was pretty, thin, a blonde with sparkling blue eyes that shone through glasses. She was always extremely well dressed. Odette loved colorful earrings which she matched with little scarves. She never left home without earrings. "I don't feel completely dressed without them," Odette would say.

Odette not only dressed with elegance, she also spoke with elegance. "Some people throw criticism in your face," Jacqueline explained. "But when Odette criticized you, she would wear gloves to soften the blow. She would say something like 'You have to think more about that, my little Jacqueline. There are other ways of doing it.'"

When it came to shopping, to choosing her clothes, Odette preferred to leave Moussa at home, friends said. If he went with her, he would push her to buy everything she said she liked. If a jacket tempted her, he would tell her to buy two or three of them in different colors. She would say she liked the blue one only, and, besides, she wanted to look around some more before buying. "I don't go shopping with Moussa because he makes me buy too much," Odette would say. It was another small sign of her independence.

In a similar vein, Odette would go without Moussa to see Auschwitz survivors she knew. That was her private world, one more sign of independence. She never told her other friends about these reunions. Such silence was typical of both Moussa and Odette. They kept their friends in distinct groups—theater people, former hidden children, camp survivors, and others—and never mixed people from the different groups socially.

Even with the camp survivors, Odette drew lines. With them she discussed their common experiences as prisoners, but said nothing about saving the lives of children before her arrest. The hidden children themselves knew precious little. They knew about their own stories, of course, but nothing about the overall operations of the Marcel Network.

The Paris theater crowd knew the least about the Abadis—little more than that Odette had been in Auschwitz. In summer, she sometimes wore sleeveless dresses that failed to cover the number tattooed on her left forearm. If someone asked, she would say she had been deported, and ended the conversation there. None of the theater people knew anything about the Abadis' clandestine work during the war because they never discussed it with them. Bertrand Poirot-Delpech, the Paris theater critic for *Le Monde*, had lunch with Moussa regularly for twenty years and never heard a word about the hidden children during that time. When the truth finally came out in the 1990s, he and other close friends admitted to being astonished by it, amazed to be learning for the first time something so important about people they had known for decades.

Moussa and Odette were very private people. They entertained in restaurants; only a handful of their friends ever got invited to dinner in their home. None of the theater people and almost none of the former hidden children ever saw the inside of their apartment. The Abadis said they rarely had people in because their flat was too small for entertaining. True. But that also helped them keep their private life private.

Moussa and Odette Abadi lived for the last forty years of their lives at 115 rue de Reuilly in the 12th arrondisement, a modest section of Eastern Paris near the Bois de Vincennes. Their home was a cramped one-bedroom apartment on the third floor. The elevator stopped on either the half landing above them or the half landing below. The entry hall led to a small kitchen to the right, then straight ahead into a combination living room/dining room taken up almost entirely by the dining room table. There was barely enough room for the other furniture—chairs and a sofa. The window of their living room overlooked a schoolyard and the Abadis loved listening to the noise of children playing there. Beyond the living room the hall led to the only bedroom, then turned left to a bathroom and an office for Moussa. Books lined all the walls.

They could have afforded larger, more comfortable quarters. Odette wanted a bigger place so that she too could have an office at home. But Moussa liked the apartment, liked the neighborhood, and wanted to stay. So they stayed.

Catherine Journoud, the daughter of Odette's close friend Jacqueline Denechère, became a surrogate granddaughter to the Abadis. While growing up, and later as an adult, she often visited their flat for meals, and recalls the experience with obvious pleasure.

"When you arrived they poked their heads through the door to see who would be first to give you a kiss," she said. "Then they stuck you in a small chair under a bookshelf. Moussa sat in the only armchair in the room, smoking a cigarette through a holder. Odette ran back and forth to the kitchen while setting the dining table, annoyed that she could not follow the conversation. Moussa did nothing to help while Odette prepared the dinner."

Moussa did the shopping for the meal. He liked to buy pistachios and baklava from the Arab merchants in the local open-air market. It reminded him of Damascus. During the meal he would play the macho man, scolding Odette for not using enough salt, or basil, or whatever. "With good humor she would go and get the salt," Catherine said. Moussa always sat at a corner of the table, pinned against a wall, unable to help Odette serve dishes or clear the table between courses, although he did work the toaster that sat in front of him on the table and he performed the ritual of preparing Turkish coffee at the end of the meal. Feminists today would call Moussa a male chauvinist—and they would be right. But, in fairness to him, the open sexism he often displayed was common in France in his day. He would, for example, tease Catherine about her small breasts. "You still have your fried eggs," he would say. "Listen," Odette would tell him. "Mine are not much bigger. Stop it."[11]

Although Moussa and Odette had very different personalities, they also shared some important traits. Like Moussa, Odette was generous to a fault. In the Nazi death camps, she often gave patients food from her own slim rations. Violette Jacquet-Silberstein said Odette cured her of jaundice at Auschwitz with an injection of glucose. Odette could have saved the shot of glucose for herself, as the sugar content in it would have helped keep her alive on her near-starvation diet. Instead she used the precious glucose to save a friend. In the decades after the war, Odette always insisted on paying the bill when meeting a woman friend at a restaurant for lunch. Usually she brought the friend a little gift as well, perhaps toilet water or a book. She showered presents on the children of her close friends.

Again like Moussa, Odette saw humor in the absurdities of life. During the Spanish Civil War, for example, she was the doctor who ended up examining patients below the belt. The other young doctors in her group rarely did that. At first she thought there was something wrong with her. Then she realized it was the other doctors, too embarrassed to examine patients' sexual organs, who had left the job to her. Odette laughed, recalling the scene. "They were the ones with the hang-ups, not me," she told a friend.[12]

Odette enjoyed a successful career. She held a number of responsible administrative posts for the state health service, starting in 1948 as a medical inspector for schools in Paris. In the 1950s, she headed the Department of the Health Laboratory for the French capital, and she retired in 1979 as the chief medical officer in the venereal disease service for Paris.

"She was always way ahead of her time," said Dr. Annick Alzoubi, her colleague at work. Odette was an early campaigner to legalize abortion, early to use psychotherapy, one of the first in France to study Chinese medicine, and a pioneer on the use of computers in medical practice. Remarkably, Odette did it all despite her own fragile health. In addition to bronchitis, her back was a wreck, permanently damaged from the beatings at Auschwitz. "I once saw the X-rays of her back," Annick said. "It was terrible. One wonders how she could live with such a back." Odette coped by undertaking yoga, massages, and workouts at the gym.

With no money problems from the late 1950s onward, the Abadis did not stint on themselves. They ate most nights in restaurants, sometimes in the most expensive ones in Paris, and stayed on vacation at the best luxury hotels in France, from Megève in the Alps to the Riviera. The Carlton in Cannes was a particular favorite. They often went by taxi the 135 miles from Paris to a five-star holiday hotel in Deauville on the Normandy coast. Moussa didn't drive a car. Odette had a license but disliked driving.

Almost every year, they took a month's holiday together. In addition, Moussa would go off for a two-week vacation on his own. "I don't want to come," Odette would tell him. "You are going to see the same people we always see there and have the same conversations with them." She also wanted time alone to rest, reflect, and tidy up Moussa's papers. Violette Jacquet-Silverstein said it was more than that. According to her, "Moussa was impossibly macho and sometimes Odette needed a breather."[13] In any event, "Moussa wouldn't stay the two weeks," Jeannette Wolgust said. "He would miss Odette and come back after a week."[14]

Odette always adored children. She risked her life to save hundreds during the war, and gave them the tender loving care of a surrogate mother. Later in life she unofficially adopted the children and grandchildren of close friends, spoiling them with presents. After she retired from the state medical service in 1979, Odette continued to dedicate herself to young people. She worked for another fifteen years as a volunteer doctor treating children at Cours Morvan, a school for the deaf in Paris. And yet, although she spent a lifetime caring for other people's children, Odette never had children of her own. The reason remains unclear.

At the end of the war in 1945, when Odette returned from the camps and resumed life with Moussa she was only thirty-one years old, well within the normal child-bearing age. Some of her closest friends think she may have been unable to have children, that she may have become infertile because of the beatings, the typhus, and the other physical traumas she suffered in the camps.

Others among her closest friends think Odette did not want children when she could have had them. She and Moussa had trouble reconstructing their lives in the decade after the war, until 1956 when Moussa moved to Paris and emerged from his depression. At that stage, Odette was forty-two. Some of these friends say Odette took care of Moussa as if he were her child. But none of her friends knew her reasons for sure.

It is possible that Odette herself did not know if she could have had children. Her friend Betty Kaluski-Saville noted that in the France of the 1950s tests for infertility in women were not as common or as accurate as they are now.[15]

Or the infertility may have been Moussa's.

Annette Wieviorka, the historian, was perhaps the only friend bold enough to ask Odette straight out why the Abadis never had children. The answer Odette gave then was probably the closest to the truth. "It was never the right time," she told Annette. "During the war it was not the right time. After the war it was not the right time. And after that, it was too late."[16]

Odette and Moussa finally got married in a civil ceremony at their local registry office in Paris in 1959, after having lived together for eighteen years. By then, Odette was forty-five. They saw no need for a religious ceremony. Odette did not have much of a religious upbringing and did not believe in God. Moussa no longer attended synagogue, nor observed the traditions of Jewish life such as the Friday night Sabbath ceremony. He claimed to have lost his faith during the horrors of the Holocaust.

Thirty years later, however, in 1989, Moussa and Odette changed their minds. They decided they wanted to be married religiously as well after all, partly to be more socially acceptable to the Jewish community, and partly because Moussa never really shook the influence of his strict religious upbringing in the Damascus ghetto. Friends said the religious ceremony was Moussa's idea and that Odette agreed for his sake.

At the time, Moussa was seventy-nine and Odette seventy-five. The two elderly Jews thought that getting a religious blessing for their longtime union would be simple. To their great surprise, it turned out to be comically complex.

They went to the young rabbi in the district of Paris where they lived, the 12th arrondisement, and asked him to perform the ceremony. "I am ready to marry you," he said, "but first you have to prove that you are Jewish." They told him the story of how they had saved 527 Jewish children during the war. But the rabbi decided that proved nothing. He wanted documents showing that the parents of Moussa and Odette were Jewish.

"Difficult," Moussa told him. "I left Syria in a hurry, and didn't take my family papers with me. Given the poor relations between France and Syria these days I won't be able to get copies now."

Odette told the rabbi that her mother had died in Auschwitz, that her father went into hiding during the war, and that the family papers got lost.

"Try anyway to obtain the papers," the rabbi said.

Try they did. And by some miracle Odette managed to get a copy of her parents' papers, what the French call a *Livret de Famille.*

The rabbi took a look, and remained unsatisfied.

"Your father's name was Rosenstock," he told Odette. "But he married a woman whose name was not Jewish."

"My mother was Jewish," Odette insisted. "It is true that her father—my grandfather—had a Christian name, but her mother—my grandmother—was Jewish and had a Jewish maiden name." In the Jewish tradition, the religion passes to the child through the mother. Thus Odette was born Jewish.

Nevertheless, the rabbi still had his doubts. "Please bring me the *Livret de Famille* of your grandparents," he said.

Moussa, who had remained calm up to this point, exploded in frustration: "How can you expect us to find documents of people who got married in the 1880s?" he demanded. "We've already explained the difficulties of obtaining papers destroyed during the last war. Going back sixty years more is much harder."

"With the help of God, you will find the documents," the rabbi said.

"God does not demand as many papers as you do," Moussa snapped. "We'll find another rabbi." Then he escorted Odette out and slammed the door.

After that they went to see Daniel Farhi, one of the better known liberal rabbis in Paris. Farhi himself had survived the war as a child by hiding with a Protestant family, but he had not heard of the Abadis before they called on him. "I was very moved to see these two elderly people who had saved so many children, and, now in the sunset of their lives wanted to get married religiously," Farhi said. He took one look at the Auschwitz number tattooed on Odette's forearm and accepted it as ample proof that Odette was Jewish. "When would you like to get married?" Farhi asked the couple. "Next Tuesday?"

During an interview with the author, Farhi first recounted in detail the absurd paper chase demanded by the younger rabbi, and then explained that the whole exercise was totally unnecessary according to Jewish law. "It is important to establish that the couple is Jewish before they can be married religiously, if they are likely to have children," Farhi said. "Whether they are religious or not matters because that determines what they pass on to their children. But if they are seventy-five or eighty, are never going to have children, and simply want to finish their lives together, none of these rules apply."[17]

Farhi proposed a Tuesday evening wedding ceremony for the Abadis because he knew there would be about fifty children at the synagogue attending a Bible class then. He wanted the couple that had saved so many Jewish children to be surrounded by Jewish youngsters when they took their marriage vows. And so they were.

Odette went to her religious wedding dressed in trousers, one of her fashion trademarks. Her friends told her it would be more appropriate if she wore a skirt. "Out of the question," Odette said. "I am going to be myself."[18]

23

Revelations

During the 1990s, the Abadis' resistance to telling the story of the Marcel Network in public gradually crumbled. It was fifty years since the war, the last decade of their lives, and they found themselves rethinking their old reasons for remaining silent.

The process began with a quirk of fate in 1993—a throwaway line by Moussa in a radio interview. He had just published his first book on his youth in the Damascus ghetto. It had won a prestigious prize (the grand prize of the Académie Française) and Radio J, the local station of the Jewish community in Paris, requested an interview about the book. On the air, the interviewer said in passing, "I believe that you hid Jewish children during the war." In reply, Moussa said only, "Yes, that's true"—three little words.[1] Then they resumed talking about the book for the rest of the program. But those few words were more than enough.

Betty Kaluski-Saville heard Moussa's radio interview. She thought the three little words were meant for her. Betty was secretary-general of the Association of Hidden Children in France, a group formed in 1992, the year before Moussa's interview, to bring together Jews who had been saved as children during the war. Betty also wrote for the association's bulletin. Moussa's story, she was certain, would be perfect for the bulletin.

Moussa, of course, needed convincing. It took Betty a year to bring him around. She began with a letter suggesting an interview. Moussa wrote back saying they should talk informally first. They met in a cafe near the Bastille, then three or four more times while Moussa checked her out. He wanted to know her background, her political views. As they got friendlier, they began to speak by phone. One day Betty's husband, Jo, answered, and Moussa warmed to him. Moussa invited Betty and Jo to the Abadi apartment and the two couples became good friends. Finally, Moussa decided he could trust Betty. So he and Odette agreed to be interviewed—but only on Moussa's terms. He would read the text before publication. Every line to be printed would have to be approved first by him.

Moussa had ample reason for being so demanding. He remembered the Lebesque interview where he was unable to control what would be highlighted and what would be played down. Furthermore, all his other reasons for remaining silent still applied. On the other hand, Moussa understood that the story of the Marcel Network might emerge someday, and, if it did, he wanted it to be an accurate version, told his way. He further realized that the terms accepted by Betty could be his last and best chance to get the story out the right way. Moussa was eighty-three years old. "He knew his life was coming to an end," Betty said. "That gave him the will to agree."[2]

Betty published an excellent summary of the Marcel Network's operations over five pages in the association's bulletin of September 1994. It covered the roles played by Bishop Rémond, Pastors Evrard and Gagnier, Maurice Brener, and Georges Garel. It also recounted many of the key incidents, among them depersonalization, the escape of thirteen boys through the window of the crypt at Dom Bosco, and the death of the Gartner brothers. At the end, Betty published a note saying, "This article was based on interviews with Moussa and Odette Abadi and published with their agreement."[3] It was the first interview with them published since Morvan Lebeque's in 1948, and, because of Moussa's terms, this time the story was more accurate and more complete.

It was, however, just a summary, in an obscure publication with a tiny audience, and far from the full story. One of their former hidden children,

Julien Engel, had long wanted Moussa and Odette to say much more. For years he had been urging them to write their own story. He said they owed it to history. Moussa kept turning him down. "I have another book in me," Moussa repeatedly said, referring to what later became his first volume of tales from the Damascus ghetto. "After that, we'll see."[4]

Getting nowhere, Julien suggested to the Abadis that instead of writing about their clandestine work, they agree to an extended recorded interview—an oral history of the Marcel Network. His idea eventually became seven hours of videotaped interviews in 1995, conducted by Annette Wieviorka, an eminent French historian, on behalf of the Fortunoff Video Archive of Holocaust Testimonies at Yale University. Again, Moussa tried to control everything. "There was a long negotiation," Annette recalled. "Moussa had very firm ideas on how the interviews should be conducted. Questions and answers were prepared. There was nothing spontaneous."[5] In addition, Moussa asked Fortunoff and Yale to give access to the tapes only to scholars or others with legitimate reasons to view them, such as families of hidden children, and to make sure the tapes were never exploited for commercial reasons.

Odette arrived for the interview in a bright yellow jacket over gray trousers, wearing her trademark earrings and matching scarf. Her hair was gray. Moussa walked unsteadily with a cane. He wore a dark pullover under a blazer. As usual, he did most of the talking. "For fifty years you refused interviews," Annette began. "Why speak out now?"

"For three reasons," Moussa replied.

"First, in France there is now an alarming rise of negativism, a denial that the Holocaust ever existed, that it is a Jewish invention. It appeared urgent to us to testify to what we saw and lived through fifty years ago.

"Second, Odette and I have come to the age where we know time is running out. We have to leave a testimony of what we have done.

"Third, many of the children we saved from certain death were too young to remember anything. They need to know what happened."[6]

The Fortunoff tapes are the fullest single account the Abadis ever gave about the work of the Marcel Network. They are an invaluable source. But for the complete story, compiled for the first time in this book, many other sources had to be consulted, among them the speeches, letters, and other personal papers of the Abadis, the OSE archives, and testimony from or about Bishop Rémond, Pastors Evrard and Gagnier, Maurice Brener, Georges Garel, close friends of the Abadis, and, of course, the former hidden children themselves.

Another major source, Odette's book about her time at Auschwitz and Belsen, *Terre de Détresse* (*Land of Despair*), was finally published in 1995, the same year as the videotaped interviews for Fortunoff.

Betty Kaluski-Saville convinced Odette to take her manuscript out of the bank deposit box where it had sat for nearly fifty years. Betty's husband, Jo, arranged to have the text put on a computer disk for her, through a friend who agreed to do the work in his spare time. The job got delayed and Moussa grew impatient. He phoned Jo to say it was taking too long. Annoyed, Jo responded that he was doing this as a favor and needed more time. Moussa, aggravated by Jo's tone, arrived immediately in a taxi to collect the manuscript, and later arranged for its publication without further help from Jo. He said he and Odette never wanted to speak to Jo again.

Jo was devastated. He regarded Moussa as a father figure. The couples were so close that they spent the New Year's holiday together. Like Victor Haim before him, Jo tried everything—apologizing, phone calls, and letters—all to no avail. Moussa would have nothing to do with him anymore. He even said he didn't want Jo to attend his funeral. Years later Jo still told the story with obvious pain. "I had a great love for them and would have done anything for him," he said.[7]

Jo and Victor were evidence that Moussa could be a challenging friend. No portrait of Moussa is complete without a reference to that side of his character. But these were exceptions. Moussa kept the great majority of his friends for the rest of his life. Among them were children he and Odette had saved, some of whom as adults became closer to them. They remain devoted to Moussa to this day, in a group that continues to honor his memory. Not surprisingly, Jeannette Wolgust was the driving force in that endeavor.

Jeannette attended the first meeting in Paris of Betty Kaluski-Saville's organization, the Association of Hidden Children. She decided that the association's bulletin would be the perfect vehicle to search for more "Abadi children," contact them, and bring them together. And so, in February 1993, Jeannette put this small notice in Betty's bulletin:

> In 1943, a man, Moussa Abadi, saved 527 children. I would like to find those children so that we can celebrate together in an official manner the 50th anniversary of the founding of the Marcel Network.

Her idea was to pay homage to Moussa and Odette for what they had done. Jeannette thought the Abadis' contribution worthy of recognition—nothing fancy but "simply to say thank you to Moussa and Odette." At the bottom of the notice she gave her address.[8]

That notice and further efforts traced Abadi children in Europe, Israel, and the United States. Betty's bulletin published a list of 165 of the children whose whereabouts were unknown. As a result, several of them contacted Moussa and Odette for the first time since the war. "We knew we were hidden, but we didn't know it was by you," they would tell the Abadis. "It was all very moving," Moussa said. "Some of them were unable to talk or eat when we invited them for a meal." The reunions also placed an emotional strain on Moussa, but the actor in him usually enabled him to put everyone at ease.

As more former Abadi children were located, they formed their own association, "The Children and Friends of the Abadis," with Jeannette as the founder and first president. The group brought together former hidden children with longtime friends of the Abadis from all walks of life. Their association has honored Moussa and Odette in many ways over the years, eventually succeeding in getting a Paris square, near their apartment, named after them. The group continues to pay tribute to the Abadis through its own website in French, http://www.moussa-odette-abadi.asso.fr/fr/home.htm, which tells the story of Moussa and Odette and sponsors conferences on the work of the Marcel Network. The organization still includes some fifty members, among them former hidden children Jeannette Wolgust, Andrée Poch-Karsenti, Françoise Knopf, Marthe Artzstein (Martoune), Julien Engel, and Armand Morgenzstern. Much to the disappointment of the three friends from the Joan of Arc convent in Grasse—Jeannette, Françoise, and Martoune—they never managed to locate the fourth girl in their little band, Denise Touchard.

When former Abadi children did find each other, their reunions, naturally, were filled with emotion. Once when Julien and George Engel visited Paris, Jeannette invited them to her home with Moussa and Odette. During the get-together the phone rang. It was Martoune. She had just found Armand Morgenzstern for the first time since the war. Fifty years earlier, they had lived together as children, with his mother and her father. Both were overjoyed and wanted to share their happiness with Jeannette. She explained that Moussa, Odette, and the Engel brothers were with her, and everyone wanted Martoune and Armand to join them, then and there. So they did. Suddenly there were five former Abadi children—Julien, George, Jeannette, Martoune, and Armand—together in the same room with Moussa and Odette. There were hugs, kisses, and tears, until Moussa broke away. He realized that Laurent, Jeannette's husband, had discreetly left the room so they could enjoy their reunion without him, the lone outsider. Moussa found Laurent and made him join the group. "Come on, son," he said to Laurent. "You are now part of the family." Jeannette never forgot that gesture of kindness. "Here I was, the wife, and I had not thought of Laurent being left out because I was so caught up in our togetherness."[9]

During the last years of their lives Moussa and Odette often met with former hidden children for dinner in a restaurant, sometimes with only one of them, other times with their spouse as well or in a group. It was always the same story. Moussa picked the place, a restaurant where the maitre d'hôtel knew him by name and would go through the ritual Moussa loved, beginning with "Good evening, Monsieur Abadi," followed by appropriate bowing and scraping, and seating at one of the better tables. Moussa would order for everyone. "You'll have the salmon," he would say. Someone would want steak. Moussa would insist on salmon. "Let them have what they want," Odette would say. Moussa would relent. With the meal came Moussa's stories, mostly about the theater. The former hidden children listened in fascination. Although Odette had heard the stories countless times, she beamed as she saw the others hanging on every word.

For her part, Jeannette never tired of telling and retelling the story of Moussa and Odette. She told it to her children and grandchildren. Her eldest grandson, then seven, was quite impressed. "What luck we had," he said. "If Moussa had not saved Granny, then there would not have been Daddy, and if Daddy had not been there, then I would not be here either."[10]

Moussa himself would not accept thanks from Jeannette's grandson or anyone else. He made the point in what became his valedictory speech, an address to a conference on hidden children held at the French Senate on May 21, 1995. Moussa said:

"When we meet hidden children again, the question they ask most often is 'How can we thank you?' My response will be brief. You have nothing to thank us for, because you owe us nothing. It is we who are in your debt. You gave us a lesson in dignity and courage. You have nothing to thank us for because we belong to a generation full of utopias, illusions, and cowardice. Our generation did not know how to protect you from disaster."

Moussa went on to say that instead of thanking the Abadis, the hidden children, and indeed everyone from younger generations, should do everything they can to aid threatened children all over the world.

"What is a hidden child?" Moussa asked. "It is a child in danger. It is a child who needs help from others. It is a child who risks death. So I ask you, I beg of you, look around yourself. Think of the children of Rwanda, of Somalia, of the children on the sidewalks of Manila, of the children of Chernobyl, of the children of Sarajevo. Then do something. They are hidden children. And you owe it to them to do something. So do something. And if you don't have the means to do anything for them then yell, scream, don't accept that in this world children can be killed a few hundred kilometers from your home."[11]

Moussa Abadi always insisted that in saving children he had only done his duty. He did more than that, of course. Do as I did, he said, in a lesson for all mankind.

EPILOGUE

Moussa began going blind in 1995. He discovered at age eighty-five that he suffered from macular degeneration, a disorder that attacks the central part of the retina, and eventually leaves the victim sightless. "We can sometimes slow down the deterioration," the doctor told him, "but we cannot cure it." Moussa wrote about his increasing blindness in a book never published, entitled *The Light of My Eyes*. The dedication read, "To Odette, the light of my eyes."

On his first visit, the doctor told Moussa, "Your left eye is finished. But I think your right eye will not give you much trouble for the next five years."[1] Moussa counted his blessings: a five-year reprieve from total blindness. But the doctor's prediction turned out to be overly optimistic. Only one year later, Moussa learned that his right eye was deteriorating rapidly.

In the taxi on the way home, Moussa and Odette leaned against each other. "I knew that the challenge which now awaited us would be one of the most formidable that we ever faced," Moussa wrote. "But I knew that we would find a way to survive this trial, just as we had survived the war, clandestine operations, deportation, and separation."

"I see badly, but I still see," Moussa told himself. "I can still read and write. For the rest, what will be will be."[2]

Before long, he could no longer read or write. In addition, he needed a cane to walk. By the time Moussa died of stomach cancer, on September 15, 1997, at the age of eighty-seven, he was almost totally blind. The disorder had destroyed his sight in only two years.

Odette was at Moussa's bedside when he passed away. She telephoned Daniel Farhi, the rabbi who had married the Abadis religiously. "Moussa has died, and I am alone with him in the hospital," she told Farhi.

"My wife and I drove immediately to the hospital," the rabbi recalled. "We saw this poor woman all by herself next to this man all by himself." Farhi told Odette she could not stay at the hospital. He made arrangements to remove Moussa's body and then drove Odette to her apartment.

"We offered to stay with her for a while but she said, 'Don't worry. I'll be fine. You can leave me.'"

The Farhis said good-bye. Odette closed the door. Then the rabbi and his wife walked down to the half landing where they waited for the elevator. It took a while to come, and while they waited they heard Odette screaming though the closed door, "Moussa! Moussa, where are you!"

"I told myself she was waiting for us to leave so she could explode," Farhi said. "She had to scream. It was an inhuman scream, full of pain. I did not go back, because I thought she had to stay alone with her unbearable pain."[3]

Odette never got over that pain. With Moussa gone, she no longer wanted to live. Odette resolved to put Moussa's papers in order, and then take her own life. For two years she sorted out thousands of papers. Eventually, the correspondence, books, interviews, speeches, unpublished manuscripts, and personal papers all went to Jeannette Wolgust, separated into two groups. Jeannette donated the general archive, including everything related to the Marcel Network, to the Contemporary Jewish Documentation Center (Centre de Documentation Juive Contemporaine) at the Holocaust Memorial in Paris. Moussa's theater archive, including notes about plays and actors, criticism, and the tapes from eight hundred radio broadcasts re-recorded on CDs, filled fifty-seven boxes that went to IMEC, a document center established by the French publishing industry.

Both are treasure troves for scholars, the first on the wartime Jewish Resistance in France, and the second on the modern French theater.

During the two years that Odette sorted out Moussa's papers, she met frequently with Catherine Breton, a psychiatrist and personal friend, and discussed her intended suicide. Catherine tried to talk Odette out of it. She thought she might succeed.

The two women were soul sisters, doctors who had long worked with patients condemned to death—Catherine with AIDS victims and Odette in the Nazi camps. Catherine spoke about the blood testing center for HIV that she created. Those found to have AIDS she treated for psychic trauma. She told Odette about the difficulty of telling these people the truth. "If I told someone he had AIDS, I was telling him that he would die," Catherine explained, because, at that time, AIDS patients had no hope. "The truth can be destructive. But if I told the patient the truth, I gave him a choice of how he wanted to live the rest of his life. I spoke a lot with Odette about this problem of what to say." Odette listened, and sometimes offered advice on how to handle condemned patients, based on her experience in the camps.[4]

A year before Odette's death, the two women decided to meet for lunch on Mondays. It was not all gloom and doom. They discussed the theater, politics, and a wide range of subjects. But the two main topics were always AIDS and Odette's intended suicide. "I wanted to engage her in the struggle against AIDS," Catherine said. She asked Odette to help her at the blood testing center. She thought that would take Odette's mind off suicide and give her life a new purpose, with a chance to help people in real need.

At the same time, Catherine let Odette talk about suicide, gave her a hearing, as part of the effort to persuade her to change her mind. Catherine said Odette cited two reasons for wanting to end her life—she did not want to continue without Moussa, and she feared that the failing health of old age would decimate her body, the way it had suffered in the camps. "She refused to go through that again," Catherine said.

Odette was tempted by the idea of working with AIDS patients. Although by now well into her eighties, Odette welcomed a new challenge.

But in the end, nothing could dissuade her from taking her own life. "I am not going to join you," she told Catherine. "I am going to commit suicide." She discussed with Catherine the pills she would take, and in what dosage. Odette said she would arrange to get the pills she needed on her own.

Catherine still hoped Odette would not go through with it. She thought Odette's other friends were also trying to dissuade her. Odette, however, had not spoken of her intended suicide to anyone else, only to Catherine. Had she known that, Catherine said, she would have tried harder to change Odette's mind.

On July 29, 1999, at age eighty-four, a year after starting the Monday lunches with Catherine, Odette Abadi took the pills that ended her life. The scene: the apartment that she had shared with Moussa. She left personal notes for all her friends, another sign of her long preparations. "I reproach myself for many things," Catherine said. For one thing, she regretted not insisting that Odette become her patient, rather than just a regular lunch date. In the doctor-patient relationship, Catherine felt, she could have done more to dissuade Odette from suicide than she was able to do simply as a friend.[5]

Some of Odette's other friends also blamed themselves for not doing more. Although they didn't know of her suicide plans, they had found her different. In the last months of her life, she was gloomy. She looked ill and tormented. Then she started refusing invitations to lunch, and kept to herself at home. When they offered to help her shop she refused, saying the cleaning woman who came in twice a week would do the shopping. After she died, they regretted not having insisted on seeing her, not demanding to know what was wrong, not giving her the will to live.

Jeannette Wolgust was one of the few to see Odette in her last months. Jeannette was worried, and phoned Odette every day to make sure she was all right. On the last phone call, Odette referred to Jeannette as "my little girl," the first time she had used that term of endearment with her. "Something's odd," Jeannette thought. She telephoned Odette the next morning at ten. No answer. She tried again at eleven thirty and again at two thirty in the afternoon. Still no answer. "I don't like this," Jeannette told her husband. "Let's go."[6]

They had a set of keys to Odette's apartment. Jeannette's husband, Laurent, opened the door. In the entry hall they found a piece of paper taped to a chair. "If you find me, call Jeannette," it said. On the buffet table they found two letters. One was for the police, explaining Odette's suicide. Another was a nineteen-page letter of instructions for Jeannette. "I must have been one of the last people to talk to her," Jeannette said. "After that she unhooked the telephone."

The instructions for Jeannette included how and when to distribute the dozens of letters Odette had written to other friends to say good-bye. One friend was in Israel on holiday. "Let her finish her vacation first," Odette told Jeannette. Another friend was visiting Avignon: "Let her see the bridge before you call her." A third was described by Odette as an old lady: "Make sure she does not find out in the newspapers." Odette even wrote her own death announcement, and instructed Jeannette to give it to particular papers.[7]

The letters contained the same typewritten message to everyone, and then a different, personal handwritten postscript to each friend. The general message said:

> My friends,
>
> Please don't grieve for me. As I am alone, free, and more than 84 years old, it is reasonable to finish with my life. In fact, I died the same time as Moussa. I had to resolve several problems—now finished—especially to edit and print out the last work [his unpublished manuscript "The Light of my Eyes"] which Moussa wrote with all his talent, humor and tenderness.
>
> I would never have been able to finish my tasks if you had not supported me so marvellously, each in your own way. I want to tell you how much you helped me by your presence and your attention—the phone calls, the letters, the meetings—and how much I admire the obstinacy of my faithful friends despite my withdrawal from society. My retreat is explained by the fact that I have lost the sense of my life and the taste of life and by the fact that I refused to take up such a large place in your existence so that your grief today would not be so intrusive.

> This is why my last thoughts will be to thank you infinitely, and, in the name of liberty, to bless you—believers, pagans and the confused—with all my heart.[8]

The personal note she added to her letter to Margareta Haim was special to her alone, as were the personal notes to all the others. Odette stressed how much she loved knowing Margareta, Victor, and their children. "I wish you and all those you love great moments of happiness," Odette stressed. She made clear she regretted Moussa's decision to break off the friendship with Victor, and asked Margareta to tell Victor that Moussa's actions did nothing to change the warm friendship Odette still felt toward him. "I embrace the two of you together," she said.[9]

In addition to the letters, Odette also arranged to distribute virtually every item of consequence in her possession to one friend or another. In the weeks before her death, she took the trouble of putting a label on each item including the name of the person to whom it should go as a memento of Moussa and herself. Julien Engel, as but one example, received several books and four framed prints of historic Parisian theaters.[10] Catherine Journoud inherited the Abadi apartment.

Jeannette Wolgust stood at Odette's coffin for a last farewell. Before they closed the coffin, Jeannette put a pair of Odette's favorite earrings in their proper place. Odette Abadi went to her maker dressed as she would have wished.

Leading French newspapers, including *Le Monde* and *Liberation*, carried generous obituaries on Odette. The magazine *La Vie* (*Life*) significantly a Christian weekly, devoted a three-page homage to her. Its headline served as the perfect epitaph for Odette. "The Mother of 527 Children," it said.[11]

✦

The streets of Paris often carry the names of eminent Frenchmen. They include statesmen (place Charles de Gaulle), scientists (square Marie Curie), writers (avenue Victor Hugo), and artists (rue Paul Cézanne).

The city also honors figures of world renown with streets, avenues, or squares named after Woodrow Wilson, Winston Churchill, and Pablo Picasso, among many others.

The tradition has led to various groups lobbying for Paris streets to be named after their favorite heroes—some great names and some virtual unknowns. City officials review the candidates and take their time in deciding. At this writing, more than a decade after the death of Princess Diana in a car crash, the decision is still pending on whether to name a Paris landmark after her.

In 2004, friends of Moussa and Odette began pushing for a street to be named after them. The Abadis had received numerous honors from the French government during their lifetimes, among them the *Légion d'honneur* and the *Medaille de la Résistance*. But their friends wanted a Paris street or square. That took time. For one thing, officials had to verify that Moussa and Odette did indeed save 527 children.

But four years later, on September 13, 2008, the advocates got their wish. Some two hundred people—friends, former hidden children, local residents, and the curious—attended the official dedication of the "Place Moussa et Odette Abadi," a square filled with trees and flowers a short walk from the apartment where the Abadis lived for the last forty years of their lives in the 12th arrondisement. Fittingly, it is a space where children laugh and play.

The street sign there—white letters on a blue background, trimmed in green on the edges—honors the Abadis as "the founders and organizers of the Marcel Network (1943–1945) which saved 527 Jewish children from deportation."

In dedicating the square, Michele Blumenthal, the mayor of the 12th arrondisement, noted that many Paris streets are named after thinkers, artists, scientists, explorers, and soldiers. "But there are other forms of heroism that merit our respect," she said. "In one of the darkest periods of our history, a certain number of men and women, at the risk of their lives, acted to save those who were hunted only because they were Jews." Then she told the story of Moussa and Odette as a prime example of such heroes.[12] Her speech and others at the dedication served as the kind of public tribute the Abadis richly deserved but, by their own choice, never received during their lifetimes.

At the ceremony, Marthe Kuperminc (Martoune) spoke for the former hidden children. "Moussa and Odette," she said, "like most other people in 1943, could have thought only of saving themselves, without a care for others. But this was not the way they saw things. Their humanist spirit, their compassion for the distress of Jewish refugees, especially the children, forced them to act."[13]

Jacqueline Denechère spoke for the friends of the Abadis. For Moussa and Odette, she said, the saving of children "was not a spectacular action, but rather a natural movement of the heart, spontaneous, irrepressible in the face of monstrous injustice. They didn't fight for glory. Theirs was a combat of conviction, in the name of solid principles—the right to life, liberty for all, and tolerance."[14]

The ceremony blended tributes from others with the words of the Abadis themselves, the thoughts they wanted to leave to younger generations.

Natasha Karsenti, the daughter of a hidden child, read out a passage from Odette's book, about the positive lesson she took with her from Auschwitz.

> We had gone through everything in the camp, hunger, thirst, torrid summers, icy winters, all forms of degradation, torture, the sight of the flames from the crematorium ovens, and death everywhere. . . .
>
> What we know now for sure is that in the worst of misery our greatness and our strength were to feel solidarity with each other. What we have learned is that absolute misery, suffering, and the permanent presence of death allows some unexpected personalities to reveal themselves and that their friendship, tenderness, and courage have sustained us, and sometimes saved us.[15]

Mayor Blumenthal, in the concluding speech of the ceremony, noted the closeness of Moussa and Odette. She said their names should be pronounced as one: "OdetteMoussa."

Then, assisted by Jeannette Wolgust and Marthe Kuperminc, the mayor pulled the cord that unveiled the street sign, as the crowd applauded.

Moussa, as usual, had the last word. A recording of passages from his valedictory speech at the French Senate in 1995 blared out over loudspeakers as the crowd dispersed. Once again, Moussa's voice implored, "What is a hidden child? It is a child in danger. It is a child who needs help from others. It is a child who risks death. . . . Do something. . . . Yell, scream, don't accept that in this world children can be killed a few hundred kilometers from your home."

ACKNOWLEDGMENTS

This book was made possible by many people who generously gave their time and shared their knowledge in interviews, among them:

Former Hidden Children—Jeannette Wolgust, Françoise Bram, Marthe Kuperminc, Andrée Poch-Karsenti, Lisette Levy, Julien and George Engel, Armand Morgensztern, and Max Poch.

Friends of the Abadis—Jacqueline Denechère, Catherine Breton, Catherine Journoud, Annick Alzoubi, Olga Fink, Marie Gatard, Betty Kaluski-Saville, Violette Jacquet-Silberstein, Margarete Haim, Régine Zimmerman, Martine Zacher, Victor Kuperminc, Georges Isserlis, Georges Loinger, Victor Haim, Robert Pouderou, Guy Foissy, Jo Saville, Theo Klein, René Sicart, Marcel Dallo, and Rabbi Daniel Farhi.

Historians—Lucien Lazare at Yad Vashem for dossiers on Bishop Rémond and Pastor Evrard, Annette Wieviorka on the Abadis, Frida Wattenberg on Maurice Brener, and Katy Hazan (archivist at the OSE) on Georges Garel.

Sons—Thierry Brener on his father, Maurice Brener, and Jean-Marc Gagnier on his father, Pastor Pierre Gagnier.

At the Catholic Diocese of Nice—Monseigneur Guy Terrancle guided me through the bishop's residence, including Moussa Abadi's office there.

Father Leon Repetto and Father Antonin Blanchi provided background on Paul Rémond. Archivist Gilles Bouis led me to documentation.

Most quotes in the book from the Abadis themselves come from two essential sources. The first is the Centre de Documentation Juive Contemporaine (CDJC) at the Holocaust Memorial in Paris, which includes the Abadi archives of hundreds of documents, among them their speeches, testimony, reports, and personal letters. The second is seven hours of videotaped interviews with the Abadis arranged by the Fortunoff Video Archive of Holocaust Testimonies at Yale University. I am grateful to the CDJC and to Fortunoff for access to these sources.

Other quotes from the Abadis come from the books they wrote: Moussa's on the theater and on his youth in the Damascus ghetto, and Odette's on her life in Auschwitz and Bergen-Belsen. Ralph Schor's book on Bishop Rémond and Lucien Lazare's on the Jewish Resistance in France were also particularly helpful. All these books are listed in the bibliography.

Special thanks go to Julien Engel, whose inspiring account of his life as a hidden child put me on to the Abadi story in the first place; to Jeannette Wolgust for leading me to many other essential sources previously listed; and to my agent, Gabriele Pantucci, for encouragement and sage advice.

Early versions of the manuscript were read by Julien Engel, Victor Kuperminc, Vanina Marsot, Roger Williams, Michael Gordon, and my wife, Nadine Coleman. All provided vital suggestions for improvement. Nadine, a former translator for the French foreign ministry, also labored valiantly improving my translations from the French of documents and taped interviews.

Rimma Solod provided the magic that restored 1940s photographs. Gilles Bastianelli created a masterful promotion video.

The team at Potomac Books—Sam Dorrance, Elizabeth Demers, Laura Briggs, Elizabeth Norris, and Melissa Jones—did me proud. One could not ask for better editors.

Any remaining errors are my responsibility.

NOTES

1. Children

1 Material for this chapter was drawn from the author's interviews with Julien Engel, Marthe Artzstein, and Françoise Knopf. Material was also taken from the personal papers of Moussa and Odette Abadi at the Centre de Documentation Juive Contemporaine (CDJC), (hereafter cited as CDJC, followed by a file number).

2. Moussa and Odette

1 See chapter 21 for Moussa's life as an actor.

2 Andrée Poch-Karsenti, *Les 527 Enfants d'Odette et Moussa: Histoire du Réseau Marcel* (Paris: Le Publier, 2006), pp. 68–71.

3 Ibid., pp. 54, 57.

4 Olga Fink, in person interview by the author, Paris, France.

5 Marie Gatard, in person interview by the author, Paris, France.

6 Jeannette Wolgust, in person interview by the author, Noisy-le-Sec, France.

7 Jacqueline Denechère, in person interview by the author, Angers, France.

8 Wolgust, interview.

9 After the fall of France in 1940, the Italians occupied a thin sliver inside France, from the border with Italy up to Menton, barely a mile away. On November 11, 1942, with German agreement, they extended their hold to the area around Nice, another seventeen miles into France. On the same day, the Germans occupied the rest of the Free Zone in southern France. Both moves came as an immediate defensive response to the threat from Allied landings in North Africa, just across the Mediterranean from southern France, only three days earlier, on November 8, 1942.

10 From November 1942, the Vichy government was compelled to work with Italian occupiers in the Nice region, slowing the repressions against Jews, and German occupiers elsewhere in the Free Zone increasing the roundups of Jews. It was at this point that Vichy began deporting whole families, including children, demonstrating that the Germans had the upper hand. It was unclear how long the Italians would remain.

11 Quotes here and on the Promenade des Anglais incident are from Moussa's speech to a conference on hidden children at the French Senate on May 21, 1995. A copy of the verbatim text can be found at the CDJC, CMXCIV–9.

12 "Moussa and Odette A. Holocaust testimony (HVT-3203)," interviewed by Annette Wieviorka, Fortunoff Video Archive for Holocaust Testimonies, Yale University Library (April 19, 1995). There are two other relevant Fortunoff tapes, marked "Odette A. Holocaust Testimony (HVT-3201)" and "Moussa A. Holocaust Testimony (HVT-3202)." The tapes are hearafter cited as Fortunoff, HVT-3203; Fortunoff, HVT-3201; and Fortunoff, HVT-3202. A copy of the tapes can be consulted at the French National Archives (CARAN).

13 "Le compte-rendu de l'hommage public à Yvonne et Roger Hagnauer, le Samedi 4 Juin 2005 à Sèvres." A report by Céline Marrot-Fellag Ariquet, in "Le Réseau Marcel," chap. 1 in *Les enfants caches pendant la seconde guerre mondiale aux sources d'une histoire clandestine*, p. 3. This is a report in honor of Yvonne and Roger Hagnauer, a couple who established a school for Jewish war orphans in Sèvres, outside Paris. The report was made public at a ceremony in Sèvres honoring the couple on June 4, 2005.

14 The first news of Nazi death camps reached Britain from the Polish Underground in November 1941. The Foreign Office was skeptical. In the spring of 1942, similar reports from other sources were received in Britain and the United States. Both governments chose not to make them public.

By the fall of 1942, rumors began to circulate in Germany about Nazi death camps. They were dismissed as enemy propaganda. Even in Allied and neutral countries, these unverified reports were greeted with skepticism by the public, including Jews. In justifying their disbelief, many people recalled the hysteria during World War I over unsubstantiated reports, eventually proven false, that German troops had hacked off limbs of Belgian children. See John S. Conway, "First Report about Auschwitz," the *Simon Wiesenthal Center Annual* 1 (1984): chap. 7.

15 Fortunoff, HVT-3203.

3. The Bishop

1 Pius XII remains a controversial figure to this day. The present Pope, Benedict XVI, has proposed him for sainthood. The Church now argues that Pius XII did more privately for the Jews than was known at the time. Perhaps. But, during the war, all that mattered was what the public knew at the time, and there is no question that the Pope's public silence then was a boon to the Nazis and a calamity for the Jews.

2 For Brener's role, see chapter 5.

3 Ralph Schor, *Un évêque dans le siècle: Monseigneur Paul Rémond (1873–1963)* (Nice: Editions Serre, 1984), p. 119.

4 Ibid., p. 22.

5 Ibid., p. 23.

6 "Monseigneur Paul Rémond," Association "Les Enfants et Amis Abadi" [Association of Children and Friends of the Abadis], http://www.moussa-odette-abadi.asso.fr/fr/remond1.htm.

7 Moussa Abadi speech, CDJC, CMXCIV–9.

8 Amy Latour, *la Résistance Juive en France 1940–44* (Paris: Stock, 1970), p. 69.

4. The Pastors

1 Fortunoff, HVT-3203.

2 Wolgust, interview.

3 Ibid.

4 Fortunoff, HVT-3201.

5 Moussa and Odette Abadi, interview by Betty Kaluski-Saville, audio tape from Jeannette Wolgust archives, (hereafter cited as Abadi, interview).

6 "Déposition de Monsieur le Pasteur Gagnier, Bd. Dubouchage, Nice" [Testimony of Pastor Pierre Gagnier], May 18, 1945, CDJC, CCXVIII–85, (hereafter cited as Gagnier testimony, CDJC, CCXVIII–85).

7 "Récit de Monsieur le Pasteur Evrard, 16 rue Vernier, Nice" [Testimony of Pastor Edmond Evrard], March 28, 1945, CDJC, CCXVIII–87.

8 Wolgust, interview.

9 Yael Abihssira, "le Réseau Abadi" (master's thesis, University of Paris I, Pantheon-Sorbonne, 1998), pp. 87–88.

5. Zazou

1 Thierry Brener, in person interview by the author, Paris, France.

2 Fortunoff, HVT-3203.

3 Katy Hazan at OSE, in person interview by the author, Paris, France.

4 Karsenti, *Les 527 Enfants*, p. 39.

6. The Germans

1 Fortunoff, HVT-3203.

2 Text of Armistice with Italy, September 3, 1943.

3 Françoise Knopf, in person interview by the author, Chevy Chase, MD.

4 Fortunoff, HVT-3203.

5 Abihssira, "le Réseau Abadi."

6 Ariquet report, p. 5.

7 Moussa Abadi to Georges Garel, October 13, 1944, CDJC, CMXCIV–9 (l).

8 Moussa Abadi speech, CDJC, CMXCIV–9.

9 Ibid.

10 Georges Isserlis, in person interview by the author, Paris, France.

11 Gagnier testimony, CDJC, CCXVIII–85.

12 Ibid.

13 Isserlis, interview.

7. Same Child, New Identity

1 Fortunoff, HVT-3203.

2 Moussa Abadi speech, CDJC, CMXCIV–9.

3 Wolgust, interview.

4 Knopf, interview.

5 Fortunoff, HVT-3201.

6 Marthe Artzstein, interviewed by the author, Paris, France.

7 Moussa Abadi speech, CDJC, CMXCIV–9.

8 Wolgust, interview.

9 Ibid.

10 Ibid.

11 No full set of fiches (identity cards) exists today. The set buried in the bishop's garden was wrapped only in paper, became water-logged, and turned into unreadable mush. Plastic wrapping was not available in wartime France.

The International Red Cross in Geneva has no record of Abadi fiches, not surprising because the guides who were supposed to take them to Geneva never left France. Instead the guides told the children they escorted to the border to cross into Switzerland by themselves. What happened to the fiches given to the guides is not known.

The Abadis' set of fiches survives, in part. Many of their cards were given to parents who reclaimed children during and after the war. Others were destroyed by the Abadis during alerts on imminent Nazi raids. After the war, still other fiches went to OSE archives, which never held more than a small fraction of the whole set. The 141 fiches remaining in the Abadis' set are available for viewing at the CDJC, CMXCIV–2. The total figure of 527 children saved comes from a list of names compiled by the Abadis. The number has been accepted as accurate by French officials and the French press.

8. Three Girls

1 Knopf, interview.

2 Artzstein, interview.

3 Wolgust, interview.

9. The Convent

1 Wolgust, interview. *Con* is slang for vagina, *fess* for backside.

2 Knopf, interview.

3 Lisette Levy, in person interview by the author, Paris, France.

4 Artzstein, interview.

5 Fortunoff, HVT-3203.

6 Moussa to Garel, CDJC, CMXCIV–9 (l).

7 Fortunoff, HVT-3203.

8 Moussa to Garel, CDJC, CMXCIV–9 (l).

9 Wolgust, interview.

10. Boys

1 Armand Morgensztern, in person interview by the author, Paris, France.

2 The *rafle du Vel d'Hiv*, literally translated as "the mass arrests at the Winter Velodrome," was the largest roundup of Jews in France during World War II. It was ordered by the Germans and carried out by French police on July 16 and 17, 1942. French police arrested 13,152 Jews, according to official figures, and held them at the Velodrome, a stadium for indoor bicycle races, before deporting them to the death camps.

3 Lucien Lazare, *Resistance as Rescue: How Jewish Organizations Fought the Holocaust in France* (New York: Columbia University Press, 1996), p. 12.

4 Ibid., pp. 202–3. The help of French Christians was particularly important in saving Jewish children. The proof of that is in the higher figure for the Jewish children under eighteen who survived the Holocaust in France (86 percent) when compared to the survival figure for the overall Jewish population in France (nearly 75 percent).

A closer look at the figures reinforces the point. Some 10,147 Jewish children in France under the age of eighteen were deported to the death camps, and 72,400 (the 86 percent) survived the war. Most of the survivors were in families that saved themselves by hiding children with parents, or other relatives, or with friends. Relatively few of the surviving children owed their lives to Jewish Resistance organizations that placed them in Catholic institutions or in Protestant families, with Garel's OSE and the Abadis' Marcel Network accounting for the largest numbers. For virtually every one of the 72,400 Jewish children in France who survived the war—both those who needed help from the Jewish Resistance and those who did not—the action of at least one French Christian somewhere along the way made the difference between life and death.

5 Moussa Abadi speech CDJC, CMXCIV–9.

6 Marcel Dallo, in person interview by the author, Nice, France.

7 Hazan, interview.

8 George Engel, e-mail interview by the author.

9 Julien Engel, in person interview by the author, Paris, France.

11. Switzerland

1 Georges Loinger, in person interview by the author, Paris, France.

2 Max Poch, in person interview by the author, St. Maure, France.

12. Close Calls

1 Fortunoff, HVT-3203.

2 Ibid.

3 Schor, *Monseigneur Paul Rémond*, p. 121.

4 Ibid.

5 Fortunoff, HVT-3203.

6 Moussa Abadi's diary, 1945, CDJC, CMXCIV–14.

13. Odette Arrested

1 Fortunoff, HVT-3203.

2 Karsenti, *Les 527 Enfants*, p. 61.

3 Wolgust, interview.

4 Fortunoff, HVT-3203.

5 Odette Abadi, *Terre de Détresse: Birkenau, Bergen-Belsen* (Paris: Harmattan, 1995), pp. 178–79.

6 Ibid., p. 16.

7 Ibid., pp. 17–18.

8 Ibid., pp. 19–24.

9 Ibid., pp. 25–33.

14. Moussa Alone

1 Fortunoff, HVT-3203.

2 Ibid.

3 Moussa Abadi speech, CDJC, CMXCIV–9.

4 Ibid.

5 Ibid.

6 Moussa saw his grandfather for the last time at age nineteen before leaving for Paris in 1927 on a scholarship. He received a certificate from the Sorbonne that qualified him as a professor of French at university level abroad. The scholarship required him to return to Syria and teach. But as soon as he could, he arranged for a second scholarship to France, this time arriving in Paris in 1933 as a graduate student. He was twenty-three and determined to stay.

7 Fortunoff, HVT-3203.

8 Moussa Abadi speech, CDJC, CMXCIV–9.

9 Ibid.

10 Wolgust, interview.

11 Knopf, interview.

12 Ibid.

13 Fortunoff, HVT-3203.

15. Auschwitz

1 Odette Abadi, *Terre de Détresse*, pp. 35–42.

2 Violette Jacquet-Silberstein, in person interview by the author, Paris, France.

3 Odette Abadi, *Terre de Détresse*, pp. 45–62.

4 Denechère, interview.

5 It is a pity that her excellent book in French was never translated and published in English. The excerpts from it that appear on these pages are so far the only English language version of her unique account.

6 Odette Abadi, *Terre de Détresse*, pp. 63–74.

16. Bergen-Belsen

1 Morvan Lebesque, "La Chasse aux Enfants" [The hunt for children], *Carrefour*, December 1, 1948, p. 5.

2 Odette Abadi, *Terre de Détresse*, pp. 77–103.

3 Ibid., pp. 127–33.

4 Ibid., pp. 153–56.

5 Wolgust, interview.

6 Odette Abadi, *Terre de Détresse*, pp. 157–65.

7 Fortunoff, HVT-3203.

8 Ibid.

9 Moussa Abadi speech, CDJC, CMXCIV–9.

10 Odette Abadi, *Terre de Détresse*, p. 172.

11 Annick Alzoubi, telephone and e-mail interview by the author.

12 Fortunoff, HVT-3203.

13 Ibid.

14 Gatard, interview.

17. Liberation

1 Moussa to Garel, CDJC, CMXCIV–9 (l).

2 Ibid.

3 Moussa diary, CDJC, CMXCIV–14.

4 Ibid.

5 Ibid.

6 Ibid.

7 Morvan Lebesque, "Les Chasseurs d'Enfants" [The hunters of children], *Carrefour*, November 16, 1948, CDJC, CMXCIV–10.

8 Ibid.

9 Moussa Abadi diary, CDJC, CMXCIV–14.

18. Reunions

1 Wolgust, interview. The remainder of Jeannette's story in this chapter comes from the same interview.

2 Moussa Abadi speech, CDJC, CMXCIV–9.

3 Ibid.

4 Gatard, interview.

5 Artzstein, interview.

6 Levy, interview.

7 Abadi, interview.

8 Morgensztern, interview.

9 Julien Engel, interview.

10 Alban Fort was a non-practicing Catholic. Germaine Fort, the daughter of a Catholic father and a Protestant mother, became a free thinker and had none of her seven children baptized. The home they ran for abandoned children was non-sectarian and privately funded. The Catholic Church had nothing to do with running the home or with placing the Engel boys there. Arrangements to hide the Engels were made directly between the Abadis and the Forts. Thus Lucien Lazare was correct in saying the Abadis saved Julien and George.

The Church played only an indirect role in their story. Odette carried working papers signed by the bishop of Nice which identified her under her wartime Christian alias of Sylvie Delattre, a social worker for the Church. These papers enabled Odette to move through police checkpoints around the Nice region when escorting children to hiding places. The Church helped directly in saving some three hundred other Abadi children by hiding them in Catholic convents or boarding schools.

11 Julien Engel, interview.

12 Ibid.

13 Knopf, interview.

14 Ibid.

19. Depression

1 Fortunoff, HVT-3203.

2 Wolgust, interview.

3 Betty Kaluski-Saville, in person interview by the author, Paris, France.

4 Hazan, interview.

5 Jacquet-Silberstein, interview.

6 Wieviorka, interview.

7 Fink, interview.

8 Régine Zimmerman, in person interview by the author, Nice, France.

20. Discreet

1 Rémond radio interview, October 26, 1945, in "L'Enfance Juive Martyre" [The martyred Jewish Childhood], CDJC, CMXCIV–11.

2 René Rémond interview with David Konopnicki, in "Le Réseau Abadi: Histoire d'un sauvetage d'enfants dans les Alpes-Maritimes durant la Seconde Guerre Mondiale" (thesis, Institut d'études politiques de Grenoble, Université Pierre Mendès-France, Saint-Martin-d'Hères, France), 2001

3 Evrard's wife, Ida, and their two sons, Daniel and Louis, were also honored as Righteous for the help they gave to the pastor. Similarly, Gagnier's wife, Hélène, was honored as Righteous for the help she gave her husband.

21. Drama

1 Moussa Abadi speech, CDJC, CMXCIV–9.

2 Victor Haim, in person interview by the author, Paris, France.

3 Robert Pouderou, in person interview by the author, Paris, France.

4 Guy Foissy, in person interview by the author, Nice, France.

5 Moussa Abadi, *La Comédie du Théâtre* (Paris: Julliard, 1985), p. 52.

6 Moussa Abadi, *La Reine et le calligraphe:mes juifs de Damas* (Paris: Christian Bartillat, 1993), pp. 74–75.

7 Moussa Abadi, *Shimon-le-parjure: mes juifs de Damas* (Paris: Parole en Page, 1999), pp. 58–59.

22. The Couple

1 Fink, interview.

2 Denechère, interview.

3 Foissy, interview.

4 Kaluski-Saville, interview.

5 Alzoubi, interview.

6 Pouderou, interview.

7 Denechère, interview.

8 Julien Engel, interview.

9 Haim, interview.

10 René Sicard died in 2009.

11 Catherine Journoud, in person interview by the author, Paris, France.

12 Catherine Breton, in person interview by the author, Paris, France.

13 Jacquet-Silberstein, interview.

14 Wolgust, interview.

15 Kaluski-Saville, interview.

16 Wieviorka, interview.

17 Rabbi Daniel Farhi, in person interview by the author, Paris, France.

18 Denechère, interview.

23. Revelations

1 Ariquet report, p. 13.

2 Kaluski-Saville interview.

3 Betty Kaluski-Saville, "Le Réseau de Sauvtage Abadi" [The Abadi rescue network], *L'Association Les Enfants Cachés Bulletin* no. 8, September 1994, pp. 2–6.

4 Julien Engel, interview.

5 Wieviorka, interview.

6 Fortunoff, HVT-3203.

7 Jo Saville, in person interview by the author, Paris, France.

8 Jeannette Wolgust interview in Konopnicki thesis.

9 Wolgust, interview.

10 Ibid.

11 Moussa speech, CDJC, CMXCIV–9.

Epilogue

1 Moussa Abadi, "Luniere de mes yeux" (unpublished manuscript), Microsoft Word file, p. 26.

2 Ibid., p. 61.

3 Farhi, interview.

4 Breton, interview.

5 Ibid.

6 Wolgust, interview.

7 Ibid.

8 Odette to Margareta Haim.

9 Ibid.

10 Julien Engel, interview.

11 Ninon Renaud "La mère aux 527 enfants," [The mother of 527 children], *La Vie*, August 26, 1999, pp. 22–24.

12 Michele Blumenthal, speech, Place Moussa et Odette Abadi, Paris, France, September 13, 2008.

13 Marthe Artzstein-Kuperminc, speech, Place Moussa et Odette Abadi, Paris, France, September 13, 2008.

14 Jacqueline Denechère speech, Place Moussa et Odette Abadi, Paris, France, September 13, 2008.

15 Odette Abadi, *Terre de Détresse*, p. 176.

SELECTED BIBLIOGRAPHY

Abadi, Moussa. *La Reine et le Calligraphe: Mes juifs de Damas*. Paris: Christian Bartillat, 1993.

———. *Shimon-le-parjure: Mes juifs de Damas*. Paris: Parole en Page, 1999.

———. *La Comédie du Théâtre*. Paris: Julliard, 1985.

———. "Moussa A. Holocaust Testimony (HVT-3202)." Interviewed by Annette Wieviorka. Fortunoff Video Archive for Holocaust Testimonies, Yale University Library, April 18, 1995.

Abadi, Odette. *Terre de Détresse: Birkenau, Bergen-Belsen*. Paris: Harmattan, 1995.

———. "Odette A. Holocaust Testimony (HVT-3201)." Interviewed by Annette Wieviorka. Fortunoff Video Archive for Holocaust Testimonies, Yale University Library, April 18, 1995.

Abadi, Odette and Moussa. "Moussa and Odette A. Holocaust Testimony (HVT-3203)." Interviewed by Annette Wieviorka. Fortunoff Video Archive for Holocaust Testimonies, Yale University Library, April 19, 1995.

Joffo, Joseph. *Un sac de billes*. Paris: J.-C. Lattès, 1973.

Klarsfeld, Serge. *Vichy-Auschwitz: Le rôle de Vichy dans la solution finale de la question juive en France*. Vol. 2. Paris: Fayard, 1983.

Latour, Amy. *La Résistance Juive en France 1940–44*. Paris: Stock, 1970.

Lazare, Lucien. *Rescue as Resistance: How Jewish Organizations Fought the Holocaust in France.* Translated by Jeffrey M. Green. New York: Columbia University Press, 1996.

Le Réseau Marcel: histoire d'un réseau juif clandestin. Documentary Film. Directed by Jacqueline Sigaar. Produced by Maria Landau and Jacqueline Sigaar. Paris: Les Productrices, 2006. Available in French with English subtitles. 52 min.

Marrus, Michaël A., and Robert O. Paxton. *Vichy et les Juifs.* Paris: Calmann-Lévy, 1981.

Paxton, Robert O. *La France de Vichy, 1940–1944.* Paris: Seuil, 1973.

Poch-Karsenti, Andrée. *Les 527 Enfants d'Odette et Moussa: histoire du réseau Marcel.* Paris: Le Publieur, 2006.

Schor, Ralph. *Un évêque dans le siècle: Monseigneur Paul Rémond (1873–1963).* Nice: Editions Serre, 1984.

Schwarzfuchs, Simon. *Aux prises avec Vichy: Histoire politique des Juifs de France (1940–1944).* Paris: Calmann-Lévy, 1998.

Zeitoun, Sabine. *L'Œuvre de secours aux enfants (O.S.E.) sous l'Occupation en France: du légalisme à la Résistance, 1940–1944.* Paris: L'Harmattan, 1990.

ABOUT THE AUTHOR

Fred Coleman's long career as a foreign correspondent included five years as *Newsweek*'s bureau chief in Paris and eight years as the magazine's bureau chief in Moscow. In France, he covered terrorist bomb attacks and the launch of the Euro. He once spent a week with the French Foreign Leigon. While working in Moscow, Coleman rode a Soviet tank out of Afghanistan. He also interviewed former Soviet president Mikhail Gorbachev and former Russian president Boris Yeltsin.

In 1978, he won the Page 1 Award of the Newspaper Guild of New York for the best reporting from abroad for magazines. The award cited a series on human rights in the USSR for *Newsweek*. Coleman's fascination with the struggle of Russian dissidents against Soviet repression led him to the similar struggle of the Abadis against Nazi atrocities.

His first book, *The Decline and Fall of the Soviet Empire*, was published by St. Martin's Press in 1996.

Coleman and his wife, Nadine, live in Paris.

PRAISE FOR *NETWORKING IS DEAD*

"This book makes networking easy and enjoyable. The authors understand that connecting with others who share your values and principles is more important than connecting with people who are simply in fields similar to yours. As business changes at an ever faster pace, it's important to build a strong network—not only so you can thrive, but also so that others can thrive through you."

—KEN BLANCHARD,
Coauthor, The One Minute Manager® *and* Great Leaders Grow

"Yes, this is another book about networking, but if you think you've seen it all (or read them all)...this one is worth adding to your shelf. It takes networking to a whole new level by talking about truly making connections in some new and time-sensitive ways that give you the edge over others who are trying to do the same and haven't read this book!"

—BEVERLY KAYE,
Founder & Co-CEO, Career Systems International,
Coauthor, Help Them Grow or Watch Them Go:
Career Conversations Employees Want

"Integrity and authenticity in communications—'being real'—cut through the clutter to create and sustain quality relationships. This book guides the building of grounded relationships that transcend the speed and quantity of hollow communications—to deliver those that matter."

—JEANNE BLISS,
President & Chief Customer Officer, CustomerBliss; author, I Love You More than My Dog

"Wilson and Mohl deftly unearth the underlying cause—'why networking is dead'—R.I.P.! It's simply because the best networkers realize it's not the WHAT or the HOW of what you do that attracts people to you, but rather the WHY that 'inspire[s] connections and more opportunities,' and that reveals your passion, which allows you to be what they term... an 'attractor of possibility.' This book will change the face of networking in some very positive ways."

—BOB LITTELL,
Chief NetWeaver; author, The Heart and Art of NetWeaving and Raising Your R&R Factor: How Referable & Recommendable Are You?

NETWORKING IS DEAD

NETWORKING IS DEAD

Making Connections That Matter

MELISSA G WILSON AND LARRY MOHL

BENBELLA BOOKS, INC.
DALLAS, TEXAS

This book is a work of fiction. Names, characters, places, and incidents are the product of the author's imagination and are used fictitiously. Any resemblance to actual events, locales or persons, living or dead, is coincidental.

BenBella Books, Inc.
10300 N. Central Expressway
Suite #400
Dallas, TX 75231
www.benbellabooks.com
Send feedback to feedback@benbellabooks.com

Printed in the United States of America
10 9 8 7 6 5 4 3 2 1

Library of Congress Cataloging-in-Publication Data is available for this title.

978-1-937856-90-8

Editing by Brian Nicol
Copyediting by Deb Kirkby
Proofreading by Cape Cod Compositors, Inc. and Michael Fedison
Indexing by Clive Pyne
Text design and composition by fusion29 and John Reinhardt Book Design
Printed by Berryville Graphics, Inc.

Distributed by Perseus Distribution
perseusdistribution.com

To place orders through Perseus Distribution:
Tel: 800-343-4499
Fax: 800-351-5073
E-mail: orderentry@perseusbooks.com

I dedicate this book to my great family—
Graham, Gavin, Courtney, David, Katie, and Winnie,
and especially, my husband, Craig, who is my muse!

—MELISSA G WILSON

I dedicate this book to my wife, Carly,
and daughters, Lawson and Erden.
They are my life and my connections
that matter most.

—LARRY MOHL

CONTENTS

NETWORKING IS DEAD

LESSON 1

DEFINE YOUR *WHY*

MEREDITH SPOTTED LANCE the minute he walked into the crowded coffee shop. His head was down, his shoulders hunched, fingers clutching the strap of his leather messenger bag tightly. Lance hated crowds.

It was, of course, one of the reasons she'd chosen the Cup of Café in the first place—to ease Lance out of his comfort zone by getting him out of his cloistered corporate office and into the real world.

At 42, Lance looked as dignified as ever in black slacks and purple dress shirt, wearing the lilac tie she'd given him for Christmas. Lance finally spotted her as he took his place in line.

A smile lit up his still-handsome face, then quietly flickered and fizzled out when he saw where she'd placed herself—in a booth smack dab in the middle of the café. She smirked as he wagged a finger; he much preferred a corner booth, out of the busy and noisy coffee shop's hub.

"Why don't we just sit on the counter and put out a tip jar?" Lance grumbled playfully as he sat down across from her, sliding a gingerbread scone across the table in her direction.

She smiled. He knew it was her favorite. "Weren't you the one who wanted to try new things this year? Wasn't 'stretching your boundaries' one of your resolutions?"

Lance fingered the side of his red and green holiday-themed coffee cup. "I suppose," he sighed, taking a sip of his coffee. "I just prefer to do my stretching in private, that's all."

"You can't grow your network in private, Lance," she scolded.

Meredith nibbled on her scone and tried to ignore the bluesy rendition of "Rudolph the Red-Nosed Reindeer" humming away on the café's speakers overhead. "You'd think they'd switch back to normal by now," Lance remarked, as if reading her mind. "I mean, it *is* the fifth of January already."

She chuckled. It had always been like that for Meredith and Lance. Like an old married couple, they could often be found finishing each other's sentences, coming up with the same ideas at the same time, partnering on a variety of side ventures despite their busy professional lives.

Lance had been Meredith's tutor while she majored in business marketing at State, and as their professional relationship grew friendlier, he'd encouraged her to join a few campus clubs to build her list of connections before she graduated.

At 36, Meredith was younger than Lance by more than a few years, but she enjoyed being mentored in various business scenarios as much as she enjoyed mentoring Lance in a variety of social scenarios—Coffee Shop 101, for instance!

How ironic, she mused as they waited for Jill, their mutual friend and yoga instructor, to join them, *that Lance had helped me start my own personal network only to turn into a professional hermit himself!*

"How are the rest of your resolutions going?" Meredith asked, subtly reminding Lance that, after all, this was his big idea for a brighter, more connected new year.

He hoisted his coffee cup to eye level and said, "Well, I'm breaking one as we speak—no more caffeine—and once this meeting with Jill goes bust, that will make two."

"Oh no" Meredith smiled, waving to Jill as she walked through the café door at that precise moment. "It was *your* idea for us both to double our business connections this year, and I'm not going to let either one of us back out of it now."

Meredith watched as Jill flirted lazily with the barista who took her order. She was in her mid-twenties and looked impeccable in fitted linen slacks and a crisp white blouse, but Meredith knew the part-time career coach was far more comfortable in the yoga pants and tank top she wore while putting her and Lance through their paces at her private gym three times a week.

"Happy New Year!" Jill declared cheerfully, joining them at the booth and hugging them both as the scent of her peppermint mocha breezed across the table. "I'm so glad you two reached out to me after the holidays. I have *just* the person to make your New Year's resolution come true."

"You amaze me, Jill," Lance chuckled.

"How's that?" Jill asked, tucking a strand of blond hair behind her ear as she set down her holiday-themed coffee cup.

Lance shrugged. "I just never thought I'd be getting schooled in business networking from the same person who taught me Downward Facing Dog, that's all."

Meredith and Jill chuckled at the same time. "That sounds like a vague insult, Lance," Jill joked, playfully slapping his wrist.

"Not at all," said Lance. "I guess that's the point of making connections, right? You never know when they'll come in handy?"

Jill nodded. "I certainly never opened a gym to make business connections, but when I realized that most of my clients were also lawyers, VPs for Fortune 500 companies, accountants, whatever, it just seemed like a natural outgrowth to start putting them together. That's how I met Dan, who should be here any minute."

"So what's Dan's specialty exactly?" Meredith asked.

Jill reached for a hefty crumb of Meredith's scone and chewed it carefully while forming an answer. "This," she finally said, using her small hands to indicate the collective of three at their booth, and the dozen or more people at the tables on either side of them. "Putting people from diverse backgrounds together."

Meredith was about to ask how he possibly monetized such a skill set, when Jill's hand shot up with a perky wave. Meredith looked toward the door to find a small, rather undistinguished man entering the café.

He behaved much as Lance had, more focused on getting his coffee than on addressing the room. He wore pleated khaki slacks and a generic powder-blue dress shirt, rolled up at the sleeves. He carried no bag, no tablet. From what Meredith could see, he didn't even have a phone on him.

When he finally saw Jill, his face turned warm and inviting with a simple smile of acknowledgement. As he walked to their booth, he made eye contact first with Meredith, then Lance, smiling at them both beneath warm green eyes.

They all stood to greet each other as Jill made the introductions. "Dan," Jill announced brightly as she gestured with open palms toward him. "This is Meredith, founder and CEO of Social Solutions. And this is Lance, head of accounting at Hospitality, Inc. Meredith, Lance, this is, well...this is Dan."

The four of them chuckled anxiously before Jill looked at her watch and said, "Well, that's it for me, gang. My work here is done. Best of luck with the meeting."

"What?" Lance asked, almost pleadingly. "Where are you off to already?"

"My Yoga for Beginners class starts in ten minutes!" she offered, making no more excuses before retreating quickly to her small but intimate yoga studio two blocks away from the Cup of Café.

Admiring Lance's reaction with a bemused grin, Dan said, "I'm surprised she stayed that long or dressed up for that matter. Jill has helped me make introductions in the parking lot behind her gym, at her reception desk, and, once, right outside the men's locker room."

The picture of Jill collaring Dan in his gym clothes clearly put Lance at ease. Dan regarded them both curiously and sipped his cup of coffee. "Jill said you both were resolved to make more connections this year, am I right?"

Meredith nodded. "Yes, Dan, both Lance and I agreed that this year was going to be the 'Year of Networking'!"

Dan reacted to her statement as if he'd just bitten into a lemon seed. "Oooh," he cautioned gently, sucking air through his teeth. "First lesson, let's completely do away with the word 'networking' while we work together. Agreed?"

Lance and Meredith shared a worried look. "But isn't that your specialty, Dan?" Lance asked. "Networking?"

Dan smiled; Meredith liked his smile. "It is, for sure, but networking has gotten such a bad name, especially in this new world of social networking. I prefer to call it what it should be, *making connections that matter*."

Meredith shared another quick glance with Lance. They both nodded, perhaps subconsciously. To her way of thinking, *making connections that matter* sounded a lot more hands on, even more controllable, than *networking*.

Meanwhile, Lance was clearly struggling with the concept. "But isn't networking technically the act of building a network?"

Dan nodded, pulling up his seat a little and growing more animated as he spoke; he clearly relished the subject matter and was interested in helping others achieve his level of success. Meredith silently wondered if that was why he was so good at it.

"It is, certainly," Dan agreed. "But rather than growing a huge network focused on sheer numbers, building a successful network is about establishing a relatively *small number* of *deep, high-quality, business relationships* based on *common values*. Or, as I call it, making connections that matter. In order to do this effectively, you must first clearly define your core values."

Lance's cheeks grew ruddy, a sure sign he was growing more and more agitated. "Small number?" he repeated, also inching forward in his seat a smidge.

He looked at Meredith and chuckled. "But that's why we came to you in the first place, Dan. Or, rather, why we approached Jill. Both Meredith and I already have a *small* network. That's the problem."

"Is it?" Dan countered. "Or is it that you have not created the *right* small network best suited for you to begin with?"

Dan paused to let his words sink in, then continued: "Think about networking for a minute. Think about its evolution. What started out as a great idea, forming relationships and putting friends and allies together in the path of opportunity, has devolved into a common act of collecting as many business cards as possible or in the case of online networking, collecting the most 'friends' and 'followers' as possible. Most people who talk about networking these days are really saying, 'I'm going to mine you for your contacts, use you until you're dry, and then move on.' Am I right?"

Meredith smiled to find Lance nodding enthusiastically. "It has grown rather selfish lately," he agreed.

Dan's eyes grew wider. "Exactly. Selfish, predatory, thoughtless, inauthentic. You go to these networking meetings and it's like speed dating—people come up to you, want to find out what you can do for them, and if you don't fit their narrow picture of what they can get out of you, BOOM!—they're onto the next person."

"So how do we fix that, Dan?" Meredith asked. "I mean, if you're saying networking is broken, how do we fix it?"

"You bring up a good point," Dan answered enthusiastically. "Before we get started *fixing* your networks, I want to know a little bit more about *why* you want to make connections that matter in the first place...I'll start!"

Lance chuckled and Meredith eased into the cushion behind her. She wasn't sure which direction they were headed or even if Dan was the proper guide for their journey, but she'd made a New Year's resolution to grow her network—sorry, make more meaningful connections—and if he could help, even a little, it was worth a cup of coffee and a few minutes of her time.

She could tell by Lance's more relaxed posture and expression of anticipation that he was feeling the same way.

Dan paused for a few moments before saying, "I was a teacher for many years. I was good at it, but I was better at helping people, one-on-one, improve their lives. That's why I went into teaching: to improve the lives of kids who might not be as fortunate as I was growing up. But it was stifling, working within the politics of the other teachers, under such careful scrutiny by the school board and the administration. Frankly, I was much more successful at putting the kids' parents in touch with a great tutor or the right guidance counselor than I ever was teaching math or science!"

Still unsure where Dan was headed, Meredith smiled encouragingly; she was eager to hear more.

"So one summer, while I was still getting paid for the teaching work I'd done that year but didn't have to go into the classroom anymore, I started a small company called Tutor Tech. It was basically me in my den with a computer, a phone, and a fax putting kids together with local tutors. Their parents paid me a small finder's fee. It was fun and I had more freedom than in the classroom.

"By mid-July, I knew I'd never go back to school. Fortunately, one of the kids' parents worked at a top recruiting firm for C-level players. He saw what I was doing for his kid and figured I could do it for him. So he hired me, full-time, to recruit. That was the first time I ever realized the power of making connections that matter. I used that power at his recruiting firm, but after a few years it was like teaching all over again—four walls and too much politics.

"It paid well though, and after living on a teacher's salary for so long, I kept my frugal habits. At the recruiting firm, my deals brought me double-digit commissions and bonuses, and I managed to save up quite a bit. I used my solid savings to go back into my own company, but this time I didn't limit myself. I started Connections Count in the same office I use today, but I barely use it. I'm too busy making, well, connections that count."

Meredith nodded; her story sounded very similar to Dan's. As if sensing this, he said, "But you're not here to listen to me talk about myself. Now I want to know a little bit more about you two. Meredith, what do you do at Social Solutions?"

"It's a social media consulting and implementation firm," Meredith said, quickly falling into the rhythm of her elevator pitch. "I talk to a client about his or her needs and then draw up a personalized plan for customizing their Facebook page, learning how to engage on Twitter and keep their content streaming, deciding which LinkedIn profiles in their company need makeovers, and building an online presence, all in a time-effective manner."

Dan smiled. "So it sounds very specialized and hands on."

Meredith brightened. "It is! I spend about a week with each client, working their schedules, touring the facility, if there is one, really getting to know them and their products inside and out. It's the only way to do what I do effectively, and it really gives me insight on how to help them. I think that's why I get so much repeat business."

Dan smirked. "Repeat business but not *new* business, am I right?"

She nodded reluctantly. "I network like crazy. Sorry, I know you hate that word, but... nothing new seems to come in. I can't figure out what I'm doing wrong."

Dan reassured her. "I wouldn't say you're doing anything wrong. It's just that repeat business is a little like swimming in the same fishbowl. After a while, you've got nowhere else to go. And people are protective, self-protective. They want you all to themselves, ready at a moment's notice to fix their problems, so it's not really in their best interest to give you a ton of new business with their friends and family."

Dan spoke to what Meredith had long suspected; she nodded in reply.

"And, Lance," he asked, shifting gears or at least perspectives. "How about you? What's Hospitality, Inc., all about?"

Lance cleared his throat and gave his elevator speech: "We're an accounting firm that specializes in the hospitality business—restaurants mostly."

Dan looked impressed. "So you've both been successful finding your niche and becoming successful there. But now it sounds like you've plateaued. Is that about right?"

Meredith and Lance both nodded.

"And Lance, Meredith explained a little why she's here; how about you?"

Lance shrugged. "It's like you said, Dan; I've reached a plateau. I'm successful at work, but I could be doing so much more for my clients, for myself. Accounting is more than just numbers; it's about making the best use of your assets. Or at least it can be if done right. I see so many restaurants close down or go bankrupt, not because they weren't successful but because they couldn't manage their money. I want to help more of them avoid that, but I can't if I don't reach out to more."

Dan was nodding vigorously. "I think we're getting somewhere. You both have very strong reasons for making connections that matter. It just sounds like you haven't been doing it the right way. So, Meredith, help me help you: What is your definition of networking?"

Uncertain, Meredith glanced at Lance, who smirked back at her with an expression that said, *Better you than me*.

She cleared her throat and said, "Well, I attend a lot of networking events. Our local chamber of commerce has a popular 'Wednesday Friends Day' event that I go to each month, and I generally make it a habit to come away with at least a dozen new introductions. Then I follow up those leads before the next month's Friends Day event."

Dan clearly looked dubious. "And how is that working out for you?"

Meredith found herself chuckling. "Well," she said in reply, "I'm here, aren't I?"

"And Lance, how about you?"

Lance looked uncomfortable. "I attended one of those events with Meredith, but...they just weren't for me. So recently I've been trying to schedule more meetings with clients. Generally I can do their accounting via phone, fax, e-mail, and the like, but I've been diligent about getting out into their natural habitat and hoping to make some connections there."

Lance paused, then sat back, indicating he was finished. Now that she'd heard their pitiful attempts at networking spoken aloud, Meredith felt even worse than before.

But Dan brightened and said, "The good news is that you guys have all the tools to build *great* connections that matter. The bad news is, I think you have your *what* confused with your *why*."

Seeing the questioning looks on their faces, Dan continued, "If you ask most people *what* they are trying accomplish or *how* they intend to accomplish it, it's something they can usually easily tell you. For instance, Lance, if I'd asked you, 'What do you want to accomplish in the new year?' chances are you'd still be talking as they closed this place down later tonight."

All three of them laughed and Meredith could almost see Lance's resistance crumble in the face of Dan's power of reasoning. "And you, Meredith," Dan continued, casting his green eyes in her direction. "If I'd asked you *how* you were going to add more connections to your present list, you could have talked me through three more cups of coffee.

"But if you ask people *why* they are doing what they are doing, their answers become far less clear. In fact, most people have *why* and *what* confused. 'I need to network in order to find a piece of business or create a new gadget' are certainly very real and practical concerns. However, if you 'double-click' on your *why*, asking a deeper *why*, new questions and opportunities appear. When your reason *why* is bigger than your *what* or your *how*, you become an *attractor of possibility*. What's more, you inspire connections and more opportunities.

"For example, Meredith, you might state, 'I am working in social media consulting because I want to help people grow their businesses more successfully and because I have seen that the Web can offer them so much more opportunity at a lower cost. I am therefore passionate about helping others get online.' Or, for you, Lance, you might say, 'I am working at this accounting firm because they focus on restaurants and I love helping restaurants become more successful.' With these reasons you become magnets for connection because you know *why* you want to make connections that matter."

Dan paused to catch his breath; his face was flushed with excitement and, Meredith had to admit, it was catching. She had never paused to consider the *why* of networking and told him so.

"I guess the *why* just always seemed obvious to me," she admitted, almost sheepishly. "I just assumed others would somehow know my *why* for doing what I do."

Lance and Dan were both nodding furiously but, it would appear, for different reasons.

"That's the problem, Meredith," said Dan. "We assume we know the obvious *why* for monetizing the process, but in fact that's not a good enough question. We need to dig deeper if we want to be truly successful at growing our best business relationships, at making connections that matter."

Lance looked from Meredith to Dan and asked, "Forgive my ignorance but... why?"

Meredith found herself nodding in commiseration. Assume or not, Meredith was pretty sure she already knew why she was meeting with Dan. Then again, she could always be wrong.

"Good question, Lance, and not ignorant at all. Just the opposite, in fact. Exploring these questions provides clarity of purpose and sets you up to build your network with purpose and persistence, because a more deeply held purpose is essential for sticking with things as you encounter the inevitable bumps in the road. The *why* of connecting is also focused on people first, opportunities second.

"If you take this first big step, you will act in an authentic and credible way as you go about your community building or, as you call it, 'networking.' Those who build successful networks start by spending at least 30 minutes weekly reflecting on their values and purpose, refining them, and assessing them to see if their actions, values, and purpose are in alignment. It's about slowing down to speed up actually."

"Thirty minutes?" Meredith interrupted skeptically. She could barely spare that much time for something critical like a business meeting or afternoon workout. For network building? She was growing more skeptical by the minute. "Why so much time?"

Dan smirked and said, "What, you want the cow and the milk on the same day?"

All three laughed. "Trust me, if we can meet, say, once a week you will know how to do this by the end of January. And that weekly 30-minute investment will be the best you've ever made. What's more, it will become a habit for the rest of your life."

Meredith and Lance shrugged. Lance said, "What next?"

"In addition to the *why* behind your need for more connections, we need to drill down to your vision. Your vision is a picture of your ideal future and acts as a powerful magnet to draw you closer to your future. Some visions are very specific, like what their office building will look like, while others are more general, outlining future direction and attributes. Either is okay."

Dan paused and Meredith took advantage of it to ask, "Do you mind, Dan, sharing with us your vision?"

Dan nodded. "My vision is to help others succeed through my unique experience with building connections that matter, which directly ties into my *why*.

"Over time and through this process, you continue to clarify and specify a future vision that expresses your purpose and values in your work and life. You should spend time weekly reflecting on your vision, refining it, and assessing if your actions align with it. Again, those people who have inspiring visions pull others along on their journey.

"The most important thing is to have a *why* that emanates from a deep passion. And that the passion must be focused and have a core around making a difference for others—not just yourself. For example, look at Steve Jobs. He had a big passion in life—to make a beautifully engineered computer. He honed his passion and pushed to get his product out to as many people as possible. He wanted to make a difference in how people experienced technology. His *why* changed the world."

Meredith found herself nodding and, surprised by the silence in the wake of Dan's explanation, looked up to find the mid-afternoon crowd mostly gone.

Now she stared out at a half-empty café, still festooned with the corporate signage wishing guests "Happy Holidays" and a blinking tree by the condiment stand.

A slightly jazzy riff on "White Christmas" played overhead as she asked, "So, Dan, now that you've completely revolutionized how we think about making connections that matter, what should we focus on next?"

"I'm glad you asked." Dan smirked, sliding his empty coffee cup away from him. "For your homework, I'd like you to define your *why*, core values, and vision in two paragraphs and/or pictures and bring them to the next meeting."

Meredith made a note on her iPhone as Lance scribbled the instructions on the back of a Cup of Café napkin. Dan then stood and said a quick good-bye. As he headed out the doorway, he turned to them and added, "And bring your list of contacts. Here is a cheat sheet, if you will, to help. I always find that putting things in writing adds to whatever you share verbally."

Dan gave the two of them one last big smile as he set down two sheets of paper with type on just one side.

Meredith and Lance looked over their respective guides, nodding their heads almost in unison. The guides simply stated:

DAN'S FIRST-LESSON TIPS

✓ Shift from traditional networking to making connections that matter.

✓ This is how you create better and more sustainable connections.

✓ Figure out what matters to you most in the work you do currently or the work you would like to do.

✓ Add to your list of what core values matter most—values such as security or freedom (many entrepreneurs choose this value), creativity, integrity, etc.

✓ Next, write down and/or find images that fit your vision of what your life will look like when what matters most to you is combined with a great network of like-valued connections, and you have achieved what you define as success.

✓ When you share what matters to you explicitly, rather than just assuming people will know what matters to you, you start building a great network and become an attractor of possibility.

LESSON 2

CREATE QUALITY OVER QUANTITY

LANCE WAS NOT generally a procrastinator. He couldn't afford to be. His job required him to think and act quickly, to notice the details and troubleshoot the problems before they began, not after they had blossomed into full-blown crises for his clients in the hospitality industry.

But he was finding Dan's homework more off-putting than he'd first anticipated. The lesson, he knew, was simple: all he needed to do was write two paragraphs defining his *why*, his *core values*, and his *vision*. Not a big deal. It was the same kind of exercise he did at Hospitality, Inc., corporate retreats every other year or so.

But this was personal. His personal network, or whatever Dan wanted them to call it, was his Achilles' heel. It was too small, Lance felt, too isolated, too internal, not dynamic, helpful, or generous enough. Not so much for Meredith, who was as outgoing, friendly, and popular as an adult could be!

He grumbled and bent down to hit the Word icon on his computer, opening a blank document and titling it simply, "Dan's Homework Assignment #1."

It felt good to be moving on something, to hear the click of the keyboard beneath his fingers and the black words filling the white page. With time running out before their next meeting, Lance decided just to grin and bear it—so he could get it over with. If he did it wrong, or misunderstood the question, he figured Dan would set him straight at their meeting.

It wasn't like he was getting graded on this stuff, right?

"Why do I want to increase my social network?" He began typing. "Because it's too small. It doesn't offer me the right opportunities and if I'm ever going to get anywhere in my professional life, I need more opportunities, not less.

"This ties directly into my core values, which include solving complex problems for, and with, like-minded people. Nothing satisfies me more than coming to a problem cold, finding a solution, and making someone's day. Finally, my vision for building a values-based network is to connect with like-valued people for our individual and mutual benefit."

Lance finished typing, hit "Save," and reread his work. He smiled but only weakly. He was done, even if the assignment sounded more like he was filling out a resume or job application than approaching a new endeavor. He wished Meredith would have taken him up on his offer to work together on this, but she'd insisted that they both do their homework alone.

Lance looked at his watch and realized he only had a few minutes to print his homework and scoot if he wanted to make his afternoon meeting with Dan and Meredith across town.

• • • • • •

The conference room was small but uncluttered—rather than using rows and rows of seats, it was set up with three small working areas, each with a comfortable leather chair and small coffee table in front.

"Is it always set up like this?" Lance asked curiously, nodding to Meredith and Dan, who were milling about the middle of the room. "I mean, this is pretty valuable space for a hotel."

Dan winked and said, "Let's just say I make it worth their while to provide me with a comfortable sitting area. Will this do, Lance?"

"It's great," Lance proclaimed. "It's just, when you said we'd be meeting at the Morecraft Hotel, I was picturing one of those drab conference rooms with the podium and rows of chairs."

Dan chuckled. "Oh, they have those, too, but I decided to make mine a little more comfortable."

"That it is," Lance said, admiring the cozy touches for their meeting. A wide array of sodas, cookies, chips, and ice lined a small buffet table, stacked with cups and napkins for their convenience. "It's like a mini-workshop."

"That's how I like to see it," Dan said, sitting down in his own seat to signal the meeting could begin. "I tend to come here a lot. My office isn't really set up for meetings, and when we meet at a client's office, it becomes more like work. This way, you're more open to interpretation."

Lance smiled at Meredith, who looked as nervous as he felt. "Will we be meeting here every week, Dan?" she asked.

He nodded. "It's my office away from my office. I hope you don't mind."

Lance sat and fingered his homework nervously.

Dan gave him a sympathetic look and said, "Lance, you look a little anxious about last week's assignment. How about we take a look at yours first and put your mind at ease?"

Lance chuckled to be figured out so easily. "If you insist." He groaned playfully, handing over his assignment.

Dan looked at it and, for Meredith's benefit, read it aloud. Lance watched his old friend's face as she heard his why, core values, and vision read to her; she was nodding by the end.

When Dan was finished reading, he put the sheet of paper down in front of him and looked back at Lance. "That's a great start," he said encouragingly before turning to Meredith. "Your turn."

Meredith looked down sheepishly at the leather laptop bag at her feet. "If you insist," she said, sliding out an 8×10 photo and handing it to Dan. When he raised his eyes quizzically, she said, "You told us we could bring a picture!"

He smiled, offering a wry chuckle. "I suppose I did, Meredith. It's just, no one's ever done so before."

Dan studied the picture carefully for a moment, smiled, and then turned it around so that Lance and Meredith could see. Lance smiled; it was a piece of stock photography he had helped her pick when she designed her first brochure years earlier.

It showed a small group of people, men and women, black and white, Asian and Hispanic, all in business suits gathered at a conference table. They were smiling and joking but clearly working on a big project together. Outside the windows of the office building the sky was dark; the three men pictured in the center had their sleeves rolled up, their ties loosened. It looked like the whole group was in for a long night of working together.

"Meredith?" Dan asked, looking sideways at the smiling office workers pictured. "Care to walk us through this?"

"Sure," she said. "I thought this picture perfectly represented my *why* for identifying my connections that matter versus just unconsciously adding people—so-called friends I don't know well or at all—in hopes that such a strategy will help me increase my success in my business.

"As you shared last week, I should collaborate with a few well-targeted people just like these who can help find more people just like themselves. In other words, these quality connections will lead to new and more quality connections. This picture also perfectly represents my core values, which are helping people help themselves. Finally, this is my own personal vision of success: a group of like-minded people working together to solve a problem."

Meredith sat back in her chair, satisfied. Lance gave her a little *good job* nod and she smiled in recognition. Dan nodded and slid Meredith's picture on top of Lance's homework.

Then he sat back, crossed his legs, and laced his fingers under his chin. "Both of you," he began cautiously, "before I begin, I want to say you're both off to a great start. I really like the creativity and enthusiasm you expended on this homework assignment I gave you last week and it's clear you put a lot of thought into it. But I think you've still got your *why* and your *what* mixed up. Let me back up and double-click on that for you so we're clear before moving ahead . . ."

Dan paused, sitting up a bit, then continued: "I think the word that's missing from your *why* answers is *because*. What I heard from you, Lance, was what you want to do—grow a network, work with like-minded people, etc. And you, Meredith, same thing—what you want to do is collaborate with like-minded people, work on solving their problems and finding solutions, etc. Those are all worthy answers, but what I'm still not hearing is the *why* because you didn't give me a *because*. I am looking for the *deeper why* beyond the surface reasons you have shared. What lies in your core that drives you to want to accomplish your goals?"

"You mean more like 'cause and effect,' Dan?" Meredith asked.

Dan nodded. "Yes, Meredith. What you guys are giving me is more of a surface answer. Dig deeper into the specific reason as to *why* you need or want other people to help you solve problems, Lance, or *why* being in a group is so appealing to you, Meredith."

Lance nodded. That made sense. Dan continued, "Remember during our first meeting, one of the *why* examples I used was this one for you, Lance. 'I am working at this accounting firm because they focus on restaurants and I love helping restaurants become more successful.'"

Lance was impressed. "You remembered it verbatim?"

Dan chuckled. "I liked it a lot, Lance, and here's why: all of us have this reason within a reason for what we do. Why am I here talking to you two today? Because I love sharing this information with folks who have so much potential really to explode these ideas off of paper and into real life. That's my *why*. Now we need to find your reason within a reason—your *why*. Lance, let's start with you. Finish this sentence: I work at an accounting firm that specializes in restaurants because..."

Lance hemmed before suddenly growing inspired: "I work at an accounting firm that specializes in restaurants because...I want to help them be successful."

"That's great, Lance," acknowledged Dan with an enthusiastic nod. "But we can go one step further. Consider this as your *why* statement, Lance: I want them to be successful because I believe restaurants are a place where people come together to share their lives and build relationships. Additionally, I like working with family-owned restaurants because they have so much more invested in their businesses. Many of these family-owned restaurants get passed down from one generation to the next. The passion these families have for their business is intoxicating. They make me feel part of their family."

Lance smiled in pleasant surprise at Dan's attempt to articulate in words how Lance felt deep down. He nodded and so did Meredith. "I've seen Lance at work, Dan," she said, "and he really does come to life when he's walking around the kitchen, especially with a mom-and-pop restaurant where he gets to show them the different ways they can save or maximize their money."

Lance felt this was true.

"Now we are starting to get to the heart of the matter for Lance," Dan explained. "His underlying *why* for connecting with more people is to help build generations of family-owned businesses, and in doing this, he is helping people build wonderful, prosperous, joyful lives. Now he has further defined *why* he wants to build a better network."

Lance was nodding and blurted, "These families move from a position of working to live to living to work in a great, innovative environment. I then become a maestro or facilitator, helping these families become the leaders in their markets!"

"Nice!" Dan said. "Now we're getting to the heart of why you're here, and now you can better understand your motivations for coming to me in the first place. You can also open yourself up to meeting the right types of people by probing deeper into why you do what you do and your vision that ties into your passion. This statement goes one step deeper into what is personally important to you and sets the context for making meaningful connections for you. It also reveals your unique differentiator that attracts more of those perfect clients you want in your network."

Dan turned to Meredith. "Your turn, Meredith. Finish this sentence for me: I am eager to grow my list of meaningful connections because . . ."

Meredith was ready, quickly answering, "Because I already work so well with others in my firm. I know that there are many talented, young, social media sensations interning at my firm and I want to learn from them because I know they have so much to offer. In return, I get the chance to mentor the next generation of public relations stars and that is exciting—and rewarding!"

Dan was nodding halfway through her explanation, letting them both know that Meredith was on the right track as well.

"Okay, Meredith, great, but let's dig a little deeper. Keep it succinct and simple, like Lance's."

Meredith thought and Lance could see the smile on her face when the lightbulb came on: "I provide custom social media solutions to small business by building intimate relationships..."

Dan smirked. "That's a great descriptor for your business card, Meredith, but let's not forget the *why* inherent in your answer. In other words, you left out the *because* from your response."

Meredith looked chagrined as she replied, "I am eager to grow my list of meaningful connections because...it is a great feeling to help others express their business in an authentic way."

This time Dan leaned forward, clapping his hands. "And?" he prompted, eager to have Meredith dig as deeply as Lance had to find her *reason within a reason.*

Thus inspired, Meredith added, "Because...I believe that much of social media is just spin, and when you help someone tell their authentic story, you are truly contributing to their success professionally and personally. And with the new young talent I have turned into a collaborative team, I combine my seasoned wisdom with their insatiable passion and ability to leverage the most cutting-edge technologies. It's a huge win-win!"

Dan's smile of satisfaction and the ease of his posture as he sat back into his seat was validation enough that Meredith was now digging deeper as well.

"This is great progress, gang," Dan said. "Your *why* isn't just about your motivation. It's about discovering a deeper, guiding purpose and a stronger set of values. Now, let's compare your visions. Lance, you first said, and I quote, 'My vision for building a successful network is to connect with like-minded people with mutual interests for our mutual benefit.' Am I right, Lance?"

Lance nodded, but now in the light of what Dan had just shared, that didn't sound like a vision at all.

"And, Meredith?" Dan continued. "I didn't memorize your vision so why don't you remind me of it again?"

Meredith looked uncertainly over at Lance. "I dunno," she confessed. "I'm not so sure mine is accurate anymore."

Dan smiled, nodding. "That's okay, Meredith. Whatever it is, there is truth to it and we'll refine it over time. After all, this is a process."

Dan's words made Lance feel better. Meredith nodded and said, "Well, I explained earlier that my vision is to 'join a group of like-minded people working together to solve a problem.'"

Dan let Meredith's vision sit there for a few moments. She quickly added, "But that doesn't sound very specific anymore, does it?"

Dan shook his head. "Actually, it's fairly specific in the sense that it aligns closely with your *why*. Lance, however, yours is a little vague; it sounds more like a homework answer than real soul searching. But that's okay. We're going to work together to refine these until you really hone your vision."

Lance nodded. "But what can we do, between these meetings, to help refine our visions?"

Meredith winked. "I think I know. This is where those 30 minutes a week come in, right, Dan?"

"That's right, Meredith. I want you to just find a quiet space, removed from your usual work space, and spend at least 30 minutes once a week reflecting on your vision, refining it, and assessing if your actions and more importantly, your connections, align with it. It's very important that you refine your visions throughout this process so that you build your network successfully, benefiting you, your connections, and the ripples of connections that are forever impacted because of wiser choices."

Dan sat back, crossed his legs, and picked a piece of lint off one shirtsleeve. "But that's more homework. For now, I want to get to the point of this week's lesson, which is to choose 'quality partners' for your network."

He then stood and approached a whiteboard affixed to the hotel conference room wall, and grabbed some markers from the attached tray. With a red marker, he drew a small circle in the middle of the board, then with a green marker, he drew a slightly larger circle around the first. Inside the first circle, he drew a "10" and outside the second, a "20." Finally, he used a blue marker to draw a much bigger circle around both the red and green circles and wrote "All the Rest" inside it.

When he was done, he put the green marker down and used the red one as a kind of pointer. He paced slowly, his dark brown loafers whispering softly on the thin conference room carpet.

"What you see on the board is what I want you to focus on this week. Here in the smaller circle, I want you to seek 10 or fewer people for this first circle. I call this your 'Primary Circle.' This second outside circle in green I call your 'Secondary Circle.' Here, I want you to seek no more than an additional 20 people."

Lance nodded cautiously, tossing a look to Meredith, who seemed equally pensive. Dan continued: "Every well-functioning network has an inner circle—a Primary Circle—and a Secondary Circle and a Tertiary Circle. Identifying these three sets of circles helps you organize your relationships and focus your energy on the right people at the right time. Your Primary Circle is critical. Within your Primary Circle should be those people who most closely align with your values and goals. These are those 'partners' with whom you will have the most frequent contact and support exchanges.

"This circle should hold no more than 10 influential people. Your outer circles represent weaker ties, but those people are still valuable. Those within your outer circles are usually great sources of information, referrals, and ideas. It's impossible to have strong bonds with too many people at one time—it becomes impossible to connect deeply with more than 15 people on a regular basis. For business purposes, I have found it is easiest to focus on just 10 people."

Lance listened with growing alarm. So far Dan had made sense—the why, the what, the how, even the vision. It was all going in the right direction. But this? This? He hadn't signed up to get together every week simply to meet just 20 or 30 new people. He needed a network, not a knitting group!

"Lance?" Dan asked cautiously, an understanding smile formed on his face as he reached over to the buffet table and cracked open a can of diet soda. "You look perplexed. Care to share?"

"I just, w-w-well," he stammered, "I can't do anything with that amount of people."

"Me either," snapped Meredith, standing up to pour herself a cup of coffee, but Lance knew there was more to it than that. She liked to pace when she was upset. "I mean, I could fill three or more circles as we speak."

Dan smiled, sipping at his soda before responding, "Yes, but...would they be quality people? Would they be connections or distractions? Friends or...filler?"

"How do you mean?" asked Lance.

"As a colleague of mine has stated, 'You're the sum total of the 10 people you spend the most time with.' Think about it," Dan explained. "Each of us in this room has hundreds if not thousands of connections—'friends' on Facebook, on Twitter, on LinkedIn and Google Plus and Pinterest, through various professional organizations we belong to, lists and blogs we subscribe to, the business cards we've collected, even old college roommates and colleagues, but...how often do we interact with them? Daily? Or more like weekly? Monthly? Or annually? In a world where social capital has value in the billions of dollars, our individual social capital needs to be recognized, developed, and sustained."

Dan paused, then took their silence as a reply. "These *thousands* of connections are not the ones we network with daily or even regularly because it would be physically impossible to do so. Instead, by focusing on a few quality connections to exchange with regularly, you will actually achieve better results faster."

"How can I achieve better results with so few people, Dan?" Meredith asked, giving voice to the same thought Lance was having. "I'm ready, I'm invested in this. I can reach two, three times that many people per day. I mean, I'm willing to invest an hour or more per day in connecting here! Isn't it all about filling that pipeline so that we reach our quotas?"

"But why?" Dan asked. "Why spend an hour or more making short-term, even fleeting connections with more people when you could spend less time having more impact on just one or two people per week? If they are the right people, then you will get to your goals faster. These people would have influence. They would connect you to others. They, like you will be doing, have started with a small *quality* group of connections to build to a *quantity* of *quality* connections!"

"But what would that look like?" Lance asked.

Dan nodded in reply. "Okay, Meredith, let's start with you. If you were to choose just 10 names to put in this first circle, who would be your first five—people you currently know—to go in here?"

Dan uncapped a black marker and waited anxiously, reminding her, "I'm not going to expand the circle, so be careful. Don't pick the biggest, most important names in your network, but those you can realistically interact with this coming week and who might benefit the most from your collaboration."

Lance found himself joining Meredith and Dan at the dry erase board, even as Meredith panicked. "Well, let's start with Lee. He runs the print shop over on Croft Street, and he expressed an interest in partnering on some marketing initiatives. But I don't know about Sylvia. She said she wanted to connect about a new business venture, but she keeps putting me off..."

It went like that, back and forth, for the next half hour. Lance was glad it was a dry erase board or Dan's hands might be permanently stained.

"It's harder than it looks, isn't it?" Dan finally chuckled, putting the cap back on his pen and taking his soda back to his seat.

They joined him, nibbling on snacks and sipping coffee.

The exercise was a valuable one but left Lance feeling less than energized. Although Meredith was stymied simply because she had so many contacts, Lance had the opposite problem: he had too few!

He was struggling trying to identify five people to put in his Primary Circle, let alone 20 to fill his expanded Secondary Circle.

As usual, Dan's green eyes homed in on his insecurity. "Lance, a problem with this week's homework?"

Lance confessed, "I just don't know that many people, Dan. That's why I came to you."

Dan nodded and said, "Actually, Lance, you're in a slightly better position than Meredith on this one."

Meredith bit. "Say what?" she chuckled. Lance did, too. After all, she was always on him to network more, meet more people, and take more chances. Meeting with Dan had been her idea from the start.

Dan held his hands up in mock defeat. "I'm saying, Lance can start from scratch, Meredith, where you'll have to kind of 'unlearn' the way you've been taught to network. For instance, whereas you're having trouble whittling down your connections to fit in your Primary Circle, Lance can choose his from the ground up. He can choose them more wisely, perhaps, going for *local* rather than *long-distance* connections and going for *less* versus *more*. It's really a mindset, this quality over quantity concentration. And unfortunately, Meredith, it's easier to learn a new habit than unlearn a bad one."

As Meredith nodded thoughtfully, no doubt wondering how her instincts for quality over quantity could have been so wrong, Lance saw an opening. "Now can you connect us to some quality people you know?"

Dan didn't answer. He smiled instead. "We'll get to that, guys, but for now I want you to go through your contact lists and actively look for people who share the values you stated for me today, and those with whom you think you could develop a better relationship. These should also be people you *believe* would have strong, vibrant networks."

Meredith nodded, making a note on her iPhone. Lance knew she'd find this part of their homework easy. After all, she had more than 150 contacts and could easily find someone to complement her values and vision. Lance knew it would be a much bigger struggle for himself. After all, his list of contacts had only eight people on it—mostly people from his church or neighborhood, all of whom he knew quite well—but he didn't think they had big networks. The rest were people in his office, such as his project team, but strangely he had never talked much about the quality of their networks within the last couple of years. They had been too busy working on projects that came their way. Neither he nor his other partners realized until recently that the opportunities that *used* to come to them monthly were now coming much less frequently. They were suffering from the downturn big-time!

Taking pity on Lance, Dan looked at him and said, "I'll get you started. First, list two people in your company who you admire but don't know very well."

Lance nodded, then asked, "What if I admire them and know them, what then?"

"We'll get to those later. First, you know how sometimes in school your teacher would partner you with someone new, just to get you out of the rut of sitting with the same people all the time?"

When Meredith and Lance both nodded, Dan continued, "This is a little bit like that. Part of my process involves taking a fresh look at your existing contacts and selectively deepening them. If you are in a larger organization, most of the people in your Primary Circle will be people in your company—at least in the beginning."

Dan smiled, looking at his watch and noting that their time together was drawing to a close. He started gathering up his things. Meanwhile, Lance felt a wave of dread wash over him. He hadn't been looking forward to these weekly meetings, but now that their first one was nearly over, he wished he could spend twice as long learning from Dan!

"The question to ask," Dan continued, "is what percentage of your current network is made up of *Givers, Takers,* and *Exchangers*. You might think Givers are the ideal connections, but in fact, your goal is to find those who are or can become Exchangers."

"What's the difference?" Lance asked. "Don't Givers exchange and Exchangers give?"

He looked to Meredith, who was nodding in agreement. They both looked back to Dan, who replied, "Not exactly. Exchangers are definitely Givers, but they are also good at making requests for support and then *exchanging* opportunities that create a more sustainable model for ongoing, *mutual* success. Exchangers are also good at *discerning* who would be other great connections—other Exchangers to whom to introduce you, to help you grow your network." Dan paused for a moment to let this statement sink in. Meredith and Lance were unusually quiet, their heads nodding, their eyes twinkling in anticipation.

"So this week, your goal is to figure out who are Takers, Givers, and Exchangers—up to 10 people who you already know and five you don't know. The latter five will be people you can be introduced to through those you know. Given that you don't know these additional five yet, write down ideas as to what professions they are in or on what levels they are in an organization.

A lot of people don't understand that you can get to those great, *additional* five through people you currently know. The process is about first finding Givers who might be potential Exchangers."

Meredith nodded, furiously taking notes, then looked up. "Can you go into a little more detail about Exchangers, Dan?"

He smiled, stood, and walked back to the dry erase board. Without another word, he wrote *Exchangers* on the board, then continued writing until he had composed this bullet list:

- Demonstrate a concern for your issues and needs.
- Work to create an equal exchange of information and leads.
- Make an effort to stay in touch with you.
- Provide assistance without talking about how much they're doing for you or without keeping score.

Lance finished taking notes as Dan turned around. He had a smile and a parting message for them. "Listen, I know this is counter to all you've learned before about networking—more is more, bigger is better. Frankly, I blame the Internet."

Both Lance and Meredith looked at him quizzically.

"Online, many people get confused because the world of social networking and social media call connections 'friends.' Even more confusing is the concept of Six Degrees of Separation. Now, sites like LinkedIn let people see who you know (your first-degree connections), who those people know (your second-degree connections), and even who *those* people know (your third-degree connections).

"Remember we talked about your Circles? Well, LinkedIn is a great example of this concept playing out in your daily work life.

"This new vista of connections can overwhelm even the heartiest of *networkers* as they see that their 5,000 first-degree connections can connect them to 3 million second-degree connections and more than 15 million third-degree connections and those second- and third-degree numbers increase daily. What was once your small network of friends and family is now a world of connections and possibilities. But it is also often overwhelming and daunting to keep up with these numbers. How do you pick the quality out of the quantity of connections you have or could be making? How can you not confuse *activity* with *accomplishment*?

"Only by focusing on a few, high-quality connections—10 or fewer at first—can you truly accelerate your goal achievement. It's paradoxical, but starting *small* to grow a *big* network is the way to go. But who are the right, quality connections people to choose to start growing first? Who is your Primary Circle?

"The answer is to *start with those you know* and ask whether each is a Giver, Taker, or Exchanger. Part of being successful with this first step is taking a fresh look at your existing connections and selectively deepening them. As I said before, if you are in a large organization, most of the people in your Primary Circle should be people in your company."

The learning duo spent the next several minutes going through their assignment and, once again, they each got a one-page list of tips from Dan. Dan left them in deep concentration looking over their notes and their tips sheets. He knew they would have their work cut out for them.

DAN'S SECOND-LESSON TIPS

- ✓ Quality trumps quantity when it comes to building a successful network.
- ✓ Because the most beneficial opportunities come from people best suited for you, it pays to take time to find the right people, who will have similar and complementary values to network with one-on-one.
- ✓ From your quality connections come more opportunities. The idea is to go deep first in order to go wide later, instead of going an inch deep with everyone in the world.
- ✓ Figure out the percentage of Givers, Takers, and Exchangers in your network.
- ✓ You will most likely find that you will be starting with more Takers than Givers or Exchangers, but be persistent. Your first step will likely be finding Givers who are interested in building "exchanging" opportunities for one another. Those people exist!
- ✓ It's not easy to trim a high-quantity network into a high-quality network, but it will be rewarding if you invest your time in doing so.

LESSON 3

DIG BELOW THE SURFACE

"YOU DIDN'T HAVE TO do that," Meredith exclaimed a few days later as her 2:30 P.M. appointment, Ariel Cruz, sauntered into the office, gift basket in hand.

But you've done so much for my greeting card company," Ariel insisted, shoving the basket closer toward Meredith on her cluttered desk.

Meredith stood and the two embraced. "That's what you pay me for," Meredith tsk-tsked, then widened her eyes at the wide array of fresh fruit and baked goodies that filled the basket.

"Have you ever thought of going into the bakery business?" Meredith asked as she joined Ariel in the seating cluster on the other side of her desk.

Ariel smiled wickedly and said, "As a matter of fact, Meredith, that's why I'm here today. Not the bakery business, but I am thinking of doing a major geographic expansion and I wanted to bounce some ideas off you."

A couple of hours later, Meredith was just recovering from her whirlwind meeting with Ariel when Chuck, her four-thirty appointment, came in. Chuck was a long-standing client who ran a local landscaping empire—an empire, Meredith realized, she'd been instrumental in building.

"Hey, Meredith," Chuck said, taking off his sunglasses and sitting down. She'd barely had time to stand up to greet him, so she stayed behind her desk.

"How is everything, Chuck? I know you said today's meeting was urgent."

Meredith tried to keep the sarcasm out of her tone. With Chuck, every meeting was urgent.

"Well, it's about the new Web site. I've still got some issues with the layout, and I was hoping I could walk you through them."

Meredith gritted her teeth and pulled up his site on the widescreen monitor affixed to her wall. She used her laser pen as the pointer as Chuck aired his latest complaints.

While they discussed color schemes and more design options, Meredith realized that this was his fifth set of revisions so far, with no end in sight. What's more, he was still an invoice or two behind, and he had yet to introduce her to that client of his—the one with the new tile business who had been expanding his locations and looking for a nationwide social media campaign to help him successfully roll out his new stores.

She had asked him about his client because she saw he was listed as Chuck's connection on LinkedIn. Chuck had chattered on and on about the great business he did with this client when she asked for an introduction, and he had said he would make an introduction, but that was three months ago. Each month she would ask, and each month he said he would "get around to it soon."

Meredith rooted around on her desk for the digital voice recorder, turned it on, pointed it at Chuck, and sat back at her desk. She watched him as he paced in front of the big-screen TV, complaining about the "new green and blue background" when, after all, he had requested it personally during his last round of changes.

Meredith had a habit of keeping a running tally of connections in her head. Her mental list had three columns: Clients, Prospects, and Referral Sources. Until she'd met Dan, she had everyone on her list as a potential referral source—people who would be open to making referrals to potential clients.

Chuck was quickly moving into the Client-only column. But that wasn't the only list she put Chuck on that day. After he finalized his changes and let her know his revised deadline, Meredith opened that week's assignment and put Chuck's name down at the top of the Taker column, especially after he ended the meeting asking if he could meet with her another day to "pick her brain" to explore, as he put it, "her gigantic network" with hopes she could introduce *him* to new business opportunities.

When she suggested that he could do the same for her, he weakly replied, "Well, I've tried, but I don't have a network like yours, so it's not really worthwhile." She was glad to put Chuck finally in the Taker category, which meant she would most likely not be meeting with him for an exchange of opportunities any time soon . . . if at all. She spent the rest of the day gaining a stronger and stronger awareness of the current makeup of her network, weeding out lots and lots of people.

Finally, Meredith was able to unwind with her last meeting of the day at Francisco's, a local bistro around the corner from her office. As Francisco himself poured her a home-brewed peach tea and buttered a hot, crisp Cuban roll, she sat admiring the wall art he had commissioned by a local painter with whom she had put him in touch.

"This place is really shaping up, Francisco," she said, savoring the flavor of the hot, buttered roll that melted in her mouth. "I can't believe you've only been open three months."

"All thanks to that YouTube channel you set up for us, Meredith." The old man smiled, sitting down next to her at the empty bar. "Last week I uploaded a video with one of our bartenders making a mojito from scratch, and oh my goodness, we had to order an extra shipment of rum for overnight delivery!"

Meredith smiled, catching herself blushing. "It doesn't hurt that the bartender in question looks just like a young Antonio Banderas!"

"You noticed, eh?" Francisco asked, as the two shared a laugh.

"So what was so urgent?" she asked playfully as he served her steaming sweet plantains and a small dish of cubed pork.

He winked and stood up from the bar. "Follow me and I'll show you."

She looked longingly at her dish but followed him nonetheless. The bistro was quiet this time of day, but she knew from experience that in only a few hours it would be bustling with live conga music and happy patrons milling about the bar and dining on the open-air patio out front.

"You remember I told you about the private dining room I was thinking about?" he asked, running a caramel finger through his bristly white hair.

"I better. We ran a contest on your Facebook page where fans could vote on their favorite layout."

"Very popular," he said. They came to a set of roughhewn double doors and, with a devilish grin, Francisco opened it to reveal a cavernous space filled with warm terra cotta painted walls and a long, wooden table surrounded by at least a dozen chairs. "Only instead of a private dining room, I'm finding customers want to hold meetings here."

Meredith nodded silently as she admired the hammered-copper wall hangings and earthen water jugs on a weathered sideboard. "What a great place for a meeting!"

He turned and took her hands. "I'm glad you think so, Meredith. I wanted to make it available to you and other clients, free of charge, whenever you need it—as long as there are not paying customers wanting the space first! That would be your fault though, given your great marketing talent!" He winked at her and smiled.

Meredith's mind was already whirling. What a great opportunity to give clients or potential clients—a unique and new destination rather than just clustering around in her office or ordering coffee at the local café.

She immediately thought of Dan and the sweetheart deal he had with the local hotel, exchanging increased business and word-of-mouth advertising for a comfortable, convenient, and compatible offsite meeting room.

Immediately, Meredith put Francisco's name at the top of her *Exchanger* list.

• • • • • •

Meredith felt at ease as she pulled her late-model Lexus into the hotel parking lot a few days later. Gone were her earlier hesitations, even doubts, about working with Dan.

Although she was still anxious to see where his "alternative networking theories"—or so she and Lance secretly called them—were leading, so far he had done something even more important—he had gotten her to change her perspective.

All week long, as she'd gone about tweeting and posting updates on her usual social media sites and returning phone calls and lunching with clients, she'd had a decidedly different attitude. She'd taken time to reflect before every meeting what she could learn about the person she was about to shake hands with, or speak with, or e-mail back and forth with.

During that week, she often found herself asking "big picture" questions, as Dan might call them:

- "Is this person aligned with my values? With my vision?"
- "Can we help each other? Or can they just help me?"
- "Are we a good fit?"
- "Will this connection matter, not just for me but for him/her?"
- "Will our connection and our knowledge, new and old, help
  others we know? In other words, could our respective or mutual success benefit others in their networks?"

Although it hadn't changed the number of appointments she made or went to, it had changed Meredith's outlook on the appointments she felt weren't up to snuff. Toward the end of the week, she found herself making fewer but better appointments.

She had also worked hard to whittle down her contact list, focusing on who was a Giver, a Taker, or an

Exchanger. The result was a revelation. She recalled three contacts in particular that had really surprised her.

Ariel was a Giver. She was forever bringing Meredith gift baskets or tokens of her affection in a very real, very personal way. But, Meredith noted, it was never in a really professional way. Ariel would throw out literally dozens of, as she put it, "possible" connections.

As a result, Meredith would find herself talking with literally dozens of people who had little or no possibility of using her services, nor did they know anyone else who might be interested in using them.

What's more, as giving as Ariel was, she was not a good receiver. Whenever Meredith tried to offer her something extra, such as an opportunity or movie tickets from another client, or even a meeting with another client, she quickly demurred. She preferred to see Meredith as a vendor, not a partner. For that reason, as generous as she was, she never quite made it to the Exchanger column.

Chuck, as she had assessed earlier, was a classic Taker. He talked a good game and was always up for jotting down one of the names she suggested as connections and having her introduce him to several people, but he never quite returned the favor. He was always going to message her with the e-mail address of that great gal who did his bookkeeping...but he failed to stay true to his word...The the name of that great and affordable caterer who specialized in breakfast meetings on the go was always on the tip of his tongue, but after working together for two years...it had never materialized.

Finally, she smiled as she realized that Francisco, her friend and ally all along, was an Exchanger. He was not only genuinely appreciative of what she'd done for him, but he was eager to exchange ideas, opinions, contacts, connections—and even a venue in which to incorporate them all!

But it wasn't just his generous offer that inspired her to call Francisco an Exchanger. It was his attitude. He was always open, enthusiastic about exchanging new ideas and information, just like she was. As Dan would no doubt put it, he was "a big picture person." Francisco and Meredith exchanged more than just opportunities—they shared the same vision and values.

Of all her most valued connections, Francisco had made it to the top of her list of five that Dan wanted her to identify for her "Primary Circle." As she parked, she looked down at her list and read the five names listed there silently to herself. A few were on the margins, but she was confident that all were good Exchangers according to Dan's definition.

• • • • • •

Meredith heard polite chatter as she entered the same hotel conference room they'd used the previous week and smiled when she found Dan and Lance seated in the comfortable chairs. She poured herself coffee and joined them.

"So," Dan asked, "what did you guys think of this week's assignment?"

Lance cleared his throat and handed over a sticky note with only one name printed on it. "As you can see, I didn't do very well. My Primary Circle has only one name in it."

He shot Meredith an embarrassed grin and she nodded in support, giving him a *chin up* look.

"What did you find so hard about it, Lance?" Dan asked.

"Well, I knew it wouldn't be easy, but I have to admit it would have been a lot easier if I hadn't met you!"

They all chuckled as Lance explained, "I mean, if someone had just asked me to list five Exchangers, I would have done so easily. That is, until you gave me a better definition of what a true Exchanger does; that made it harder. It appears that most of my contacts are, frankly, Takers."

"Mine too," Meredith interjected, handing her list over to Dan when Lance had run out of steam. "I had trouble whittling it down at first, but I realized that not many of my contacts are actually 'connections that matter,' given your definition last week."

Dan took the assignments and nodded, barely glancing at the names before he slid them onto the low-slung coffee table beside him. Meredith and Lance shared a look and, Dan being Dan, he smiled, catching them.

"The names aren't really important to me," he said, leaning forward in his seat. "What's important was the exercise of seeing the people you know through a fresh lens—an objective, fresh pair of eyes.

"Most people," he went on, "get hung up with the external trappings of the people they already know, making huge assumptions and sweeping conclusions about people in their lives. Everyone has an *authentic* story that lives below the surface of their job, their hairstyle, and the clothes they wear. It's your unique story that evolves from your *why* we talked about earlier. Have people in your Primary Circle who are Exchangers or have the potential of becoming Exchangers and you can generate new conversations and find people you already know who have similar values and purpose around what they are trying to create in their companies, local communities, or even the world."

Meredith thought of this as Dan paused to let his latest "lesson" sink in. As much as Ariel was a Giver and Chuck a Taker, she would still hate to stop working with them, connecting with them. Would that make her a Taker if she cut them off simply because they hadn't made it into her Primary Circle?

Dan added, as if he read her mind, "Just because you put someone into a category that is not that of an Exchanger, they don't have to be removed from your network altogether. You can move them to your Secondary Circle where you connect less frequently or even your Tertiary Circle where you check in maybe once a year. The important thing is that you have your Primary Circle in place so that you can leverage those *exchanging* relationships into great and ongoing opportunities."

"So how do we get to know their stories better?" she asked Dan. "I mean, I'm thinking in particular of a few people who I thought were great contacts but aren't, but could be... how do I find out for sure?"

Dan beamed. "I'm really glad you asked that, Meredith, because that leads me right into next week's assignment. Before you reach out to any contacts this week, before you pick up the phone to call them or click your mouse to e-mail them or tweet at them or race downstairs to meet them, I want you to spend a couple of minutes 'researching' them."

"How do we do that, Dan?" Lance asked.

Dan shrugged and Meredith could tell that he figured a part of the lesson was for them to find out for themselves. "How do you do anything, Lance?" Dan said instead. "Google them. Look at their profile on LinkedIn. Look at their connections, their Web site, their blog, their Twitter, Google+, or Facebook page—the races they ran in or the charity events they attended or... the wedding photos they have on their Tumblr site.

"We think we know the people we work with, but we don't. We could know more. It's all out there, and the more you know about the social side of someone, the better you can connect to that part of them—the part that is human and wants to connect back at a deeper, more sustainable level. That's what building social capital is all about—not just for you—but for the people with whom you partner as well.

"For instance, Meredith, chances are you could look closer at each of the five names you currently have on your list and discover that some of these folks don't really share your vision or your values. They only seem like good Exchangers. By the same token, you could probably find folks just outside of your Primary Circle—maybe somebody in your Secondary Circle—who does in fact align more closely with the way you do business. But you have to know their stories first. Dig below the surface of what you think you know."

Meredith liked that—digging below the surface. As much time as she spent with her clients, contacts, and connections, what did she really know about them?

Dan went on, "The more you get to know your contacts, I want you to start having conversations with your potential partners to explore new possibilities and see if you can have conversations with more substance. Skip the small talk and dig a little deeper to sincerity.

"Given that making connections that matter is about finding people with shared values, interactions must be substantive and values-connecting, not superficial. Part of this means being a bit more open and authentic than you may be used to being. Part of this is asking great questions that take your conversations to a deeper level. It's also about having more conscious conversations."

Meredith nodded, watching Lance do the same. "That could take some getting used to," she admitted. "I tend to keep people at arm's length, if only out of respect for them."

"Absolutely," Dan agreed. "We all do, but this is about making deeper, not more, connections. Let your instincts guide you. If you think a connection is strong enough, the right questions can only strengthen it. You'll see. It's like a wall comes down and opens you both up to a new relationship. That's all we're looking for here—newer, deeper relationships."

Meredith was thinking of Francisco, and how much deeper their connection could be if she could just get him to talk about himself a little more: his background, his family, his energy, and why community is so important to him.

She made a mental note to do so, but Lance was already thinking ahead.

"So," he asked, avoiding Meredith's eyes, "are we ready to be introduced to some of your contacts, Dan?"

Meredith smiled slyly. She knew what Lance was getting at. His circle was empty; no doubt he wanted to fill it with some "proven" connections from Dan!

For his part, Dan smiled humbly but shook his head firmly. "Not yet," he said, standing to signal the meeting was over. "Keep digging deeper with your current list first."

Dan started to gather up his things but then stopped suddenly. "Oh, I almost forgot something. Your network is dynamic. What I mean by that is your circles will expand and contract. It's all about being ready, willing, and able to exchange. You see, some people will be too busy transitioning in a job or moving, to name a few examples. Perhaps they are not *able* currently to be part of your Primary or Secondary Circles. Just remain flexible."

With that final instruction, Dan pulled out the familiar two white sheets of paper with the tips for this session and finished packing up his computer, notepad, and pen. He hugged both Meredith and Lance before he left them sitting, silently staring at their respective guides.

DAN'S THIRD-LESSON TIPS

✓ Digging below the surface is all about having conscious conversations with your potential Primary or Secondary Circle partners to determine where they best fit in your network.

✓ Listen with your eyes. Determine who should be in your network by what people do rather than what they say they will do.

✓ Be curious and do your research. Before you jump in headfirst in making your connections, find out more about them—especially through their social media channels.

✓ Your circles are dynamic. You will find that people will come and go in your circles. Remain flexible.

✓ Be prepared by constantly keeping an open eye for new circle partners. Keep a mental list and written list of Givers, Takers, and Exchangers.

LESSON 4

HAVE YOUR AUTHENTIC STORY READY TO GO

LANCE COULD BARELY believe his ears. This was it! Dan was finally ready to make the introductions that he and Meredith had both been waiting for. Clearly, as they sat in the cozy hotel conference room exactly one week later, Meredith was disbelieving as well.

"Are you sure this isn't a trick?" she asked as Lance nodded furiously.

Dan chuckled, sitting back in his chair. "Now, why would I trick you two?"

Meredith shot Lance a *what now*? look. Lance grinned. "Well, Dan, it's just that you made it sound like we'd need to find the holy grail before we could get a connection out of you, and it's only been a couple of weeks."

Dan smiled back, but his tone was serious as he replied, "I said I'd make an introduction, Lance. What you do with it is up to you."

Lance wasn't sure he liked Dan's tone. So far, every week there had been a lesson. Was the connection this week's lesson? He listened as Dan said, "Okay, Meredith, for you I've got a great contact. Her name is Carol Livingston and she's VP of social media marketing for Running Start."

"The sneaker company?" Meredith asked, sitting up in her seat a little taller.

Dan nodded and handed Meredith a business card before turning his attention to Lance. "And Lance, you're in for a big treat. It just so happens that Peter James, one of my clients, works for the Principle Group's restaurant division."

Lance's eyes grew wide. When Meredith shot him a questioning glance, he quickly explained, "Principle Group runs the Papa's Pasta Parlor chain. Wow, Dan, this could be *huge* for me."

Dan smiled humbly and stood. "Both Carol and Peter are expecting you, and I've done my best to make the proper introductions. From here on in, it's up to you two. I wish you the best and look forward to hearing how it goes next week."

Dan left the room and Lance sat stunned, staring at the business card Dan had handed him before leaving.

"Papa's Pasta Parlor, huh?" Meredith said, admiring the familiar green and red logo in the corner of the card. "Lance, just think what could happen if your firm landed that account."

"I can't," Lance confessed.

Meredith snorted playfully as she pulled her iPhone out of her stuffed purse. "Why not?" she asked.

"It's too intimidating!"

She shook her head and smiled as she began dialing numbers. "Who are you calling?" he asked.

"Dan's connection, of course," she whispered, holding up a manicured finger as someone answered on the other line. "Yes, hello, Meredith Mathers for Carol Livingston, please."

There was a pause before Meredith replied, "Yes, I was referred by Dan Paterno, of—oh, you do? Great! Okay, well certainly; tomorrow at 4:00 P.M. sounds perfect. Yes, I have the address right here. Thanks so much and I'm really looking forward to it."

"That was easy," Lance exclaimed as Meredith made a quick notation in her phone's calendar feature before sliding it back in her purse.

"Dan's name really opened that door, I'll tell you. I was this close to getting shut down before I mentioned him, then it was as if the floodgates of happiness opened."

Lance nodded, turning the Papa's Pasta Parlor business card over and over in his fingers. "Your turn," Meredith nudged gently.

He grinned but with a sour feeling in his stomach. This was why he'd agreed to meet with Dan in the first place—not so much for his connections but for the confidence to capitalize on those connections.

At the moment, he was feeling supremely unconfident.

Still, there was no time like the present, and he knew Meredith was eager to leave and start preparing for her meeting. If she left him to his own devices, Lance knew—and he supposed Meredith did as well—he might never follow through.

Before he could lose his nerve, Lance slid out his phone and dialed the number on the card. It was a direct line to Peter James's office, and the receptionist answered with a clipped, "Hello and welcome to Papa's Pasta Parlor marketing division, how can I direct your call?"

"Peter James, please," said Lance.

"I'll direct your call," said the woman, causing Lance to panic. He'd assumed that, like Meredith, he'd make an appointment with Peter's secretary.

"Peter James speaking," said a gruff voice.

Lance stammered, "Mr. James, yes, this is Lance Hardy, I'm a friend of Dan Paterno's?"

"Yes?" said Peter James briskly, the name clearly not opening the kinds of doors Meredith had led him to believe—at least, not yet.

Lance shot Meredith a *what now?* glance and said, "Yes, well, Dan thought that maybe you and I should get together and talk over some possibilities . . ."

Meredith gave him a thumbs-up sign, but Lance wasn't so sure. Peter said, "Sounds good to me, Lance. How about this afternoon? I usually break for lunch about 2:00 P.M. I could meet you in the corporate cafeteria downstairs. I'll be the only one wearing a tie!"

"That'd be fine, sir, yes," Lance said to a dial tone.

"Yikes," he groaned to Meredith as they stood to leave the room. "I was hoping for a little more time to prepare."

Meredith gave him a conspiratorial pat on the shoulder. "Sometimes, Lance, more time just means more time to worry."

• • • • • •

Peter James wasn't kidding. Not only was he the only employee in the Principle Group cafeteria wearing a tie, but he was older than the other employees gathered there by a good twenty years.

"Welcome to the Kiddy Zone," said Peter gruffly as the two shook hands after Lance made his way over to Peter's table in the corner.

With a napkin still in his hand and food still in his mouth, Peter offered Lance a seat. Lance's stomach rumbled; he had assumed they'd have lunch and he hadn't had anything to eat before their early afternoon meeting.

"Is everyone here so young?" Lance asked, taking a seat and eyeing the garlic bread on Peter's plate.

"Most are younger," Peter complained, pushing his plate away. It was clear he'd already eaten and was eager to get the meeting started. "So, Lance, how can I help you today?"

Lance was nearly thrown by the question. He had assumed Dan's name would immediately clue Peter in to what he was there for, and why. "W-w-well, Mr. James," Lance stammered, "I work for Hospitality, Inc. As you may know, we specialize in doing accounting for chains like Papa's Pasta Parlor and—"

"I don't," Peter said, staring back at Lance.

"I'm sorry?"

"I don't know that you specialize in doing accounting for fast-food chains."

His tone was pleasant, his jaw firm, his eyes clear and bracing. And yet, there was something...confrontational...about Peter's statement. Lance thought for a moment and said, "Well, now you do!"

He was hoping for a little cocky humor, but the joke fell flat. He and Peter simply weren't connecting. The vibe was awkward and growing more so by the minute.

"I suppose I should start over," Lance hemmed.

Peter shook his head and said brusquely, "How about I try? What brings you here today, Lance, really?"

Despite Peter's abrupt tone, the question was a good one, and sincere. Lance risked an equally sincere answer: "To be honest, I've never eaten in the Papa's Pasta Parlor cafeteria before!"

He'd meant it as a joke, a way to diffuse the obvious tension this abrupt and unfortunate meeting had created, but either Peter James wasn't a joking man or Lance just didn't tell jokes very well.

Peter nodded and gathered his things. "I appreciate you coming to see me today, Lance. I hope that next time we meet, we can both be better prepared."

• • • • • •

Dan chuckled when, the following week, Lance related the story in an admittedly pitiful tone. Quickly apologizing, Dan said, "Lance, trust me, I'm not laughing at you, just with you. We've all been there, right, Meredith?"

"Yeah, like last week," Meredith said despondently.

Dan arched one eyebrow and, as he turned to look at her, so did Lance. "But I thought your meeting got off to such a great start," he said to her.

Meredith merely groaned. "Yes, the meeting got off to a great start, but eventually I discovered I just didn't have anything in common with the woman. Of course, it's not her fault."

Lance chuckled. "Maybe you should have met with her secretary instead."

Meredith nodded. Dan interjected, "Actually, Lance, you make a good point. Sometimes it's better to have a meeting with someone you click with, even if you don't necessarily have something to offer each other—other than good conversation, that is."

Lance chuckled. "Actually, Dan, after Peter James left, I *did* have a good conversation with Jack, the guy who ran the salad bar."

"Salad bar?" asked Meredith.

"Hey, I said I'd never eaten at the Papa's Pasta Parlor cafeteria before. I wasn't going home without crossing that item off my bucket list!"

This time, Dan seemed to be laughing. "What did you two talk about?" he asked.

"Who, me and Jack, the salad bar guy?" Lance asked. When Dan nodded, Lance admitted, "I asked him why everybody who worked at the Pasta Parlor seemed so young. Jack said that their recruiting staff was twice the size of any other department, and that everyone who worked there was pretty much fresh out of college, but that turnover was extremely high. I asked him why he worked there, and he said he was working his way through school, majoring in, guess what?...economics. I handed him my card and told him to call me when he graduates next semester! I want to see if I can help him get an interview with my company."

Meredith clapped her hands appreciatively as Dan nodded. "See there, Lance, you made a connection after all."

As he finished his story, Lance realized that he'd learned much more from Jack than he had by meeting with Peter. Dan seemed to be in agreement.

"Now, let's think about that for a minute, Lance," said Dan. "Why do you think you got along so well with that cafeteria worker, Jack, and not so well with the executive I set you up with?"

Lance replied, "I can't really tell you. Maybe I didn't feel so pressured once Peter left the cafeteria or I didn't expect anything from Jack. And, really, he didn't know me from Adam or that I ran a company that might one day hire him. We weren't there trying to get anything from one another, we were just there to...make a connection."

Dan nodded knowingly. "Going into a first meeting without someone with any expectations is tough to do but much more beneficial. More specifically, having the belief that *anything is possible* is the best way to approach a meeting. This belief will drive a better attitude and set of behaviors. I have seen, for example, where an encounter with no expectations has lead to one of the biggest deals of someone's career. Both of you, I'm sorry that these connections were a little out of your comfort zone. Peter and Carol are both great connections, and I sincerely want you to follow them up with a second meeting...just not yet."

Meredith and Lance looked at each other, confused. "So, wait," Meredith asked. "That first meeting was...a setup?"

Dan shook his head fiercely and waved his hands in surrender. "Hardly, gang; none of us have time for setups. However, I wanted you to meet with two connections who were outside of your comfort zones so you would realize how important it is to be prepared under any conditions. Connections can be made anywhere, anytime. And although we've been working hard at exploring your current connections to dig deeper, today I'd like to talk about the importance of having your authentic story ready to go, especially for situations where you are less comfortable, like what happened this week. One way to form powerful human connections is through stories. Powerful, strong, human, personal stories."

"Like what?" joked Meredith. "Nursery rhymes?"

Dan wagged his finger playfully. "You know better, Meredith. These are *your* stories, why you do what you do, what you can do for others, and what makes you tick. Lance, you said you got stumped when Peter asked why you were there that day. If you'd had your authentic story ready, I guarantee you could have told it simply, easily, sincerely, and the meeting would have had a drastically different outcome. Do you believe me?"

Lance nodded. "I believe that if I'd been as comfortable around Peter as I was with Jack, then yes, I would have made a more powerful connection."

Meredith nodded. "I agree. But we can't just wait for the other person to make us feel comfortable. We have to create a comfortable atmosphere. I think telling stories that create connections can help us do that."

Dan nodded eagerly now. "Sometimes you have to prime the pump a little, Meredith. The more confident and comfortable you are at making connections and sharing engaging stories that resonate with those you meet, the more powerful those connections become. I recommend you have your stories thought out and ready to go when you meet new people so the connections you make are thoughtful and focused on your mutual stories. Valuable connections are all around you and many times the difference between making or missing a mutually valuable connection is your ability simply to articulate who you are, what journey you are on, why you are on it, and what you need to take another step forward. When you have your story ready, you are also more prepared to draw out the stories of others because you know what to ask."

"So how can we do that, Dan?" Lance asked.

"Well, first of all, you need to prepare your stories. They start with your vision and passion. We talked about your individual visions and passions earlier. Then you tie these into a specific experience you have had that illustrates more *who* you are over *what* you do for a living. Lance, you already said you connected so well with Jack, the cafeteria worker, because you had no expectations of each other, no pressure. But weren't you happy when you heard that he was studying economics?"

"Absolutely," Lance replied.

"Why?" Dan probed.

"Because suddenly we had something in common and I could help him."

"Exactly!" Dan and Meredith shouted at the same time.

"Is this a good example of a story?" Lance asked hopefully.

"Yes," Dan added. "You shared *how* you helped a soon-to-be college graduate effectively and in doing that, you showed more about *who* you are—someone who cares about others and takes the time to go out of your way to help. Your story shows others that you are someone who would make a good circle partner."

Dan paused a moment before turning to Meredith and asking, "So, Meredith, how do you think your story might sound? Don't recite it for me yet. You'll have all week to work on these so no pressure, but...what would you want to tell me if we'd never met?"

Meredith shot a glance toward Lance before turning back to Dan and extending a hand. "I'm Meredith," she announced confidently. "And I love to help young people get better starts in their careers. This began after I helped my brother, who was having tremendous difficulty getting into law school, study for the LSAT—Law School Admission Test—and because of my help, he ended up not only getting a great score, but he got into his dream school. Since then I have developed a passion for helping any young person when I can. With that passion, my vision is to create a wonderful team of young, up-and-coming social media sensations who work with me to help companies jump successfully into this new world of social media. With this stellar team of seasoned veterans with top strategy skills that I have developed combined with the bold energy of a team of talented and collaborative young social media professionals, my firm has the differentiator that creates a competitive edge and, as a result, attracts the most amazing client list possible."

Dan leaned forward and high-fived Meredith. "Good job!" He smiled and turned to Lance. "Your turn, pal."

He watched Lance squirm in his chair but then sit forward, clear his throat, and begin. "I love to help family-owned restaurateurs blend their love of family and good food with great, state-of-the-art restaurant designs so they can compete in one of the most competitive marketplaces out there. My vision is to expand my practice into other locations around the country so that hundreds of similar families will be able to grow their restaurants generation after generation. In turn, people who are served by those families will experience amazing cuisines as well as world-class service and, most of all, a loving family environment."

Lance stopped. He waited for Dan to speak. Dan's head was down, cupped in his hands, making both Lance and Meredith grow anxious with doubt. Then, suddenly, Dan lifted his head. He smiled, flooding Lance's heart with pure relief. "Good," he finally exhaled. "You should both now be much more prepared for unexpected connection opportunities in the future."

The three of them ended their meeting with Dan's usual dissemination of tip sheets. Lance and Meredith were particularly excited to move forward by first making sure they absorbed what they learned from their current session.

DAN'S FOURTH-LESSON TIPS

✓ Great stories build connections as people identify with your experiences on a personal level.

✓ Be bold and confident. Share your story and then ask your connections
to share theirs. Sharing your stories also builds rapport and trust.

✓ Acknowledge and share your appreciation for one another to create
further connection.

✓ Allow yourself to help others. Don't feel as if you're being too generous or giving away too much with nothing in exchange. Keeping score won't do you good.

✓ Creating your authentic story is about combining your passion with your vision and connecting these to a story that shares powerfully who you are rather than what you do or have done. Work at it until you have your authentic story ready to share.

LESSON 5

GIVE FIRST

MEREDITH WAS READYING HERSELF for that week's meeting with Dan when her cell phone trilled an alert for an incoming text message. "Sorry, folks," Dan had written only a few moments earlier. "A family emergency is forcing me to postpone this week's meeting but not this week's lesson: Give First."

Meredith looked at the phone, half-relieved she wouldn't have to trek halfway across town but more than a little disappointed that she wouldn't be able to get more introductions. In fact, she and Lance had made a pact that this was the week they would pin Dan down on giving them more introductions to people in his network.

A follow-up e-mail explained: "This week, you should first go back and connect with one of your Primary Circle partners and give first by asking what is one thing that partner would like your help with. By giving first to those key people in your network, you set up a powerful environment for a reciprocal relationship, rather than one that is one-sided. If you have chosen the right Primary Circle partners, you will then find that your efforts have fallen on fertile soil for continuous networking, meaningful connection, and creating an exchanging relationship. Also, download this week's guide."

Meredith responded with best wishes for a quick resolution to Dan's family emergency, then sat back at her desk. Her office was pleasant with bamboo wallpaper and a light green and brown palette of colors and accessories. A large picture window faced the industrial park below, where a small but beautiful open space with benches and bronze sculptures by a local artist was bordered by a row of majestic oak trees.

Finding herself with a free hour—make that nearly two hours, given the commute to Dan's favorite hotel—wasn't something Meredith experienced often. Instinctively, she thought of the dozen and one things she could, possibly *should*, be doing. But she'd devoted herself to Dan's program for the last month, and she wanted to make sure it took by following all of his lessons.

Dan had given her and Lance no reason to doubt him so far, and she didn't want to lose a week's worth of solid work simply because nobody was looking. She had ignored a flood of that morning's e-mails and her workaholic tendencies and instead focused on what

Dan had sent her: "By giving first to those key people in your network, you set up a powerful environment for a reciprocal relationship, rather than one that is one-sided. Also, download this week's guide."

First and foremost, Meredith considered herself a giving person. That's why she'd gotten into social media in the first place. It was the first time in the history of marketing and promotion where giving was in the actual job description! That is, if you did it right.

She wondered, though, in her eagerness to make strong connections if she always thought of the other person. If she had to put herself in a category, would she assess herself as a Giver, a Taker, or an Exchanger? Although she would have loved to consider herself an Exchanger, and in most cases she was, like many small-business owners she was sometimes forced to be a Taker. It didn't happen often but often enough to give her pause with Dan's new assignment.

Feeling slightly sheepish, Meredith turned back to her e-mail from that morning. Dan wanted her to give to an existing contact, not someone new, and the fastest, simplest, most random way to do that was to see who'd written her that day.

Seventy-four e-mails. That's how many she'd received since logging off of her computer the night before. Seventy-four names to help, to give to, but the minute she saw an e-mail from her colleague Anne asking for a little hiring advice, she made her choice.

She e-mailed Anne back and set up a quick lunch date. Before they met, however, Meredith stood up from her desk and headed out the door. She had some work to do in her HR Department before her meeting.

• • • • • •

"So, how's the entrepreneurial life treating you, Anne?" Meredith asked as she sat down on a bench in the small park between their two offices. Anne was a former employee who, several months earlier, had made the leap to form her own boutique advertising agency.

"I wish I could say I was hiring for growth," said Anne, a petite blonde in white slacks and a navy blazer. "It's just hard to find good team members who you know are team players."

Meredith nodded and joined Anne in line at Doug's Dogs and Donuts, a popular lunch cart that parked in the park each morning and left each afternoon. They'd had many lunches there when Anne still worked for Meredith.

"So, tell me a little about what you're looking for," Meredith said as they sat back down with the daily lunch special: a hot dog, soda, and a cake donut for $2.99. Meredith bought, taking Dan's lesson to *give first* literally.

"I need two people, actually," Anne confessed, wiping a smidge of ketchup off her lower lip before setting the second half of her hot dog back in its shiny foil tray. "One is for an administrative position, and the other is creative."

Meredith nodded. "In my experience," she said gently, "creative support can be as valuable as creative-creative."

Anne blushed. "No, you're right, Meredith. I'm just trying to prioritize what's going to help me with my current client load and keep the folks I do have happy while filling the pipeline for the next few months."

Meredith nodded. How many times had she been in Anne's shoes? Stuck between a rock and a hard place and an unpaid invoice or two away from closing her doors—and her very dream—forever?

Meredith opened her valise and pulled out a thin stack of resumes. She'd highlighted the contact information on each of the six she'd brought along, and pointed this out as she handed them to Anne.

"What are these?" the young entrepreneur asked earnestly.

"Last month I hired a new assistant. She's wonderful, but . . . so were these six people. The decision was a hard one, and I'd be proud to recommend any one of these people."

Anne looked up from the slim pile and asked, "Don't you want to hold onto these?"

Meredith nodded, then grinned. "Sure I do." Company policy was to hold onto resumes for at least six months and to hire, if possible, based on a previous talent search rather than starting from scratch. As a former employee, Anne knew this all too well.

Anne frowned, looking down at the resumes. "Er . . . I don't know how to say this, Meredith, but will these folks even respond if I mention that my starting salary is at least five grand lower than yours?"

Meredith smiled. "Not all, Anne, but it's worth a shot. Like I said, we began the initial candidate search a few months back, so if any of these folks are still available, my bet is they'll be willing to negotiate. But more important, the reason they're in this pile in the first place is because they impressed me as team players, folks who—like you, like me—come to work for more than a paycheck. So I think you'll find a gem in this pile, trust me."

Anne smiled, looking reassured. Meredith felt good. She'd been sincerely disappointed she hadn't been able to hire all the candidates who'd made it to the final round before choosing her last assistant. She was glad that, at the very least, one of them might now find a job with someone like Anne, who would not only appreciate but reward a solid team player.

Anne filed the resumes away in her own distressed leather messenger bag before looking up sheepishly. She swept a blond lock behind her ear and said, "Well, that takes care of the support person, hopefully, but about the creative..."

Anne let her voice drift off and Meredith rested a hand reassuringly on her shoulder. "I don't have any resumes for that, unfortunately, but what I can do is what I do best: tap into my contacts. Before this meeting I put a call out on Twitter, LinkedIn, Facebook, and through Google+, and when I get back to the office I'll get on the phones and start working my personal connections, business owners or recruiters or other creatives who may be between jobs. Don't worry, Anne. We'll find you somebody."

Anne looked grateful but still tense. "I know talk is cheap," Meredith added as they both stood and tossed their foil wrappers in the nearest trashcan, "but I care about you and your success, Anne. I've been where you are, and although it's not always pleasant, it's a learning experience."

"But why are you doing all this for a competitor, Meredith?"

Meredith shrugged. "I'd like to think we're friends first, Anne, competitors second." Anne smiled and nodded in agreement.

In the car on the quick drive to Lance's office, where she had an afternoon appointment, she spoke to friends and colleagues via the Bluetooth built into her steering wheel. In addition to the resumes she had handed Anne, she was fairly certain she had a few leads in the creative department as well.

"Hey, do you mind if we walk a little?" Lance asked, meeting her at her car as she pulled into the employee parking lot of Hospitality, Inc.

Meredith, who had come fresh from her lunch date with Anne and still had her walking shoes on, smiled and said, "Great idea!"

"I've just been sitting all day," Lance explained as they started onto the paved track that surrounded the commercial park where Lance's building was located.

"So, what did you think of Dan's assignment?" Meredith asked as they settled into a brisk, if comfortable, pace.

"I was a little offended at first," he answered, mirroring Meredith's own initial *how dare he suggest I'm not a giver* reaction, "but then I realized he was right. We could all stand to give first and receive second, you know? And since I don't have a huge list of contacts like you, the only folks I could give to were on my inner circle."

He gave her a playful nudge as he continued, "Then I got to thinking about last week's meeting with Dan's contact, the grump at Papa's Pasta Parlor? And how I'd written it off, but then I remembered Jack, the kid in the cafeteria. He'd given me his cell phone number, which I figured I'd never use, but I called him and he answered right away. I asked him if he was doing any interning, and he said he'd considered it but with class and work, he wasn't sure he'd have the time. I asked him if it'd be okay to call around on his behalf, maybe find him an opportunity where he could get credit for his next semester. He seemed pretty jazzed, so I've been working on that all day."

Meredith was impressed. Not only had Lance shown some major initiative calling this kid up out of the blue like that, but he seemed genuinely excited about it.

"Any luck?" she asked.

He shrugged. "I think I got him a slot doing night auditing for Barry's Bistro downtown."

"Yeah?"

"They're a client and I know they're really active with the university Jack is going to, so...they seemed excited about the prospect. I think Jack did, too, when I told him. They should meet next week to iron out all the formalities."

"Another Italian place, huh?" Meredith joked. "Poor kid's gonna get typecast."

"Well, at least this one's moving him out of the cafeteria. My client tells me most interns get hired on before they graduate, so... here's hoping."

They walked for a little while until Meredith asked, "So, I have to ask, just between you and me, what do you think you'll get out of this partnership with Jack?"

Lance smirked. "You first, Meredith. How will moving heaven and earth to find two employees for your competitor help you?"

Meredith thought for a few steps before responding. "I like Anne and I've been where she is. We worked well together and I think once she's up and running and clear of her first few years of business, we'll be able to partner on something. What's more, she seemed immensely grateful for what I'd done and I don't think you can go wrong with generating that kind of goodwill."

"Same with me," he confessed. "I just liked Jack and I felt for him. He seemed so smart and quick and motivated, and there he was stuck in the cafeteria, you know? I know we've all been there, we've all paid our dues, but so many people have helped me along the way to where I am now so I thought I'd try to be one of those people to him."

Meredith nodded; his answer was so sincere, how could it be wrong?

"I wonder, though," she offered, "what Dan will think of it."

Lance smirked. "I guess we'll have to wait until next week to find out!"

The two spent the rest of the hour going through Dan's guide, which Meredith had printed out for both herself and Lance. They were very happy to see they had done well with the task of giving first, even though Dan had not been with them to set the foundation for their efforts. They agreed this task was easier than they thought and that giving had lots of intrinsic rewards they had not expected.

DAN'S FIFTH-LESSON TIPS

- ✓ You must first connect by showing you are a Giver versus a Taker.
- ✓ Once you give first, you set into action a potential for exchange and build your skills as an Exchanger.
- ✓ Choose at least one person a month to give something to—time, treasures, talents, or thoughts are all options. It could be volunteering your time, mentoring someone, or sending someone information you believe they would benefit from knowing. It could also look like sponsoring something by offering financial support. Be creative with your giving.
- ✓ Give wisely. Give not to receive but to offer value. Giving wisely is about giving to someone you strongly believe would benefit from your gift, someone who will appreciate your gift and be likely to either reciprocate now or in the future to you or someone else.
- ✓ To get started, all you have to do is ask one of your partners what one thing they would like your help with. A very simple move on your part will set a foundation for a powerful environment.

LESSON 6

UPGRADE YOUR NETWORK—FIVE LEVELS OF EXCHANGE

"WOW," Dan exclaimed the following week after Lance and Meredith had summarized their "Give First" lesson. "I was worried that I was letting you down by canceling last minute like that, but... it seems you went above and beyond the call of duty on this one."

Lance smiled, basking for a moment in Dan's enthusiasm. "So," Dan added, "any updates for me?"

"I'm glad to announce that Anne hired one of the support staff she needed from the stack of resumes I handed her," Meredith said. "And she's got interviews next week with two creative staffers from the connections I wrote to on Twitter and Facebook."

Lance was suitably impressed with Meredith's experiment in giving, as was Dan. When it was his turn, Lance explained, "Jack was approved for the internship at Barry's Bistro. He'll be doing their books at night and getting college credit toward his MBA, so it won't affect his job with the Pasta Parlor chain or his GPA. He's pretty stoked about it. Truth be told, so am I. I'm hoping that, one day, he'll come work for Hospitality, Inc."

"Now you're talking, Lance," Dan exclaimed, standing from his seat with an approving nod. "I'm glad to see you both not only got into the spirit of giving but were so happy and enthusiastic about it. Truly, the sign of a real Exchanger is one who is sincere and generous with his or her connections. You really can't fake the goodwill that fuels a solid, ongoing exchange between two great connections."

Dan was pacing in front of a tall stand set up next to the dry erase board at the back of the room. To follow his movements, Lance had to shift slightly in his chair. The stand held a giant sketch pad. On the first page, written in black marker, were the words *The Five Levels of Exchange.*

As Dan paused in front of the pad, Meredith cleared her throat and asked, "So, Dan, we're on Week Six of your little program now. Do you think we're finally ready to meet some more of your connections?"

Dan smiled. "I know you think you're ready, Meredith, and certainly you and Lance are poised to make powerful connections in the near future. Look how well you both did with the giving experiment, and how much it meant to you both. But now I propose something even more specific, something more hands-on that you can use to make meaningful connections that matter."

He paused, looking from the title on the sketch pad first to where Lance, then Meredith sat. "Just imagine what kinds of meetings you could have if you were an expert at taking any good potential Primary Circle partner through what I call the Five Levels of Exchange."

Meredith gave Lance a look. He asked, "Is that like Six Sigma?"

"Actually, Lance, it's a model I created that identifies the evolution of the most effective exchanges successful circle partners could offer one another. Going through this process moves building your network from a haphazard and often unconscious activity into a much more conscious and proactive process.

"So in today's lesson, I'm going to teach you the Five Levels of the Exchange."

Meredith and Lance exchanged looks before quickly pulling out their messenger bags for a way to take notes. Meredith was quick to retrieve her iPad, but Lance took a little longer to get his laptop up and running, a blank Word document finally filling the screen.

When they were both ready, Dan turned to the next page in the giant sketch pad. The words *Level 1: Social Exchange* were written on the page.

Dan pointed to them and said, "So, let's start with Level 1, or what I call 'Social Exchange.' This step is the foundation of building a strong relationship. You may also think of it as emotional intelligence, which is the ability to understand emotions and use them to promote emotional and intellectual growth in yourself and others.

"People are increasingly receptive to emotional honesty, and they're looking for someone who not only says what he or she really feels but is also an empathic listener. Emotional support builds trust and naturally allows the relationship to progress along the Exchange Model."

After a slight pause, Dan flipped to the next page. It read *Level 2: Information Exchange*. He began: "Once at least some kind of emotional exchange has been established, people are more willing to volunteer information. But let's face it, people are overwhelmed with data and information. Think of all the sources you yourself have from which to gather information. The key here is useful but easy-to-obtain information versus valuable, not-as-well-known facts and statistics."

Lance looked to Meredith, who was busy typing. Before Dan could continue, he cleared his throat and asked, "Well, what type of information, Dan? Can you give us a for instance?"

"Sure," Dan said, turning to them both. "You both just engaged in an extreme case of information exchange in the Give First exercise. Meredith gave those resumes, based on her Level 1 Social Exchange with Anne. And you, Lance, gave information and contact numbers for a valuable internship to Jack based on your earlier Social Exchange in the cafeteria at Papa's

Pasta Parlor. But information can be anything: a tip, a review, a business card, a Web link. That's the type of information we're talking about here."

On the following page were printed the words *Level 3: Knowledge-Wisdom Exchange.* Dan said, "Now, the next natural progression in relationship-building is knowledge. So I called Level 3 *Knowledge-Wisdom Exchange.*"

"But, didn't we just cover that with *Information Exchange*, Dan?" Meredith asked before Lance could form the words.

Dan replied patiently. "There's actually a pretty big difference between knowledge and information. Information is typically pure data and facts; knowledge involves a personal experience, lessons learned, experiences, insights, and ideas.

"So, for example, if you give someone a tip, the name of an event you heard of but have not attended, or articles you have heard about but have not read, you are sharing information. Knowledge support, on the other hand, signifies a growing level of trust. Examples of knowledge-sharing could be experiences shared in mastermind groups or mentoring relationships. So, for instance, Lance, all you gave Jack so far is information: a contact at the college, a chance at an internship, the connection to make it happen. But let's say you really find yourself clicking with this kid and he pursues a relationship and begins exchanging experiences he has had and you share your insights and experiences that complement his. Well, your conversation could evolve into a knowledge exchange where you mentor him and take him under your wing."

Lance nodded toward Dan and chuckled, "Hmm, why does that sound familiar?"

They all laughed. "Exactly, we're having a knowledge exchange right now. But you can see how if you didn't trust me or I didn't trust you, we all might be a little less forthcoming with the type or amount of knowledge we convey. If you are doing this correctly, it adds an element of wisdom. Here, you are sharing that 20 percent that can yield an 80 percent return. Best-practice-sharing is an example of wisdom support."

Lance raced to type in Dan's words as Meredith did the same. The rustling of paper against paper caught his attention, and Lance risked a rare glance up from his laptop. Dan had flipped the last sheet of paper over to a new one.

Level 4: Connection Exchange was written on the next page. Dan pointed to it and said, "Connecting two people you know who do not know one another is leveraging your network, creating a ripple effect for those you connect as well as yourself. If you have made a strong connection through a great introduction, the people you connect will remember you for this and you will grow your social capital."

The final page said *Level 5: Opportunity Exchange*. Dan pointed to this page with particular pride. "Finally, gang, we get to Level 5 or what I call the 'Opportunity Exchange.' Here is your chance to be recommended or introduced to a wonderful new business opportunity—whether it's a new piece of business or a new job. Getting leads, referrals, and introductions that evolve through this hierarchy of ongoing exchanges of support throughout your circles is your ultimate goal. The reason I created these Five Levels of Exchange was to help people realize that you can't think of *closing* deals before you effectively *open up* your relationships through a dynamic *exchange* with the right people."

Lance nodded, taking copious notes on his laptop. Meredith finally finished typing her own notes into her iPad. Dan waited patiently, busying himself by closing up his pad and folding the stand that came with it. When Lance looked up, Dan had his equipment bundled and ready to go, waiting by the door.

"Are we done for the day?" Lance asked. His watch told him only half an hour had passed while Dan had been teaching them the Five Levels of Exchange.

"Not quite." Dan shook his head. "I'm done, but your work is just beginning."

Lance laughed heartily, but Dan wasn't known for his jokes. "So what are we supposed to do?" he asked.

"For the next half hour," Dan began, handing them their usual one-page guides for their current session, "I want you two to practice these levels with one another. Walk through all five levels and see how your exchange plays out. Next week, we can revisit how it went and, hopefully, keep putting these relationship-building skills to good use!"

• • • • • •

Lance and Meredith found themselves once again at their local coffee shop office away from their offices. Meredith was sipping away at her chai tea latte with soy as she began the exchange, "So, Lance, I know you think I am so much better at this anti-non-networking process than you are, but to tell you the truth, I am very shy. In fact, when I was a little girl, I was known as 'the shy middle sister.'"

"Really?" exclaimed Lance. "It's hard to believe. Everyone I know thinks of you as the most outgoing, assertive leader in your field!"

"Well, I am a good actress," Meredith said with a sigh. "You don't realize I am shy because you don't see me every day. If you did, you would see that I spend most nights recuperating from my busy days. Haven't you ever wondered why you don't see me much between conferences or my speaking engagements? I need that downtime to recover. Anyway, what I know is that this type of one-to-one exchanging with a limited number of key, qualified people is so much better for my personality type than entering most conferences or networking events and having to work the room."

"Really, Meredith? Wow... well I'll tell you, learning this new insight about you gives me a little comfort—I'm not as much alone in this process, so to speak!" Lance smiled. "Okay, so let's try Level 1: The Social Exchange. Would your shyness story count as a good beginning?"

"Absolutely! In fact, telling it to you now, I suddenly see why I should integrate that into my authentic story."

"I agree." Lance nodded. "You had me hooked from the beginning. Good emotional connectivity."

"Well, it is authentic," Meredith stated soberly. For the first time ever, her smile revealed a veil of pain underneath it. Lance reached out and grabbed her hand.

"Now I understand what makes you tick even more and why you love to help and mentor others," he replied reassuringly. "Now, let's move on to the next level of exchange—Level 2: Information Exchange."

"Yes, let's!" Meredith bounced back to the present with her usual perkiness. "For the Information Exchange, let me offer you a site I just discovered today. It's called 'InMaps' and it's offered by LinkedIn. It offers you the opportunity to visualize the clusters of contacts in your network graphically and zoom in and out to see the trends—for example, who the 'bridgers' are in your network—linking you to groups of connections."

"Great! I love the sound of that! Have you heard of the new tool CardMunch? It's also a LinkedIn app. It allows you to take a photograph of someone's business card after meeting at some business function. From there, you can send a request to link to them on LinkedIn. It helps with keeping track of turning contacts into connections that matter."

"We're on a roll!" Meredith clapped her hands together enthusiastically. Then she leaned in, took a deep breath, and continued, "Okay, now for Level 3: Knowledge Exchange. I would share that my experience with social media is showing me the best thing we can do to keep up with this fast-paced social world is to choose just one online place where we do most of our connecting. For me, it's LinkedIn—the business Facebook."

Lance nodded before contributing, "Ah, well for me, it's LinkedIn, but even more so the group I just started. One of the guys in my office asked me to start a finance group for restaurant owners. I was surprised to see that within the first couple of weeks, I have more than a hundred people who have asked to join."

"Really? Maybe I should consider a group."

"Well, why don't I look at areas that aren't represented yet on LinkedIn that might turn into an opportunity for a group that addresses an unmet need? I would be happy to share my insights and offer suggestions."

"Deal!"

"Great. Moving right along, Level 4: Connection Exchange."

"Hmm, I've been thinking about this," Lance reflected. "Ever since we started working with Dan, I've been thinking about Karen, our social media director, and you. Originally, I thought it would be a waste of time to connect you two because we aren't looking for any help in our media strategy. But now I realize that you two just need to know each other. Karen is passionate about what she does and shares your philosophy of work. I think you guys need to connect."

"That's great," Meredith said, with a knowing tone in her voice.

"Indeed," remarked Lance. "It could also lead to a Level 5 Exchange: the Opportunity Exchange. Here, I realized today when I was looking at my second-degree connections on LinkedIn that there is someone I want to meet that you have within your network, Meredith. It's actually your colleague James's brother who works over at McConbrey Brothers Restaurants—one of the biggest high-end restaurant chains in the country. I would like to meet him to see if our accounting firm might be of support in helping them with a second opinion on their tax returns this year. We have found that by offering prospects a second opinion on their last year's tax returns, we have often been able to identify some pretty significant tax savings."

"Well I think they would at least want to hear your story and consider a second opinion," said Meredith. "I'll see what I can do." She paused while Lance took a moment to sit up straighter, smiling more broadly than she had seen him smile in a long time. Evidently, he was hitting his stride. She continued, "Finally, for me, I see that someone just connected with me with whom you have a third-degree LinkedIn connection."

Meredith paused for a moment while she pulled the information off of her LinkedIn app on her iPhone. "It's a woman named Debbie Scher. She's the CMO of a company I've been trying to get into for two years. It looks like your direct report, Sarah Abrams, is connected to her."

Lance was busily writing down Meredith's request. "Okay, got it. I'll go back and see what I can find out. Looks like we've got a bit of work to do, but all in all, wow! It's a lot easier having this structure in place."

"Yes." Meredith smiled. "It's also strange we have not done this before. It's like that proverb, 'the shoemaker's children go barefoot,' which is about how we often neglect taking care of those closest to us. Let's do it differently from here on out. And now that we actually have things stirring in our respective pipelines, 'let's make hay while the sun shines,' which is another good proverb!"

With that, the two of them stopped for a moment before packing up their things to look once again at the guides Dan had handed them at the beginning of their meeting. They both wanted to make sure they memorized each exchange level.

DAN'S SIXTH-LESSON TIPS

- ✓ Practice the Five Levels of Exchange, first with someone you know.
- ✓ With Level 1, focus on creating some kind of emotional connection. This happens when you take the time to figure out what matters most to your exchange partner. Make it personal for yourself.
- ✓ In Level 2, focus on information sharing, where you offer relevant data that would be of value to someone with whom you want to build further rapport.
- ✓ With Level 3, share your personal experiences (knowledge) and key insights regarding those experiences (wisdom) with those in your network.
- ✓ Level 4 advances your exchanges to an even more powerful level when you start to make connections that matter. Here, you discern which targeted connections could make a difference in your network circle partners' lives.
- ✓ Level 5 is where the action happens—where you make warm introductions and/or referrals. Here, you are creating opportunities that can lead to recurring exchanges of opportunities for you and as many others in your network as possible.

LESSON 7

LEARN TO MAKE GREAT INTRODUCTIONS

MEREDITH AND LANCE were already seated comfortably in the hotel conference room when Dan came bouncing through the door. He looked more dressed up than usual, his dress slacks crisper somehow, and his white shirt more fitted, his tie a real eye-popper.

His smile was beaming as he shut the door behind him and stood in front of the two chairs where Meredith and Lance had plopped themselves, looking harried but buoyed by the previous week's assignment.

"Hi," he bellowed, two tones deeper than his usual voice. He then shoved his hand in Meredith's direction. "My name's Dan and I'm here to help you!"

He shook her hand energetically, then turned to Lance and repeated the procedure. Lance and Meredith shared a conspiratorial look as Lance covertly twirled his index finger around his temple in the universal sign for *somebody's going cuckoo* while Dan was taking his usual seat.

"Now," Dan said, sighing heavily as he loosened his tie and unbuttoned his top button, "why do you think I bounded in here today, acting like a crazy man?"

"Uh," Lance offered, looking at Meredith uncertainly, "you wanted to show us what we probably look like when we were networking?"

The three shared a good laugh. "Almost," Dan confessed, wagging a playful finger, "but not quite."

Dan turned to Meredith and seemed to be waiting for a response. Almost on instinct, she guessed, "Well, perhaps today's lesson has something to do with...making a good impression?"

Dan nodded, sliding the laptop bag off his shoulder. "Yes and juxtaposing that good first impression with good *introductions*. Further, I'll share with you how introductions have become the new referral."

"Interesting!" said Meredith slowly.

"I don't get it," Lance retorted, shifting in his chair and shaking his head side to side.

"Don't worry, Lance. I'll bring you along by showing you what I am talking about," responded Dan with a gleam in his eye.

There was a small coffee table between their three oversized chairs, and Dan quickly booted up his notebook computer, plugged his power cord into an outlet in the floor, and started jamming away at his keyboard.

His new MacBook Air was sleek with a large screen, and he smiled when the program he selected opened. With his smiling face bathed in the bluish-whitish light from his screen, Dan explained, "Today, I am going to make formal introductions for each of you to two trusted people in my Primary Circle.

"What's really exciting," he continued, "is that these connections will be tailor-made for you, and I'm going to make the introduction literally right before your very eyes."

As he was speaking, Dan pulled a pad of sticky notes from his computer bag, wrote a name down on the top one, then handed it to Lance. On the second sheet, he wrote down a name and then peeled the note off, handing it to Meredith.

She read it immediately; it said, "Lee Seymour."

Meredith wasn't sure whether to be excited or disappointed. Dan continued, "What we're doing now, what *I'm* doing for you two today, at this point in our relationship, is helping you build better relationships from the start. So, yes, it's only one name for now, but trust me, it's for your own good."

Meredith itched to ask a question that was on her mind, but Lance beat her to it. "Not to sound ungrateful," he said to Dan, "but... why just *one* connection?"

"For now, it's the only thing to do," Dan explained patiently. By the look on his face, Meredith was certain that actually wasn't enough for Lance.

"And here's why, Lance," continued Dan. "A good relationship builder doesn't overwhelm his partners with too many connections. One good connection, one strong connection that has been carefully screened and just as carefully targeted, is going to be more than enough if you handle it right. Remember *quality* over *quantity* when it comes to building your Primary Circle? Well, the same holds true for building *out* when you first get started in this process of making connections that matter. When I came in today, I started out in my first connection with you showing you how many people start connecting with others. They probably don't intend it, but they are way too pushy. I came on like that to help you experience the powerful difference there is between introducing yourself and having someone known and respected by someone you want to meet introduce you effectively. I am going to show you what great introductions look like."

He paused, adjusted his computer screen and projector, and then pushed a button on a remote control that automatically pulled down a projection screen in the back of the room. With a few more adjustments, he had the screen on his notebook computer transposed onto the wall at the back of the room, making it much easier to see.

"So what I'm doing now," he explained, logging onto LinkedIn, "is showing you the profiles of the people I'm connecting you with. Meredith, let's start with you."

Meredith inched forward in her seat unconsciously, even though the screen was more than big enough to provide her with a crystal-clear view of what Dan was doing. She watched as his virtual mouse pointer clicked on Lee Seymour's LinkedIn profile.

Meredith quickly scanned Lee's online profile. She was the CEO of a local chain of nurseries called Lee's Trees & More. Meredith instinctively smiled. She drove by one on her way home every day. It was odd to put the pieces together as Dan scrolled through her online profile, even as she pictured the busy nursery at an even busier intersection.

Lee sold much more than trees: she ran a busy landscaping business and sold personally customized Adirondack chairs right by the side of the road, with old-fashioned, hand-lettered price tags. Some of the chairs looked like hot dogs, some like hot rods, all were charming and many was the time Meredith had sat at a red light, staring at one, tempted to put on her blinker, pull in, and buy one for her back garden.

"Meredith," Dan was saying, "you'll see how I targeted Lee specifically for you for a variety of reasons. Look at her profile, the charities she's involved with, her list of connections. She's as passionate about what she does as you are, but she's clearly reluctant to go electronic. I spoke with her last week and all her marketing is hard copy, real-time. None of it's virtual or digital. Meredith, I think you could certainly help realize her vision in a way that aligns with the brick-and-mortar world she's created for herself—and quite successfully at that."

When Dan paused, Meredith asked, "You said she was reluctant, Dan. How reluctant?"

He smirked, opening a new e-mail on the giant screen in the back of the room. "Did I say reluctant?" He chuckled. "More like...agnostic. But you'll see, you two have a lot in common. Now I want you to see how I'm doing this from inside the LinkedIn system. This way I can attach your profile, Meredith, as well as a few select references."

Meredith watched as Dan handpicked two of Meredith's 45-plus LinkedIn references. Then he quietly began composing his LinkedIn letter of introduction. "The qualities that I think will resonate most with you, Lee," Dan typed in the e-mail field as Meredith and Lance watched, "are her top two strengths—being a good listener and being great at building strong, long-term relationships with top leaders. But don't let my recommendation be the only one you receive on Meredith's behalf. Here are two other recommendations that Meredith has received..."

As she watched, Dan found a reference a former client had given two months earlier: "Meredith is a joy to work with and we only wish we would have called her sooner. We would have started growing our new target markets even faster. Meredith is one of the best marketing strategists we have ever worked with because she 'gets us' and works to make sure we are 100 percent satisfied every time we hire her and her team."

Next, he found an older but similarly glowing reference from another previous client. These were attached to the original e-mail, which Dan asked Meredith to approve before he sent. "Now, Lance, let's look at your connections and find some references that showcase your top strengths and passion."

As Dan followed the same procedure for Lance as he had for her, Meredith could picture Lee Seymour opening up her letter of introduction from Dan. Not only would it be coming from a trusted source, but it would also have the power of two additional recommendations and an instant, bona fide link to Meredith's LinkedIn profile.

Talk about making a good introduction, Meredith thought to herself.

DAN'S SEVENTH-LESSON TIPS

- ✓ Well-done introductions translate into referrals. Don't become overly aggressive at first, looking for the winning sell or ultimate result. It's just the beginning.
- ✓ In today's online world, take advantage of LinkedIn—review your profile and make sure it is ready for optimal sharing and viewing by others.
- ✓ Ask for recommendations for current and previous positions from people in your LinkedIn connections who know you well, and offer to write one in return for them, too!
- ✓ When you scour your connections, you don't always have to do it with the mindset of "who can help me?" Leave some room to be able to identify how your connections could help out someone else you know. What goes around comes around.
- ✓ If you find yourself in need of introductions, look at your connections' circles on LinkedIn or identify a target pool of people you'd like to meet and then see what mutual connections you share.
- ✓ Introductions can be made in person. At live events, take advantage of the chance to learn more about others by playing matchmaker, such as Jill did when first introducing Dan to Meredith and Lance. Research the attendees or speakers who will be at the events you will be attending ahead of time. You

may even want to ask a mutual connection there to introduce you for the sake of getting to know that speaker or presenter!

- ✓ Open up a relationship by first exploring similar interests or values
beyond business.

LESSON 8

EXPAND YOUR CIRCLES OF CONNECTIONS

"I CAN'T BELIEVE how many times I've driven by here," Meredith said a few days later, as she was led into the inner sanctum of one of Lee's Trees & More's most popular franchises. Admiring not only the plants but the accessories, the garden gnomes, and Adirondack chairs, she gushed, "I need all of this!"

Lee pointed to a padded Adirondack chair in a back sitting area while taking the one opposite. Meredith's was shaped like a catcher's mitt and surprisingly comfortable. Lee's was shaped like a barbecue grill. Next to it was a small end table with wire legs and a mosaic tiled top. On top sat a lemonade pitcher and two glasses.

While Lee poured the pitcher into a Ball jar drinking glass, Meredith admired the older woman. She had white hair, soft and straight down to her back; she was dressed in vibrant colors that matched the outside seating area she had chosen for their meeting. There was a vibrant green awning hanging over a lush back deck. The entire back area was bursting with color from every type of flower and tree she thought she had ever seen in every garden she had ever been in.

Meredith looked over at a small desk up against the back wall. "What an amazing outdoor office!" Meredith gushed, taking her first sip of ice-cold lemonade.

"Don't I wish," Lee said with a wave of her hand that sent several sterling silver charm bracelets clinking together on her thin wrist. "I have my daily desk and a chair back at our corporate headquarters downtown," she explained, "but when I found out where you lived I thought I'd show off my little arboretum. I use it as a showplace during the off-season and a mini wedding chapel during the summer."

"It's darling." Meredith blushed.

Lee pinned her with an inquisitive glance. "I can't say I was surprised when I got Dan's e-mail," she explained, setting her lemonade aside. "Truth be told, I've been looking for a social media specialist for some time. I'm just concerned that whoever I choose needs to share at least a few common goals with me and have a bit of a passion or interest around my work."

Meredith nodded enthusiastically. "Frankly, Lee, I do what I do for people who are as serious about their business as I am...and I do love all things related to nature! Neither of us has the time to waste any, and if you're not ready, or eager, or trusting of my services, then I certainly don't want to waste any of yours."

Lee nodded appreciatively as Meredith realized that without Dan's introduction and the trust that had helped break down walls on her behalf, she would have never been able to speak so freely with Lee this way.

"One other thing, though." Lee paused and cleared her throat. "I do have a niece who has begged me to let her do an internship focused on social media, which she has been studying in college for two years now. She has her own blog and is constantly sending us e-mail links with great stories and pictures and . . ."

"Don't say another word, Lee. I would love to get your niece involved." Meredith smiled to herself. "I mentor at least six kids a year. She could be a big help working on your campaign and maybe even getting you to blog!"

"Really?"

"Really!" laughed Meredith.

Lee leaned toward Meredith with a big smile. Meredith took that as a cue to move the meeting along. "So, Lee, how ambitious do you want your social media strategy to be, I mean, no matter who eventually handles it?"

Lee nodded thoughtfully. "I see it like I see the rest of my business—slow and steady. I'm not interested in setting the Internet on fire and, frankly, I'd be concerned that I wouldn't be able to provide the level of customer service my guests appreciate if I did get too busy."

Meredith smiled. "One of the ways I approach a client's social media campaign is from the outside in. In other words, look at me. I've driven by this place hundreds of times but just couldn't get motivated enough to pull over. What would have given me that extra nudge? A blog post I'd read of yours? A free gardening pamphlet you offered online? A weekly newsletter? A gardening tip in the local *Weekly Reader*? My gut tells me that the personal approach is, really, the only approach to target the customers you really want."

Lee had visibly relaxed as Meredith spoke—a good sign!

"You can't imagine how good it makes me feel to hear you say that," Lee offered, reaching once again for her tall glass of lemonade. "So often marketing gurus, and I use that term loosely, are all about conquering the world and getting as much attention as they can. I just want to help provide a sanctuary for fellow nature enthusiasts or gardeners and bring a sense of peace to their lives—and backyards."

• • • • • •

"It was such a revelation," Meredith gasped when, a few days later, she, Lance, and Dan met at their regular place, at their appointed time. "You had said Lee was an 'agnostic,' Dan, but she wasn't doubting me as much as my profession. Once we were able to connect on a personal level, all those walls of resistance came down. We're meeting later today to brainstorm the design of her blog."

"Lee? Blogging? I never thought I'd see the day," Dan remarked.

"She didn't either," Meredith gushed, "but once I was able to show her a few similar blogs—creative, noncommercial, helpful sites that actually open a door to creative expression through gardening and planting—she couldn't get enough!"

Lance was nodding right along and Meredith paused to take a breath and let him discuss his meeting. "So," he said, picking right up where she left off, "I couldn't agree more with what Meredith was saying. The man I met with, Mr. Francis, runs that giant waterfront restaurant on the wharf. The one with the lighthouse in the parking lot. Well, I knew you said he was targeted when you e-mailed him, Dan, but I didn't realize just how targeted. He confessed that he was considering opening a second restaurant over in Cobia County, and wanted me to run the numbers for that establishment."

Meredith and Dan both realized the importance of such a ground-floor opportunity and congratulated Lance unanimously. "What's interesting to me is that although I've done this before a few times, I've never been given carte blanche to sit there with the blueprints in hand and make actual, hard-copy decisions with the owner right there at the drafting table. I mean, we're talking about what kind of ceiling fans to use, how many fish tanks he can afford or should invest in. It's the most creativity I've been able to enjoy with a client in, oh, I don't know...years. I really appreciate it, Dan."

"We can't thank you enough," Meredith seconded.

Dan shook his head thoughtfully. "Come on, guys," he began. "Do you really think it was my introductions that made all the difference? Think carefully before you answer."

Meredith did. "What I think, Dan, is that your introduction collapsed the time it took to build trust between them and us. I think I speak for Lance when I say that we both appreciated your preview of each person, to say nothing of your introduction, and found that going in with the groundwork already laid for us made for a much more trusting exchange between us and the prospects.

"Personally, Dan, I was able to connect with Lee in a way I've never experienced before. Practicing the Five Levels of Exchange with you and Lance beforehand helped me figure out how to ask Lee for help and how to offer her my support."

Meredith took a rare breath, looking to Lance for support. His beaming smile sped her onward: "I realized that although I consider myself pretty good at making connections, and Lance and I talked about this very thing last week, for whatever reason, I hadn't been asking specifically for help with introductions like the one you made for me with Lee.

"Instead, I tend to spend more time with my connection exploring the types of people I want to meet. More specifically, I spend *a lot* of time identifying the industries they should work in—to be most beneficial to me, I mean—and the titles they should hold and even the psychographic aspects, such as 'people who love to learn' or 'people who regularly attended conferences,' etc. I found that, with Lee, I was more connected on a personal level, live and in person, and going into the meeting from a knowledge exchange basis really helped me focus on her needs. Well, I guess I should say, *our* needs."

Dan nodded appreciatively, then turned to Lance. "And Lance, how do you think this kind of targeted, specific, one-on-one introduction versus a mass e-mail, pick-a-business-card-out-of-a-fishbowl approach helped you?"

"I think this guy was loaded for bear when I walked in," Lance confessed. "By that, I mean the recommendation was so targeted, was so personal, that he was genuinely interested in seeing how we could help each other. I can't imagine what this type of consultancy can do for my business—the kind of value we can add to our portfolio by helping clients from the beginning of their business plan then all the way to after they're up and running."

Dan nodded, noting the obvious enthusiasm in Meredith and Lance's tales. "I'm really pleased to hear how well these two meetings went, particularly to hear how eager and enthusiastic and *open* you two were to using what you've learned. Working through the Five Levels of Exchange is all about practicing to develop a *state of mastery*.

"And you've seen that, really, these same Five Levels of Exchange are the main secret to any good relationship."

Dan's brow furrowed as he complained, "It's really too bad schools don't teach kids early on this very important set of skills. I predict that someday schools will incorporate these skills in their curriculum but for now, at least, people who get tools like this can use them to improve their networking success—their ability to make connections that matter!"

Dan began getting fidgety, a sure sign, Meredith knew, that the meeting was about to end. Before it could, she looked at Lance. In unison, they both asked, "What's next?"

After his usual bemused chuckle at how often Meredith and Lance thought alike, Dan answered, "Well, gang, the next step is all about practicing networking exchanges with others."

Lance chuckled. "Yeah, Dan, but what others?"

"I'm glad you asked," Dan said. From inside his ever-present computer bag, Dan pulled out two laminated sheets of paper. On them were printed a list of ideas for expanding their networks:

Places to Expand Your Circle of Connections

1. ***Internet.*** Use keyword searches for your industry to find thought leaders. When you get to know an influencer through his or her work, you might e-mail that person or seek them out through social media. You can send them a note supporting their ideas and begin

establishing a loose relationship. Social media especially has opened the doors to connecting with people who would be otherwise difficult to reach.

2. *Periodicals.* Search for both online and offline publications, newspapers, books, and article directories. These are great ways to find potential influencers, and many of them may have contact information within those publications.

3. *Conferences and lectures.* When you attend a conference, keynote, or lecture, do you introduce yourself to that person whenever possible? If not, you're missing a great opportunity.

One idea is to write a question related to the talk on the back of your business card and approach the speaker after the event. Talk with the speaker, sharing that you enjoyed their speech and that you wrote down a question you'd like to discuss for a few minutes at some point in the next several weeks. Follow up and keep any discussion to the short time you promised. This shows your respect of that person's time and can set the stage for future exchanges.

4. *Volunteering.* Volunteering pays off in connections when it's done from the heart. When you volunteer for a group or organization that you strongly believe in, a few things will happen. One, you're likely to support that group or organization for the long term, allowing you to create better connections. Two, when you do

meet an influencer and establish a connection at a volunteer level doing something you both love, that connection will be even stronger and more meaningful to the influencer. Some of the best opportunities in business and life come from connections based on personal interests.

5. ***Program committees.*** Join an industry association and get actively involved in the program committee. This is a great place to connect with influencers in your industry on a regular basis as you book them for events. You will also create continual value for the group with quality programming and have further qualified access to group members.

6. ***Alumni groups.*** Alumni groups on LinkedIn especially offer a great place to build social capital with people who attended your alma mater.

7. ***Traveling.*** Use airline travel to its fullest! A lot of great conversations can be struck up at 35,000 feet. However, just be careful to respect your seatmate's desire to be left alone.

8. ***Leisure activities.*** People sometimes mistakenly believe that they can only meet influencers in work-related situations. On the contrary, in many cases great connections are made in social settings where people tend to feel comfortable sharing more. Extending yourself socially gives others a more complete picture of who

you really are. For example, let's say you are the guy or girl who plays in a band and is in sales. You become much more memorable. As with volunteering, some of the best connections are made when personal interests are shared. Not all of these people are influencers, but they can become friends, which adds balance to your network. And you never know when these friends can connect you with others of influence.

9. ***Current Connections.*** With LinkedIn now growing by one million weekly, your network grows exponentially in the same amount of time. On LinkedIn, your connections may keep their networks hidden. Sometimes, what it takes is an in-depth conversation with a current connection to be granted access to their hidden connections. Again, it will be the way you approach and handle the exchange that will determine your success in getting introductions to your network's first- and second-degree connections.

Dan also left them with another sheet of tips.

DAN'S EIGHTH-LESSON TIPS

- ✓ Be open-minded and adventurous when you expand your connections. That guy on the treadmill next to you could be your new friend—and possibly a future partner.
- ✓ Take advantage of social media. Many users of social media share a mutual interest—they are there to meet new people and connect. They realize not every single "follower" or "friend" will be the gateway to a business opportunity, and that's perfectly fine. They appreciate the various levels of exchange. Actually, the more you engage, the more you will eventually attract like-minded people.
- ✓ Ask for help with introductions. It's okay—as long as you keep practicing the Five Levels of Exchange!
- ✓ Listen and think about how you can help someone you are connecting to before you make a request for yourself.

LESSON 9

MAKE YOUR PROGRESS AND COMMITMENT VISIBLE TO OTHERS

LANCE SAT IN THE LOBBY of Frozen Food Stuffs, the massive restaurant chain supplier whose corporate offices were just outside town. He was dressed casually in pleated slacks and his crispest white dress shirt, working in a new pair of loafers he'd bought online.

He recognized the face of Erin Zack as she approached him in a crisp suit of ironed linen. A pale green blouse beneath the snug jacket set off her eyes. He'd seen her face, of course, on many magazine covers in recent months. After all, although she was just in her early thirties, she was already considered by many to be a thought leader in the hospitality industry, and Lance had been following many of those thoughts for months, never guessing her office was located less than an hour's drive from his own.

"Thanks for offering to meet me on such short notice, Erin," he said, standing and offering a hand.

"Glad to, Lance," she replied in a voice that sounded as young and exuberant as a college sophomore's. "I have to say, it's not every day I get such an interactive, richly detailed, and fully researched introduction. I didn't know I'd been in half those articles, let alone that anybody had read them all."

Lance tried, and failed, not to gush. "Oh, I love your premise that frozen foods don't have to taste frozen, and your stance on 'rubber chicken' is really refreshing. I also tout the production model used here at Frozen Food Stuffs."

Erin sat across from him in the spacious, sunlit, atrium-style lobby of the sprawling corporate offices and smirked. "It's funny you should mention that, Lance. I was speaking with someone in management over at Papa's Pasta Parlor and they mentioned they'd heard about us from your company, of all places."

Lance blushed and confessed, "Like I said, when I spot a new trend, game changer, or thought leader, I like to pass it along."

Erin studied him carefully. "I'm sure you understand that's pretty rare in our industry, Lance. Pretty rare in any industry, from my point of view."

Lance shrugged. "I believe the best way to get valuable information, knowledge, and especially wisdom is to exchange it, Erin, don't you?"

He could hardly believe his ears. He was sounding just like Dan. Erin smiled, toying with a lock of her curly auburn hair. "That's my philosophy anyway, Lance. I just wish more of our colleagues shared it. Do folks at your office share your value of sharing and collaboration? If they did, I can't imagine how much more effective it would be to work in that environment."

Lance looked for a moment into Erin's bright, probing green eyes. Was she asking him if there was a potential job opening at his company or was she just one of those rare, great "connectors" Dan seemed so good at finding? Lance decided that she was the latter and responded, "In my office, lately at least, I've been practicing Dan's process and found that the more explicit I am about *how* I connect with others, the better the results I achieve."

Erin looked puzzled. Lance paused a moment, thinking, and then continued. "For example, the other day I helped a colleague figure out how to go online and promote an e-book our marketing department had recently created for our potential and current clients. I had learned a couple of new Google+ and Twitter marketing strategies from someone over in our IT department who has been moonlighting as a social media marketing coordinator for a local restaurant chain. I shared my newfound online marketing ideas and they were well received. Then by tweeting and sharing just a couple of well-chosen tweets, our e-book was downloaded more than 200 times in less than half a day! Now, our whole office is tweeting and sharing updates on LinkedIn and Facebook and we're getting calls now that are a result of that free e-book being passed around the Web. Our prospects are coming to us rather than us always having to seek them out. And best of all, sharing with my colleagues has resulted in a number of other ideas about sharing our expertise on the net, such as the creation of an industry-focused group on LinkedIn and a series of monthly webinars we are all contributing to—even a possible radio show on Blog Talk Radio!"

"Wow! That sounds viral all right!" said Erin, choking back a laugh.

"Yes. What Dan helped me realize is that the shoemaker's children shouldn't go shoeless."

"Huh?"

Lance continued, "In other words, I start my networking right where I am planted currently—in my own office and within my own company. The process of making connections that matter begins right where we each work every day. This realization has helped me learn and grow and learn and grow again, to build a network that is sustainable." Lance paused again, realizing that his usual shyness, especially with people he did not know or did not know well, was nowhere to be found at the moment. In fact, he felt comfortable speaking with Erin. She was just sitting there nodding her head throughout the several minutes it took to tell his story.

Lance was momentarily distracted by the clicking of heels growing louder and louder. He looked up to find a male receptionist leaning down toward them. "Can I get you and your guest anything, Ms. Zack?"

"Lance?"

He asked for bottled water and she nodded. "Make that two, Jeffrey, and thanks."

Erin turned back to Lance. "Wow! That was a wonderful story! It puts a context around the building of networks I never thought about much before. It really makes me want to go back and start connecting with certain people in my company to see what *we* can make happen for each other and, of course, for our whole company!"

"Yes," said Lance with a nod. "Not one of us is better than two or more of us working toward a common goal that we all can benefit from. Dan also helped me realize that I am not only my own brand in this interconnected world, but I also represent, now more than ever, my whole company's brand. Further, anyone in the company who is on the Web now does the same thing. Talk about reputation management!"

"True," added Erin. "It's more important therefore that each of us becomes 'awake in the network,' if you will."

The two paused for a moment lost in their own thoughts of the implications of their conversation. Erin finally spoke up quietly, “Lance, I’m curious, how did you find such direct contact information for me?”

Her tone implied that she was, in fact, curious rather than dubious. He blushed a little and confessed, “Well, like I said, Erin, I keep a close eye on thought leaders in our industry. I set up a Google Alert featuring your name, and one day last week it alerted me to a string of tweets you were making about a new article you had been interviewed for in *Hospitality Monthly*. You posted an excerpt on your blog, so after I read that I read through some older posts, and you had mentioned taking a day off to attend the local Brewer’s Fest here in Smithfield. I figured if you were that local, we must share a few connections and I found a few on LinkedIn. After that, it was merely a matter of getting past the gatekeepers in your office!”

Erin laughed breezily as they both accepted the bottled waters Jeffrey brought for them. “You know,” she admitted, “I don’t often read, let alone respond to, unsolicited e-mails but yours was so targeted. I never realized there was a company and experts like you and the many others in your company who exist solely to help restaurants, fast-food chains, hotels, and others in the hospitality industry do their paperwork. You offer such a niche service and I did some checking, too, and, really, you guys are one of the only companies doing what you do in my area and I like to deal with people locally. It’s much more satisfying to me.”

Lance gave her some background. “It’s because we met through a local industry conference we attend twice a year. We are a group of introverted guys who found one another because of the fact that we are all shy. We realized after about a decade of going to conferences together, spending hours talking about our industry's leading challenges, even well into most nights while our colleagues were at bars socializing, that we had built quite a brain trust of talent. The least shy of our group, Sam Warner, came up with the idea of forming our own company. He asked us to consider the idea and give him time to present a business plan. When he returned to the next conference with an amazing plan, we unanimously agreed to unite and harvest the many opportunities none of us could create on our own. Now, five years later, we have almost 100 employees and growing. I myself started as a junior bookkeeper for Pattie's Patties, a small fast-food chain with only six restaurants. After that, I was head accountant for the Tijuana Flats Mexican franchise, when Sam presented the concept of joining Hospitality, Inc."

Erin was nodding her head enthusiastically by the time he had wrapped up his mini-memoir. "Mine was about connections too," she explained. "I started with the frozen foods division of Choc-o-Loco Ice Cream before being recruited for R&D for the Fro-Go-Yo chain of frozen yogurt stands. A few years after that, my old boss from Choc-o-Loco, who had moved to this company, contacted me and asked if I wanted to join him, and I started in the food truck division."

Lance and Erin discussed the pros and cons of their jobs for a few more minutes, until she began looking at her watch. Taking the hint, Lance stood and said, "Well, I've taken up enough of your time."

"Hardly," she said, remaining seated. "I'm just waiting for Mr. Broderick to come. He's head of our finance committee, and is interested in talking to you about how Hospitality, Inc., works . . ."

• • • • • •

"So I have to ask," Dan began later that week after Lance had finished sharing the tale of his latest Exchanger connection, "did you get the account?"

"Signed, sealed, and delivered." Lance smiled, feeling a supportive squeeze from Meredith on his left forearm. "And I couldn't have done it without you, Dan."

Dan shrugged and waved a hand dismissively. "Not at all," he said confidently. "I really think you two are underestimating yourselves here. You had skills for opening up relationships to close deals *before* I met you. Yes, some were weaker than others and not prioritized to give you the best edge out in this new, networked world. But you both have been embracing the beliefs I have shared about making connections that matter and have leveraged those beliefs with both my connections and yours to *re-create your network*."

He paused and turned to Meredith. "Between Lance and his new account and you landing the Lee's Trees social media campaign, Meredith, it looks like you two will be busy for the foreseeable future."

"Yes, but...that's a good problem to have, right, Dan?" Lance asked.

"For sure," he hemmed, "but it's still a problem."

"How so?" Lance heard Meredith ask as he reached for his notebook; he sensed a lesson wasn't too far in the offing.

"Well, guys, let me ask you—how about your current Primary Circle? New business is always good but not at the expense of your current Primary Circle partners."

Meredith shook her head. "Between this new account and a few of the other new connections you set me up with, Dan, I confess I haven't been keeping up with my Primary Circle as often I should be."

"Me either," Lance said. "But mine isn't as big as Meredith's."

They all chuckled. "Be that as it may, Lance," Dan explained, "whoever's in your Primary Circle is there for a reason. Think how hard we worked on whittling that list down, working on the pros and cons of who should be on it. We don't want all that work to go to waste, do we?"

Lance felt it was a rhetorical question but shook his head anyway.

Dan continued. "Today, I want you both to take just a moment and think about what your Primary Circle partners have given to you so far."

Meredith nodded. "You're right, Dan. Monica introduced me to her colleague just the other day, and

Francis set up a meeting with his publicist next week. And I haven't had time to thank either of them yet."

Lance agreed. "I've got two meetings coming up next week, both of them referred to me by members of my Primary Circle, and I haven't really followed up either. I guess I figured because they're in my circle, they know that."

"But how could they, Lance?" Dan asked pointedly. "The point of being an Exchanger is to exchange constantly, now and later, not just to grab what you can and run, assuming the other person knows how grateful you are. Let them know it!"

"But how?" Lance asked.

"You should make a point of taking time monthly, or at the very least every other month, to go back and thank those who have helped you in your network. It's just as important to let them know the results of the connections they set up for you as well. Just like companies that find that 20 to 30 percent of their customers bring them 80 percent of their business, you will find the same to be true of your Primary Circle partners as well.

"You will also find that it would be much harder and take longer to build those great connections continually with new potential Primary Circle partners than to go back to your partners to see who else you know to connect them with and vice versa. In other words, it's going to be much easier to leverage your existing Primary Circle than create a new one."

"So, it's a little like a company continuing to train and nurture old employees versus hiring new ones?"

Lance asked, thinking of how his future might have been different if he'd been made to feel more welcome, even appreciated, at his earlier jobs before deciding to cofound Hospitality, Inc., with his colleagues.

"Exactly!" Dan said. "Most so-called networkers think the grass is always greener on the other side of the fence. But you and I know that watering our own lawn is the best way to achieve success. And to do that, you've got to take your Primary Circle literally. By that, I mean they are your first point of contact and should be treated as such. You should include them in the good news and the bad news. That's how great relationships are formed."

"But won't we be bugging them?" Meredith asked. "I mean, even though they're Exchangers, will they want to know every little detail of our connections? I'm not sure I would."

"No, of course not," Dan agreed. "But don't you like to hear when something you've done, some effort you've made, pays off? If you don't check back in with these people, it's the same as if they've given you a gift or thrown you a party and you never sent a thank-you card. They might not need to know the good news right away, but after a few weeks they'll start to wonder, 'How did that meeting I set up for Meredith go?' That's the time to tell them. Feedback loops are important!

"The problem with many of us is that we *assume* they already know or are too busy to care or even already understand how much we appreciate them. Remember, by making your connection activities more explicit than implicit, especially around the process I've shared with you, it helps those strong partners become even more successful with their results and new opportunities.

"One of the ways you keep others engaged with you is to keep them informed about how what they gave you has made a difference in your life and share, specifically, the outcomes of their efforts. These feedback loops go a long way to build trust and further opportunities for exchanges. Having a conversation that creates great energy and then 'goes dark' for a month is a recipe for losing momentum and credibility. Therefore, I suggest you organize and manage your relationships so that you follow up with people when you said you would.

"But," he added, "you shouldn't feel the need literally to measure how many minutes you spend each year with each person in your Primary Circle. This is too literal, but it can definitely be helpful to have a simple calendar tool or technique to let you know when it's appropriate to drop in on your Primary Circle members with some good news or simply news.

"The most important recommendation is to invest in a database—Microsoft Outlook is fine for this, for example—that allows you to note your interactions and commitments with your network. A simple list of those in your network, along with actions and current outcomes, will allow you to see who you are supporting, and who you are neglecting."

Dan paused to let his words sink in. He saw they were busily jotting down notes to follow up on their new connections and opportunities. The conversation continued through afternoon drinks and concluded with both of them committing to follow up first thing the next morning. Dan congratulated the two of them for persistence, but more importantly, for their commitment to following up. He left them both more lively and excited than he had ever seen them in the time they had been working together. When he handed them the day's lesson tips, they immediately began reading, oblivious to the growing noise from the afternoon work crowd. They didn't even realize until a half hour later that Dan had gone home.

DAN'S NINTH-LESSON TIPS

- ✓ Don't neglect your Primary Circle connections. Make a point to follow up, whether they have made a significant impact on your current opportunities or not. You don't want to lose them in the long run, do you?
- ✓ Don't feel obligated to let them know every little detail. Share important events, good and bad, to build a relationship, but create deeper relationships by sharing more than you would with those who are not in this closer circle.
- ✓ Continue to explore new connections.
- ✓ Invest in new tools, including a customer relationship management (CRM) system, to help you manage and follow your connections, such as Nimble or Microsoft Outlook.
- ✓ Create personalized lists on sites like Twitter, Google+, or LinkedIn. You want to keep the intimacy of your relationship.
- ✓ Never forget the simple power of saying "thank you!" Your network contracts and expands, but you don't want it to dissolve.

LESSON 10

INSPIRE OTHERS

"HAPPY ANNIVERSARY!" Meredith raised a glass as Lance walked into the private dining room of one of their favorite restaurants. She chuckled as he looked behind him, perhaps suspecting a married couple was following him inside the private room complete with candlelight and a table set for three.

"Am I missing something?" he asked, taking a seat across the table from her and spreading a white linen napkin across his lap.

"It's been three months since we first met Dan," she explained, putting down her glass of red wine. "That makes this an anniversary dinner."

"In that case..." He smiled, reaching for the open wine bottle in the middle of the table. "Let's celebrate!"

In fact, there was much to celebrate, as both well knew. For herself, Meredith had never been more successful. The journey hadn't been without its bumps and bruises, but she was a far better businessperson—frankly, a far better person—because of it.

She watched Lance as both of them awaited the guest of honor. He seemed more confident than ever, and she certainly knew his business was booming as well. He'd gotten two promotions in the last three months, due in large part to the connections he'd made and the new business he'd brought to his company, Hospitality, Inc.

Her thoughts about Lance were interrupted by his soft clapping as he stood up to welcome Dan. Though their mentor blushed at the rare display of emotion, Meredith felt compelled to stand and cheer as well.

She was one breath away from singing "For He's a Jolly Good Fellow" when Dan shushed them good-naturedly.

They sat back down as Lance poured him some wine. "At least let us offer you a toast," Lance said.

Dan blushed but made no further objection. "Here's to Dan," Lance began. "We wouldn't be here without you. What you've taught us about the magic of human relationships has truly changed our lives."

He raised his glass as Meredith joined him, eyebrows arched. She was impressed. Three months ago, she doubted he'd have had the confidence to say anything so well—or so exuberantly!

Dan seemed overwhelmed as well. "Wow, you two," Dan said after he put his glass down. "I have to say, I'm impressed. It's like, well, it's like night and day from our first meeting."

They all chuckled, but Meredith was curious. "How so?"

Dan slid his menu away. "Well, have you ever seen a deer in headlights?" he asked with a smile. "Seriously, though, you were both so convinced you knew networking up, down, and sideways!"

Meredith shook her head playfully. "Now, that's not entirely true, Dan."

"Yeah," Lance chimed in. "If we knew everything there was to know about networking, why would we have come to you in the first place?"

"Good point, Lance." Dan nodded. "I guess what I meant to say was, you thought you knew the language of networking, the letter of the law when it came to making connections. And now, I can sense that you're making truer, more valuable connections than ever before, am I right?"

"Absolutely," said Lance. "Believe it or not, my supervisors have started calling me 'that connection guy' at work. Me? Mr. Two People in His Primary Circle?!"

"But not anymore, right, Lance?" prodded Meredith.

"My Primary Circle is overflowing now." He laughed. Then quickly he turned to Dan. "But I've kept the number low enough where I can still make personal contact once a month, just like you said."

Dan nodded appreciatively as Meredith began, "Well, I can sympathize with Lance because I've never had more connections. And before, connections were never my problem, but acting on them was. Now I would say half my time is spent making quality exchanges, which in my business...well, that *is* my business."

"Yes, Meredith, but was that your business before you came to understand the true power of connecting?"

She thought about that for a minute, tempted to say "Yes," right away. But actually, that wasn't the right answer. "I thought people were my business before, but now I know that connecting with people—sincerely exchanging with them—is the fastest path to success in our networked world."

Dan nodded with satisfaction as the waitress came into the private dining area. She introduced herself and took everyone's orders, then quietly left.

Dan seemed to take the pause as a teaching moment and sat up in his chair a little as he said, "I'd be remiss if I didn't ask both of you what the difference is in how you used to approach networking with what you know today about the power of building strong, exchanging relationships. Lance, could you start? Because I think you've gotten the most out of this mini-course?"

Lance nodded energetically as Meredith smiled, if only to herself. Three months ago, he would have been begging her with his eyes for her to go first. Now there he was, up front and center, ready to share.

"I think the first thing you taught me was to trust the process," Lance began. "By that I mean, before the trusting the process, I first asked, 'what can I get?' You taught us that we have as much to give and that in giving, we actually are receiving. But even further, you showed me how to move from giving and receiving to setting up ongoing *exchanges* that make the difference between creating a *good opportunity* to creating an *ongoing series of good opportunities*. That was a breakthrough moment for me and, I think, the reason I've had so much success.

"I also think you gave me the confidence—and Meredith helped with this, too—to embrace my expertise. I forgot that I work for Hospitality, Inc., because I love the restaurant business so much. Or more specifically, love the people who work in restaurants. They're a particular breed and once I realized that I'm a particular breed, and that we're all in this together, I was really able to flourish."

Lance's cheeks were flushed and he looked to both sides for approval before continuing: "I mean, take the frozen foods account I just closed. I would have never, not in a million years, had the confidence or even the knowledge to track down Erin and approach her about our possible connections. And look how that ended up: Hospitality, Inc., is now providing paperwork solutions for the company *and* Erin and I are coauthoring a magazine article about, of all things, 'The Power of Great Connections'!"

"Lance," Meredith gushed and hugged him. "You didn't tell me that!"

"I just found out," he said, blushing in her sudden embrace. "But that's just it. Little things like that happen every day for me now."

"Me, too," Meredith agreed once Lance turned the floor over to her. "Now I actually look forward to checking my e-mail because I know someone is going to be answering a question or offering a solution or even asking for a solution. Now I have real connections on Facebook, Twitter, and LinkedIn, and not just a bunch of random friends or followers. It's like there's this new energy to the connections I make, and a true bond between myself and the connector that I never understood or maybe never appreciated before."

Dan nodded thoughtfully as the waitress brought their food. They thanked her and ate quietly for a few minutes before Lance mentioned, "You know, it's funny, but I see in my friends a lot—I mean, *a lot*—of the same attitudes you and I had three months ago, Meredith."

She put down her fork and nearly squealed. "I was just going to say that. I call myself 'Mini-Dan' now because I'm constantly lecturing my friends and family about the way they view making connections. I literally stopped a man from giving me his business card the other day and insisted he give me his LinkedIn public profile URL instead."

They shared a good chuckle over that. Lance nodded, pushed his plate away, and said, "My friends just don't get it. A coworker, a mom of two, told me yesterday that because her husband traveled, she wasn't able to go to events where she could build her network. I made her sit down with me and look at my LinkedIn profile and my connections. I told her that was how I was going to spend less than an hour of my time Wednesday night, responding to comments and queries and requesting and giving introductions. I explained that I would consider the evening successful even if only one person responded. She looked at me like I was crazy, until the following day when we were at the same client meeting—with one of those LinkedIn connections!"

Dan was nodding, almost clapping, as Meredith watched him wipe his lips and put his napkin over his dinner plate. He smiled as she said, "I dunno, Dan, it's like we know this secret and they just don't speak the language..."

"A secret," Dan interjected reverently. "Yep, that's exactly how I felt when I first learned how to make connections that matter. It was like I had a great big secret that made me different and, frankly, gave me an edge—not something I should share with others."

Lance and Meredith looked at each other, clearly stunned. "B-b-but, didn't you figure this out on your own?" Lance asked.

"And if it gives you such an edge," Meredith added, "why would you share all this with... *us*?"

Dan smiled and sat back a little in his leather seat. "It might surprise you to learn that once upon a time, I worked in an office like most of the rest of the world. Before I started teaching and then later recruiting, I was at a software company that seemed no different from a million others just like it 10 years ago. But this one was different, because it was run by a man named Jim Wilkins. You don't know the name, but trust me, this is one of the most powerful men I know.

"And wise, too. As much as he valued my work for his company, he could see that my real strength lay in people. He put me in human resources, then sent me out on the road to colleges, recruiting people. I never really came back. I think in a way, Jim didn't want me to come back. He was my first client, and the work I did for him early on—making connections with software designers, illustrators for their game division, buyers in the malls—kept me on my feet until I could find a second client, and a third.

"But it wasn't the freedom Jim gave me that changed my life; it was this secret process of making connections that matter that he shared with me that really revolutionized the way I approached meeting people, making friends, and forging relationships that last. When I was a teacher, working and engaging with kids and parents, I used Jim's process. I also used it when I started my tutoring and later when I was recruiting. It consistently made a big difference in my success."

Meredith was impressed by Dan's story. She had seriously thought he was the originator of the process he had taught them. What's more, she still had one question. "But you still haven't told us, Dan, why you're allowing us to learn this process if it gives you such a competitive edge?"

"I have to," he said, smiling. "My mentor, Jim, told me that the price of admission to this little mini-course I now teach was this—you have to now go out and find two people to mentor in the process of making connections that matter. In my case, once I started with my first two pay-it-two-wards, as Jim would put it, I felt elated. Then after Jim passed away, I made a promise to myself that I would carry on the good work he began."

"That's it?" Lance asked.

"That's it?" Dan reiterated. "That's a lot, Lance. And, to answer your question about competitive advantage, Meredith, I know it seems counterintuitive, but this great secret grows in value only when it is shared widely. Additionally, the pie of exchanging relationships only grows, resulting in even more opportunity for everyone connected. Just think, gang, now if I ever need anybody with expertise in the hospitality or social media worlds, I'll know just who to call."

Meredith and Lance shared another look. This was all so new, and just when she thought there could be no more surprises.

"But why us?" Lance asked, reading Meredith's mind. "How did you pick us to share this information with?"

"Just as important," Meredith added, "how did you know we'd be receptive to it?"

Dan's beaming smile was like dessert after a rich meal.

"Through my introduction to you, I learned that you were both open to learning. It turns out that truly successful people are always learning. They are honest with themselves, have a drive to be better, and can handle or thrive through the inevitable ups and downs that come with trying new things.

"I got a tip that you two were both cut from the same pattern, so I felt my time would be well invested in mentoring you. What you needed most, I found, was a dose of inspiration. That's what turned it all around for you. Once you realized how powerful your story could be, and what it might mean to others, you both got so inspired there was no stopping you."

Meredith considered Dan's words. He was right!

"That's where you come in," he concluded. "Your story, progress, and results will be inspiring to others who are stuck and, if they are open to it, you can help them turn their passions into actions."

He paused, sitting forward in his chair and pinning them with a serious expression. "So, are you up for it?"

Meredith found herself nodding without hesitation. Next to her, Lance was nodding exuberantly as well.

As they left the restaurant that night, she felt a pang of regret as she shook Dan's hand. She didn't know when she would see him again and said something about her concern. But Dan replied assuredly, "Don't worry, Meredith. I put both you and Lance into my Primary Circle. Hopefully, you did the same! But, don't forget...pay it 'two-ward!'"

As they watched him drive away, Lance turned to Meredith. "Now what?" he asked, with both a serious and amused tone in his voice. They both realized the hefty weight behind his seemingly innocuous question.

"I guess now we've got to go out and find two people like us who know nothing about networking and—"

"Correction," Lance interrupted, walking her to her car. "Two people like us *who think they know everything* about so-called networking."

They both laughed before parting ways. Lance was right. Once upon a time, Meredith had imagined she knew all there was to know about networking. Now she realized all she'd known was how to make lots of connections, hoping that some of them, with little effort, would turn into referral sources or at least lead generators.

Now, as she drove away from the restaurant that night, she thought how much her life had changed since learning the power of story and, just as important, the power of making meaningful connections and setting up the right environment for mutually beneficial, ongoing exchanges of opportunities.

Suddenly, she couldn't wait to find a willing pupil to share the most powerful lesson of all: Making Connections That Matter!

DAN'S TENTH-LESSON TIPS

- ✓ Keep refreshing yourself on the Five Levels of Exchange.
- ✓ Be conscious of who is in your Primary Circle.
- ✓ Keep a mental and written list of Givers, Takers, and Exchangers to ensure you are connecting with the best like-minded and like-valued people.
- ✓ As you set out to make connections that matter, listen and give first, share your authentic story, and you become an attractor of possibility and opportunity.
- ✓ Adopt the pay-it-forward attitude, whether it's in making introductions, teaching someone how to make connections that matter, writing recommendations, or exchanging information and knowledge—especially about how to build connections that matter.
- ✓ Don't keep this method to yourself. Inspire those who you recognize will value it and share the lessons and process.

ACKNOWLEDGMENTS

FIRST WE WOULD like to thank our great team at BenBella, run by Glenn Yeffeth, for their wonderful support on this project. It was truly a collaborative process, one that defines what publishing should be—supportive, engaging, motivating, and even challenging.

Next, we thank John Willig, our agent. John, you saw our vision and championed it all the way. You also embrace our value of partnership, helping us move seamlessly through the maze of publishers trying to make sense of this new digital world. We thank you for your faith in us, and most of all, for your constant sense of humor!

FROM MELISSA: Thanks to all those great colleagues who have supported my efforts in Networlding, primarily Jocelyn Carter Miller, who originally introduced me to Larry, and who is my coauthor on Networlding. It was invaluable for me to learn how to make connections that matter with you at both Motorola and Office Depot. I also thank the folks at CDW, specifically Lauren McCadney. My experience gained in working your national team of CDW sales professionals to build beneficial, sustainable relationships was successful because of your amazing support. Thank you also to Andres Tapia, who helped me when he was the Chief Diversity Officer at Hewitt, understand that diversity of all kinds in your network (age, gender, thought, and more) enables you to achieve greater results for the common good.

Finally, thank you to Networlders throughout the world who kept me focused on building out the model of Networlding over the past twelve years. This includes my coauthor Larry, who helped me refine, test, and develop a better model for building networks inside and outside of companies like Motorola, American Express, and many small to midsized, fast-growth companies.

FROM LARRY: A huge thanks to my coauthor Melissa—her spirit, determination, and support have always been an inspiration to me personally and professionally. To my business partners Terry Barber and Carol Chapman, thank you for helping me find my own voice and for taking this incredible journey to inspiration together.

When Melissa and I started working on the concept of intentionally creating vibrant networks, it was a fairly new area of study and practice. Thank you to all my colleagues at Motorola, American Express, and Children's Healthcare of Atlanta that supported my attempts to innovate in the areas of creating communities, leadership development, and talent management. All of the opportunities I have been fortunate to have are a direct result of the wealth of connections I have made over the years. Thank you to all the exchangers in my network that have guided me, connected me, and encouraged me. Much of what I learned was from you!

Finally, I got myself on the right career track while at Motorola and my transformation was made possible by the community of people in the business learning functions and at Motorola University. A special thanks to Leo Burke, Mary Bottie, Jim Austgen, and Bill Wiggenhorn for taking a risk on an electrical engineer with a desire to make a difference.

ABOUT THIS BOOK

Are you…

…hoping your next networking event will be "the one"?
…collecting mountains of business cards?
…having countless breakfasts and lunches?
…thinking that you give much more than you get?

Then your way of networking is…DEAD.

With social networks, teleconferencing, and webinars, you are able to meet more people in more ways than ever before. But how do you create new possibilities through connections that matter? *Networking Is Dead* offers a new approach to fundamental networking misconceptions through an entertaining and knowledge-rich business story. In it, you meet Lance and Meredith, business colleagues who both consider their networking skills mediocre at best. Lance is the shy accountant and partner of a firm that specializes in restaurants. Meredith is the founder and owner of a social media marketing firm. Both of them seek direction to build their networks more proactively. Their search leads them to Dan, a specialist in creating and building what he calls *connections that matter*.

In this compelling book, authors Melissa G. Wilson and Larry Mohl show you it's the *quality* rather than the *quantity of* connections that counts.

You will learn ten lessons to help you build an effective process that:

- Deepens existing relationships and makes meaningful new ones;
- Connects across your own company to strengthen your business;
- Finds people with similar values to embark on mutually beneficial opportunities; and
- Leverages your connections instead of being overwhelmed by them.

Networking Is Dead is an engaging story that provides a specific road map designed to help you take purposeful and productive action immediately.

Networking is Dead. Literally. Make connections that matter!

INDEX

M

N

U

V

W

Y